D1257529

Twilight Rails

Also Published by the University of Minnesota Press

Twilight Rails

The Final Era of Railroad Building in the Midwest

H. Roger Grant

University of
Minnesota Press

Minneapolis
London

Portions of chapter 2 previously appeared in different form as "'Iowa's Brightest Railway Project': The Creston, Winterset & Des Moines Railroad, 1907–1920," *Iowa Heritage Illustrated* 89 (Fall 2009): 100–109. Portions of chapter 7 previously appeared in different form as "The Ozark Short Line Railroad: A Failed Dream," *Missouri Historical Review* 100 (July 2006): 197–211.

Original maps created by Philip Schwartzberg, Meridian Mapping, Minneapolis, Minnesota

All photographs and illustrations are from the author's collection unless credited otherwise.

Published by the University of Minnesota Press
111 Third Avenue South, Suite 290
Minneapolis, MN 55401-2520
http://www.upress.umn.edu

Library of Congress Cataloging-in-Publication Data
Grant, H. Roger, 1943–
Twilight rails : the final era of railroad building in the Midwest / H. Roger Grant.
    p.   cm.
Includes bibliographical references and index.
ISBN 978-0-8166-6562-4 (hc : alk. paper) — ISBN 978-0-8166-6563-1 (pb : alk. paper)
1. Railroads—Middle West—History. I. Title.
HE2771.A14G73 2010
385.0977—dc22

                                                                    2009046767

Design and production by Mighty Media, Inc.
Text design by Chris Long

Printed in the United States of America on acid-free paper

The University of Minnesota is an equal-opportunity educator and employer.

17 16 15 14 13 12 11 10   10 9 8 7 6 5 4 3 2 1

To Don L. Hofsommer
longtime friend and fellow railroad historian

Contents

Preface

W hy this book? In some ways this study came about accidentally. When I was serving as a visiting professor at the University of Missouri–Rolla during spring semester 2005, I decided that one of my research activities would involve the Ozark Short Line, a largely unbuilt railroad that was planned to connect Rolla with several communities to the south. I knew about this railroad as the result of my passion for collecting public timetables; years ago I acquired what I thought was a bona fide schedule of the Ozark Short Line, but then discovered it was a promotional folder. Although I wrote a short history of this ill-fated project, I had no further plans. Later, while rummaging through files in my Clemson University office, I discovered photographs and notes that I had gathered on the short-lived Creston, Winterset & Des Moines Railroad. Indeed, I had last focused on this Iowa short line when I was a senior at Albia Community High School. More than forty-five years had passed, so it was time either to finish the work or to discard these materials. It soon struck me that the Ozark Short Line and the Creston, Winterset & Des Moines shared striking similarities: both were business failures; both had come about at the end of the railroad-building craze in the Midwest—the "twilight" years—and both had been projected as electric interurbans. Then I recalled that I had written about aspects of the Akron-based Akron, Canton & Youngstown Railroad, another carrier born late in the construction period.

My interest in railroad projects that occurred during the final push to flesh out the railroad map has grown. In the Midwest this covered the period from approximately 1905 to 1930, the year in which the stock market crash of 1929 started to adversely affect the economies of the region and nation. With a vision of the past, the knowledge that the Motor Age would make short-haul steam and electric railroads largely unneeded (and unprofitable) suggested a wholly unfounded optimism for many of these twilight ventures. Yet, I quickly sensed that the builders were not so foolhardy and that their ventures had positive economic dimensions.

To add to my three railroads, I needed to identify representative "twilight" carriers in the other states of the Midwest. I thumbed through old issues of *Poor's Manual of Railroads* and *Official Railway Guides*, and I used contacts at a meeting of the Lexington Group in Transportation History to learn of other possibilities, and to get reaction to my working list of companies. After my conversations with the Lexingtonians I decided that the Ettrick & Northern and the Illinois, Iowa & Minnesota and Chicago, Milwaukee & Gary railroads were ideal candidates, one a late appearing short line and the other a partially built belt line.

While I considered suitable cases studies, I needed to make certain that I had appropriately defined the Midwest. My graduate school mentor, Lewis Atherton, wrote a marvelous account of small towns in the region, *Main Street on the Middle Border* (1954), and he considered the Midwest states to be Illinois, Indiana, Iowa, Michigan, Minnesota, Missouri, Ohio, and Wisconsin. His selections more or less coincided with what has been called the Corn Belt. An earlier study, *American Regionalism* (1938) by Howard Odum and Harry Estill Moore, reached the same conclusion about what was the Midwest. For decades the U.S. Census Bureau placed Illinois, Indiana, Michigan, Ohio, and Wisconsin as the East Central Division, and Iowa, Minnesota, and Missouri as the West North Central Division. Some might quibble about the states that I selected. Andrew Cayton and Peter Onuf, for example, in their book, *The Midwest and the Nation: Rethinking the History of an American Region* (1990), focused on the five states of the Old Northwest (Illinois, Indiana, Michigan, Ohio, and Wisconsin) and at times they added Iowa and Minnesota. Occasionally the eastern sections of Kansas, Nebraska, and South Dakota, portions of a roughly defined Corn Belt, have been included. *The American Midwest: An Interpretive Encyclopedia* (2007) considered the Midwest to cover an even larger expansion of the nation's midsection, adding Kansas, Nebraska, North Dakota, and South Dakota. If I accepted this geographic expansion, I might have chosen four additional case studies: the Leavenworth & Topeka Railroad (1918–31); Midland Continental Railroad (1912–70); Mound City & Eastern

Railway (1927–40); and the never completed Yankton, Norfolk & Southern Railroad that finally gave up in 1928.

As this project was developing, I thought about twilight rails on a national basis. It would have been relatively easy to find examples, especially from the Great Plains and the South. My recent book, *Rails through the Wiregrass: A History of the Georgia & Florida Railroad* (2006), chronicled a carrier that was organized in 1906 and several years later began running between Augusta, Georgia, and Madison, Florida. But from a practical consideration, I doubt if I could easily defend the half dozen or so case studies scattered throughout the country. The much larger geographic coverage would also need to be more topical in orientation, offering fewer opportunities to explore the "human side" of twilight railroad ventures. I hope I have captured the essence of eight mostly forgotten midwestern carriers. An attractive feature of the region is that twilight railroad projects coincided with the zenith of interurban construction, an alternative form of transport much less extensive on the Great Plains and in the South. Moreover, the Midwest featured greater complexities in terms of people and patterns of settlement. The case can be made that midwesterners, more so than others elsewhere, were passionate about improving transportation. Even before the Railway Age, residents of the Old Northwest had championed steamboats and canals and, to a somewhat lesser degree, turnpikes and plank and wagon roads.

Together, these state-by-state studies of particular midwestern railroads tell a much larger story of how new carriers developed and affected their environments. Conclusions reached about twilight railroads in the Midwest can likely be applied elsewhere, and much can be gained by an examination of what took place in America's heartland at the close of the rail-building era.

Acknowledgments

benefited from strong support in the preparation of this book on latter-day railroads in the Midwest. Significantly, my Kathryn and Calhoun Lemon Professorship at Clemson University provided research funds and allowed for a reduced teaching load. This academic chair helps to explain why it has not taken an exceptional length of time to bring this work to fruition.

Like the eight railroads that this study examines, this book could not have been completed without the help of numerous people. I appreciate assistance provided by the staffs of the Archives of Michigan, Lansing; John W. Barringer III National Railroad Library of the Mercantile Library, St. Louis, Missouri; Bay County Historical Society, Bay City, Michigan; California State Railroad Museum, Sacramento; Elkhart County Historical Museum, Bristol, Indiana; Ettrick Public Library, Ettrick, Wisconsin; Gibson Memorial Library, Creston, Iowa; Minnesota Historical Society, St. Paul; National Archives, College Park, Maryland; R. M. Cooper Library, Clemson University, Clemson, South Carolina; Michigan Historical Center, Lansing; Railway & Locomotive Historical Society Archives, Sacramento, California; Regional History Center, Northern Illinois University, DeKalb; State Historical Society of Iowa, Des Moines; Special Collections, Murphy Library Resource Center, University of Wisconsin–La Crosse; Western Historical Manuscript Collection, Missouri University of Science and Technology, Rolla; and the Wisconsin Historical Society, Madison.

I also thank these individuals: Gregg Ames, St. Louis, Missouri; Ronald Bloomfield, Bay City, Michigan; John F. Bradbury, Rolla, Missouri; Ralph Breakenridge, Macksburg, Iowa; Thomas Burg, Merrill, Wisconsin; Arly Colby, Barron, Wisconsin; Cindy Ditzler, DeKalb, Illinois; G. Y. Duffy Jr., Port Huron, Michigan; Arild Engelien, Trempealeau, Wisconsin; T. J. Gaffney, Port Huron, Michigan; William Howes Jr., Jacksonville, Florida; Art Johnson, Park Ridge, Illinois; George W. Knepper, Stow, Ohio; Gary Lenz, Winsted, Minnesota; Graydon M. Meints, Kalamazoo, Michigan; William D. Middleton, Charlottesville, Virginia; David Pfeiffer, College Park, Maryland; Larry Polsley, Blanchard, Iowa; Richard Saunders Jr., Clemson, South Carolina; Mike Schafer, Lee, Illinois; Carlos Schwantes, St. Louis, Missouri; Darwin Simonaitis, Elkhart, Indiana; the late Richard Simons, Marion, Indiana; Charles H. Stats, Oak Park, Illinois; Robert Storozuk, Algonquin, Illinois; Thomas T. Tabor, Muncy, Pennsylvania; John Wickre, Newport, Minnesota; and Diana Zornow, Bristol, Indiana.

And there are more people to acknowledge. Christine Worobec and David Kyvig provided food and shelter during my research trip to DeKalb, Illinois. Don Hofsommer, professor of history at St. Cloud State University and a close friend, encouraged me in this endeavor and helped me make initial contact with the University of Minnesota Press. Keith L. Bryant Jr., another longtime friend and former colleague at the University of Akron, reviewed the manuscript with great care. My wife, Martha, also read the manuscript and immensely improved it, which is surely devotion above and beyond the marriage contract.

Introduction

Twilight Rails

A universal truth in the story of American railroads involved the joy associated with the arrival of the first train on a new railroad. Prior to all-weather roads and the triumph of internal combustion vehicles, railroads were magic carpets that bound localities and the nation. "The railroad system of the United States is a great piece of commercial machinery, essential to everyone in this complicated modern civilization," observed Howard Elliott, president of the Northern Pacific Railroad, in 1913. "Without this piece of machinery, there could not be the volume of business—agricultural, manufacturing, and commercial—that there now is." Even if a community had access to what was popularly dubbed the "steam car civilization," common wisdom held that the more rails the better.[1]

This feeling of euphoria with new or additional rail service lingered into the early decades of the twentieth century. It is hardly surprising that when, in 1910, the "inland" county-seat town of Ava, Missouri, at last joined the railroad network, the residents cherished that moment. "At half past nine o'clock last Sunday night the old Ava died and the new Ava was born," wrote the delighted editor of the *Douglas County Herald*. "The welcome 'toot' of a locomotive whistle was heard as the first train of the Kansas City, Ozarks & Southern Railway came slowly down the hill from the John A. Spurlock homestead, and stopped in the midst of a cheering crowd at the depot." Added

Transportation timeline: 1900–1930

1900	Illinois Central Railroad engineer John Luther "Casey" Jones is killed at Vaughan, Mississippi
1901	Olds Motor Works introduces first automotive assembly line
1902	American Automobile Association formed
1903	First heavier-than-air flight
1904	Northern Securities decision
1905	Publication of *Treatise on Roads and Pavements* by Ira O. Baker
1906	Hepburn Act
1907	Ohio Electric Railway organized
1908	First Model T Ford
1909	Opening of the Pacific Coast Extension of Chicago, Milwaukee & St. Paul Railroad
1910	Mann Elkins Act
1911	Charles Kettering develops the self-starter
1912	Completion of Key West Extension of the Florida East Coast Railway
1913	Dedication of Grand Central Terminal in New York City
1914	Opening of Panama Canal
1915	*S. S. Eastland* disaster, Chicago, with 845 lives lost
1916	Peak mileage reached for steam and electric railroads
1917	Federalization of transportation under the U. S. Railroad Administration
1918	New York State Barge Canal completed
1919	U. S. Army truck convoy crosses country on Lincoln Highway
1920	Transportation (or Esch–Cummins) Act
1921	Abandonment of Colorado Midland Railway
1922	Railroad Shopmen's Strike
1923	Chrysler Corporation organized
1924	Congress charters Inland Waterways Corporation
1925	First Ford Tri-motor ("Tin Goose")
1926	Air Commerce Act
1927	Charles Lindburgh pilots *Spirit of St. Louis* across the Atlantic Ocean
1928	Completion of the Great Northern's Cascade Tunnel
1929	First Annual Cleveland Air Races
1930	Greyhound Corporation formed

First Exe M.C.O&S March 13 1910

the writer, "And from a gondola car at the rear end of the train stepped a cold, tired, but very happy man, a man whom in the face of abuse and discouragement had pegged away for years until he had made his dream come true. J. B. Quigley, almost blind, had accomplished what Ava had been hoping for and scheming for twenty years to secure—he had completed a practical railroad connecting Ava with the outside world."[2]

Throughout the final years of major railroad construction, such excitement was widely repeated and knew no geographical bounds. Two years after the fifteen-mile Kansas City, Ozarks & Southern opened, and about three hundred miles to the north, hundreds of residents of Page County, Iowa, celebrated the first train that steamed along the seventeen-mile Iowa & Southwestern Railway. "The train came [into Clarinda] at noon, loaded with people from Blanchard and College Springs. About 130 were loaded up from here, and started on a free railroad ride," reported a Clarinda newspaper. "The train went slowly and the road was found in good condition, better than any expected in fact. A short stop was made in College Springs and a short stay in Blanchard. The enthusiasm of the people of those two towns is unbounded." This was a predictable response, especially for individuals who lived in or near College Springs, the largest town in the Hawkeye State without a railroad, because "the farmers were compelled to haul their products and supplies from ten to fifteen miles to the nearest railroad" and the community's struggling Amity College wanted to improve travel opportunities for faculty, students, and visitors.[3]

Shortly after the Kansas City, Ozarks & Southern Railway opened in 1910 between the Missouri communities of Mansfield and Ava, the road's first major excursion took place. Although merry riders wore their "Sunday best," many passengers were forced to make the trip standing in a flatcar or a gondola borrowed from the connecting Frisco Railway. *Courtesy of John F. Bradbury Collection.*

The celebration that came with gaining a railroad might involve a ceremonial spike, a free meal, or other festivities. In the case of the completion of the fourteen-mile Hooppole, Yorktown & Tampico Railway in 1909, a gala fete featuring food and drink commemorated the opening of the line from the heretofore isolated western Illinois communities of Hooppole and Yorktown to Tampico, which the Chicago, Burlington & Quincy (Burlington) served. "The program called for a gold spike to be driven by [Mayor] John Daley of Hooppole," noted a writer in 1940. "Thrifty tillers of the soil resented the use of a trinket so costly as a gold spike, and when the celebration began, they were vastly relieved to find it was only a bit of rusty iron covered with gilt." But a "golden spike" it was for happy farmers and villagers. At last area residents had their railroad.[4]

In the formative years of the twentieth century, many Americans may have thought that the national railroad map had finally jelled. Still, there were those citizens who believed that there was insufficient trackage. Unlike Europe, where in 1900 there were about 2,200 inhabitants to every mile of railroad, in the United States there were only 392, even though mileage had exploded after the Civil War, especially during the 1880s. On the eve of the war, mileage stood at 30,626. It reached 52,922 by 1870, climbed to 93,267 a decade later, and then soared to 163,597 miles in 1890. Building continued, but not at such a blistering pace. By 1900 the country had a network of 193,346 miles of steel rails and five years later it had grown to 218,101 miles. Construction then spiked in 1906: "More miles of railway have been constructed in the United States during the year 1906 than have been built during any year since the wonderful era of railway construction in the later eighties." Then in 1916 the network peaked with a cobweb of 254,037 miles. Between 1905 and 1916, and even until the Great Depression of the 1930s, a significant amount of construction occurred in the Great Plains and farther west and also in the South. Nationally, these additions consisted of trackage installed by major carriers as "stems," "cutoffs," and "feeders"; independent short lines; and the occasional terminal switching road. Examples abound. In 1911 the Minneapolis, St. Paul & Sault Ste. Marie Railroad (Soo Line) finished a seventy-three-mile link between the Wisconsin communities of Boylston, south of Superior, and Frederick, northeast of St. Paul, Minnesota. This addition forged the shortest route between the Twin Cities and the Twin Ports of Lake Superior, allowing the Soo to compete favorably with the Chicago, St. Paul, Minneapolis & Omaha (Omaha Road); Great Northern; and Northern Pacific railroads. Or consider the final major addition to the steam railroad mileage in Indiana. In 1918 the Indianapolis & Frankfort Railroad, an affiliate of the mighty Pennsylvania Railroad, completed a forty-one-mile line between Frankfort and Ben

Davis that gave its parent company access to Indianapolis from the north. This was also an active time for major roads to add stretches of second, even third or fourth, track to their primary lines.[5]

Not to be ignored was the "splendid optimism" about railroad construction that prevailed during the early part of the twentieth century. The comments made in 1907 by former Iowa governor William Larabee were widely quoted: "No railroad had ever been built whose earnings were not greater than estimated before the road was built." While a farfetched statement, the Larabee opinion was commonly held. Enthusiasts should have considered the more balanced remarks made a few years later by the Public Service Commission of Ohio: "The railroad and public-utility business of the country presents all phases of growth and development, ranging from the embryonic enterprise of doubtful expedience and uncertain success to enterprises which are so wisely conceived, so firmly established and so judiciously managed as to furnish, in their securities, investments almost as safe and more remunerative than Government obligations."[6]

Early in the twentieth century, the highly developed Midwest still encountered dedicated railroad promoters and active civic boosters. Between 1900 and 1920, mileage rose in the eight-state region from 64,010 to 71,633. Although hardly a breathtaking expansion, the construction allowed some rail-starved communities to end their isolation. Arguably, mileage might have been far greater had not the electric interurban craze swept the region, especially in Ohio, Indiana, and Illinois. During this period, midwesterners experienced the spectacular increase of this recently perfected transportation alternative, resulting in a somewhat unconnected grid of 8,081 miles. Remarkably, this total was more than half of all interurban mileage built in the nation. For some places "these latest harbingers of a higher state of civilization" solved any shortcomings of the then existing patterns of steam railroads. "If your town had been left out or stuck on a branch line, you had another chance with the trolley."[7]

The public saw the interurbans providing additional benefits. Passenger travel was clean, avoiding the nuisance of smoke, soot, and cinders. Also, farmers did not need to fear hot embers from passing steam engines setting their fields, pastures, or wood lots ablaze. Unlike several railroads in the West, midwestern carriers used spark-producing coal rather than oil to fuel their locomotives. Then there was the matter of noise. When racing across the countryside, steam locomotives clanked against the rails, but interurban cars, resembling earlier canal boats, were virtually noiseless. Relating to service, electric roads typically dispatched cars more frequently than their steam counterparts, and at speeds as great as, or greater than, trunk roads offered on their branch and secondary lines. Patrons liked that cars stopped almost everywhere, and fares were commonly lower. For individuals who wanted better delivery times for package and less-than-carload freight shipments, interurbans made a real difference. In 1908 an Indiana journalist noted that in Lebanon, which a few years earlier had received an electric line, "the rapid service of the traction 'express' allowed the furniture dealer to sell chairs with the same certainty of delivery as though he had them in his own stock room." Interurbans also bolstered land prices. "Real estate along electric lines in northern Ohio has nearly doubled in value since they were built," observed a businessman from Oberlin, Ohio, in 1913, "and the first question a prospective buyer of a farm asks is, 'Haw [*sic*] far is it from an electric line?'" Interurbans provided perceived advantages for managers and investors, including less maintenance on motive power, and the sale of excess electricity to commercial and residential customers.[8]

Whether a steam or electric railroad was built, arguments for construction during the twilight years were usually the same. Individuals wanted to reduce their isolation and combat the tyranny of distance, longing to "bring a market to every man's door." Citizens had already enthusiastically adopted the telegraph and telephone, communication technologies that had done much to annihilate time and space. Although improvements had been made in road-building machinery, materials, and practices, public thoroughfares often remained wanting, especially during the "mud season." Highways usually lacked any sort of hard surface and in wet periods were veritable mud holes. Out of the national network of 2.2 million miles of roads prior to World War I about two million miles consisted of dirt construction. The Midwest had the dubious reputation of being the center of the "mud road states." Iowa, for one, early in the twentieth century had less than 2 percent of its 102,000 miles of public roads improved with broken stone or gravel. "This week a farmer WALKED 4 miles to town with a basket of produce," commented a Hawkeye State editor in 1909. "This week a farmer's wife drove to town with her butter, and most everybody in town heard of it because it was about the only country butter received here the past week." The reason why these occurrences were remarkable was simple: "Verily, the bad roads have well nigh cut off the country from the town, and the town from the country." Then there were railroad customers that wanted to unsnarl the freight congestion in urban centers. A new steam or electrified heavy-duty belt road could create a more efficient flow of traffic, reducing costs and shipping headaches.[9]

As the twentieth century developed, rails continued to benefit most everyone. Support for additional lines involved not just the anticipation of better transportation facilities. One Iowan expected more: "Larger population, cheaper fuel, railway competition and inducements to factories to come and locate here." And a new railroad "will help our churches, our schools, all our present industries, our stores and hotels." Interestingly, there was no widespread feeling that a railroad would be a *negative* force, a quasi-public entity likely to commit acts of corporate arrogance. This contradicts the observation made by historian Michael Kammen that by this time "the railroad shifted from being a symbol of dramatic and unimagined progress to representing abusive and regressive economic power."[10]

Unsurprisingly rail-building proposals, large and small, persisted. Few citizens were shocked when they read about gigantic projects; in fact, some wacky proposals developed in the region and elsewhere in the nation. Immediately before the outbreak of World War I, the grandest of all twilight-era schemes received considerable ink, namely the Pan American Railway that would stretch from Alaska down to the tip of South America. The length would be nearly thirteen thousand miles and the cost more than $300 million ($6.3 billion in 2008 dollars). The route, though, would use about seven thousand miles of existing steam lines. Through sleepers between Nome and Cape Horn, of course, never appeared or were really wanted. A much shorter, yet nevertheless grandiose project involved the Chicago-New York Electric Air Line Railroad. On September 1, 1906, backers celebrated the turning of the first dirt for a double-track interurban designed to be built *directly* between the Windy City and Gotham with no grade crossings with other railroads, no gradients of more than .5 percent and with minimal track curvature. Once completed, the company planned to dispatch frequent, high-speed, electric-powered trains for a ten-hour trip that would cost passengers just ten dollars. But the Air Line sputtered, building by 1912 only twenty miles on the La Porte Division in northern Indiana and not the 742 miles announced.[11]

Nevertheless, during these final years of major construction, spectacular railroad undertakings were completed. Much was made of the Pacific Coast Extension of the Chicago, Milwaukee & St. Paul Railway (Milwaukee Road). Under the corporate banners of several subsidiary companies, the Milwaukee Road built a 1,400-mile line between South Dakota and Washington that opened officially on May 14, 1909, and cost a whopping $234 million ($5.5 billion in 2008 dollars). The line featured breathtaking bridges and long tunnels as it crossed four mountain ranges—the Belts, Rockies, Bitter Roots and Cascades—on the way to deep water. Much shorter but still expensive was the 156-mile, $30 million ($661 million in 2008 dollars) Key West Extension of the Florida East Coast Railway between Miami and Key West, spearheaded by oil titan Henry Morrison Flagler. The construction of this line that "went to sea" involved challenging bridge, fill, and embankment construction. When

ELECTRIC RAILWAY JOURNAL.

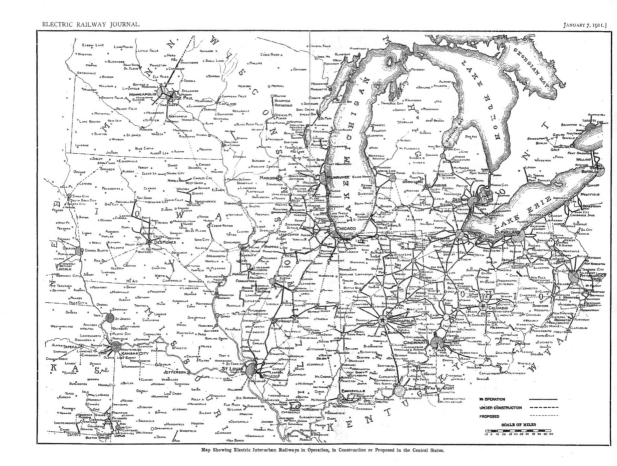

Map Showing Electric Interurban Railways in Operation, in Construction or Proposed in the Central States.

The extent of electric railway operation, construction, and proposed construction in the Midwest is displayed in this map that appeared in the *Electric Railway Journal* on January 7, 1911. Although the map contains errors, the Creston, Winterset & Des Moines is shown as being proposed between Creston and Winterset, Iowa, and the St. Joseph Valley in Indiana is marked as partially completed.

it opened on January 22, 1912, commentators considered this "impossible" project or "Flagler's Folly" to be one of the greatest engineering achievements of the modern era. Opined *Scientific America*, "[it is] one of the most difficult works of railroad construction ever attempted."[12]

Lunatic fringe or sensible, a conundrum of sorts existed for promoters of these latter-day railroads. Should tried-and-true and ever-improving steam locomotive technology be selected or should electricity become the power source? A lively debate ensued. "The electric engineer contends that the steam locomotive, with all its history and magnificence, is destined to be consigned to the scrap heap. The steam railroad superintendent of motive power insists that steam operation is best for long hauls." Yet this was really not a critical matter for most steam roads, although in 1912 the Milwaukee Road selected electric power or "heavy traction" for hundreds of miles of its recently finished Pacific Coast Extension. Admittedly, some carriers faced public pressure to retire their smoky, noisy engines in urban locales, and this sentiment led to scattered electrification of commuter lines and terminals. As time passed, railroads could also choose "wireless traction," specifically, recently introduced gasoline-powered motor cars for passenger and freight runs, and even battery-propelled passenger units. It would be during this time that some steam short lines electrified, making them bona fide interurbans. There were other roads, including some that were new, that seriously contemplated this latest propulsion technology.[13]

In these midwestern studies of twilight carriers, five of the eight roads considered electric power: Akron, Canton & Youngstown; Creston, Winterset & Des Moines; Electric Short Line; Ozark Short Line; and St. Joseph Valley. This simply had *not* been an option for roads contemplated or built prior to the end of the nineteenth century. Only the St. Joseph Valley embraced the cutting-edge technology, and it electrified just a small segment of its completed line. Still, several roads, including the St. Joseph Valley, utilized gasoline motor cars, although they depended on steam for freight operations and occasionally as a backup for passenger movements. The Electric Short Line

N. Side Square
Plymouth O.

Throughout the Midwest, communities during the final years of railroad construction welcomed electric interurbans. In 1904 well-wishers gathered on the public square in Plymouth, Ohio, to see the arrival of the first electric car on the seventeen-mile Sandusky, Norwalk & Mansfield Electric Railway. Later this company extended its trackage eight miles south to Shelby.

The railroad corridor of a twilight-era short line might slice through an existing community. A photographer captured the recently laid rails of the Chicago, DeKalb & Rockford Electric Traction Company (later Chicago, Aurora & DeKalb Railroad) in the farming village of Maple Park, Illinois, circa 1907. A few years later the owners managed to electrify this line between Aurora and DeKalb. *Courtesy of Embree Collection, Regional History Center, Northern Illinois University.*

was somewhat different, using gasoline units in freight service along with steam. The reason most commonly reported for rejecting electricity was the cost. In 1909 the contractor told sponsors of the Iowa & Southwestern that the price tag for an interurban that could handle freight equipment suitable for steam–road interchange was about $75,000 ($1.7 million in 2008 dollars) more than for acquiring two small, secondhand steam locomotives. Since the backers had struggled to raise the $345,000 ($8.1 million in 2008 dollars) to build their little road, the additional amount, in their minds, was prohibitive, preventing the service that they so desperately wanted.[14]

This debate over propulsion provided opportunities for promoters to embrace innovation. An outstanding illustration comes from the career of Herbert Bucklen, who literally built the St. Joseph Valley and made every important decision. Here was a man who had revealed his eagerness to try new ways, whether it was a drugstore soda fountain in the 1860s or a battery-powered rail motor car in the 1910s. After all, the twilight years were a time of technological marvels and new railroads could become demonstration places.

As was the case with the general development of the nation's rail network, there was no master plan for construction during this final wave of building. Where holes existed in the railroad map, efforts to undertake a project were most likely to occur, and the mileage involved was often relatively small. If service in a particular area was poor, inconvenient, or expensive, building a competing line might seem desirable. When a strategy existed, it involved managing mushrooming freight and passenger congestion, not for an integrated network of railroads but for an individual carrier. The period before World War I saw the rebuilding of portions of the infrastructure, mostly main stems and terminals. Capacity limitations had become so acute that in 1907 an officer of the Car Service Association told his associates that "the truth of the matter is the railroads of the United States are simply swamped with business that no power on earth can remedy outside of natural conditions. The legislature and congress cannot do it, neither can any one man. There must be greater terminal facilities, more cars and a patient public."[15]

The nature of twilight railroads varied greatly; no single type dominated. In reality these carriers were no different from previous enterprises, a phenomenon demonstrated in the case studies. Two of these roads, Ettrick & Northern and the Ozark Short Line, were designed to connect inland areas with a rail outlet. Two other short lines, Creston, Winterset & Des Moines and the Electric Short Line, claimed the same function, but sought to provide connections at either end. Another two, namely the Detroit, Bay City & Western and St. Joseph Valley, fit the category of actual or would-be links in a regional or inter-regional steam or electric railroad network. They were longer than average short lines, although they fed heavily on local traffic. The Illinois, Iowa & Minnesota, later the Chicago, Milwaukee & Gary, was intended to be an extensive interstate belt line, a road that was expected to relieve freight congestion in greater Chicago. Still another twilight carrier, the Akron, Canton & Youngstown, was created to serve several industrial customers. In time, though, this urban switching operation evolved into a strategic link in the rail grid of the Midwest through control of a much longer connecting steam road.

The financing of these twilight-era carriers was likewise diverse, just as the sources of capital had varied for earlier railroad projects. As in the past, predominately rural carriers relied on local tax subsidies to provide direct aid, and on farmers and town dwellers to donate land for rights-of-way, stations, and other purposes. In some instances these individuals joined in the actual building process, contributing their labor, animals, and equipment; after all, a railroad meant convenience, growth, and prosperity. This attitude, according to one midwesterner in 1911, was a pronounced departure from the past.

Before the Chicago, Aurora & DeKalb Railroad became a bona fide interurban in 1909, the company employed a vintage 4-4-0 American Standard steam locomotive and a wooden passenger and baggage car, or "combine," for service between Aurora and DeKalb. The crew of a mixed train, with its lone revenue stock car, rests on a village street in Kanesville, Illinois. *Courtesy of Embree Collection, Regional History Center, Northern Illinois University.*

"How I remember what a howl went up when they came along surveying a railroad. Last year I happened to have some interest in surveying a right of way through our country, and I noticed the great change. Farmers were willing to make all kinds of concessions to get a road through a little closer to them. Not many years ago to secure a right of way meant a fight, both in the courts and with fists, but now it can be had almost for the asking." More urban-based roads, though, might receive little or no direct financial assistance from the public, as in the case of the Akron, Canton & Youngstown, whose backers raised their own funds for real-estate and construction expenditures. Whether rural or urban, a variety of people, who were usually within the projected service territory, bought stock, either as an investment or as a demonstration of support. Some investors surely felt the power of peer pressure to make financial commitments, just as many Americans would be persuaded during World War I to participate in Liberty Loan drives. Bonds were more likely to be sold in major financial markets. Almost always an investment house or bank became involved, and these institutions might well have connections in Europe, especially Great Britain and Holland. Although foreign outlets mostly disappeared with the outbreak of war in 1914, private financial institutions continued to fund capital needs up to the start of the Great Depression. The village or farmer railroad, however, might struggle to place its bonds; the market for securities in small roads was limited and considered speculative. Also, competing carriers might thwart the financing of what they viewed as nuisance roads. The Creston, Winterset & Des Moines, for one, encountered this hostility from both the powerful Burlington and Rock Island railroads. Indeed, such opposition occurred nationwide. As the *Catskill Mountain News* said in early 1907 of the recently opened Schenectady & Margaretville Railroad, "It takes no small amount of determination and indomitable courage to carry on a contest for the right of way, charters, etc., for a new line of railroad at the present time, for there are nearly always concerns in existence that will fight the project to the last ditch." Luckily, twilight rail construction took place in a time of relative prosperity, years that coincided with a positive economic cycle. Except for the Panic of 1907, which temporarily depressed the money market, confidence prevailed. Factories, mines, and businesses bustled; communities thrived; and urban dwellers acquired homes, modern appliances, and fashionable clothing. Their rural neighbors purchased land, replaced barns, and bought farm equipment. And they all might have invested in railroads.[16]

Also replicating earlier railroad endeavors, the leadership role varied. Some twilight carriers, usually the smallest, were products of community nurturing. Both the Creston, Winterset & Des Moines and the Ettrick &

Northern might best be described as "farmers'" roads. The vast majority of other projects depended heavily on the business skills of a handful of individuals. Such were the experiences of the Akron, Canton & Youngstown; Detroit, Bay City & Western; Electric Short Line; Ozark Short Line; and the St. Joseph Valley. No wonder the Detroit, Bay City & Western became known as the "Handy Line," after the four Handy brothers who built the road, and the Electric Short Line was quickly dubbed the "Luce Line" that recognized founders William Luce and his son Erle. The Rockford Route, though, had over time a more extensive executive and investment base and never really became strongly identified with one or two men.

Proponents of twilight-era schemes often thought that their endeavors were the last best hopes for their communities to obtain rail service. At times this sense of urgency and inexperience in railroad matters could lead to flawed management, dooming a paper project or a completed road. When a Chicago consultant examined the faltering Iowa & Southwestern in early 1915, he found troubling that the "records have been very poorly kept—in fact, most of them have been lost." But that was only part of the story. "The road is utterly lacking in organization, the only paid official being the agent at Clarinda, who is also the auditor." The company, too, did not employ a roadmaster to administer the physical plant. "It is very wasteful to operate the property without supervision as at present, for it is inconceivable that it can be so operated without incurring a loss more than sufficient to secure and pay for competent oversight." Moreover, the local owners had failed to exploit potential customers in Clarinda, losing an estimated 2,000 cars annually to the Burlington, its only competitor. The Iowa & Southwestern did not pay much heed to the report, likely explaining why the road folded two years after a failed reorganization in 1916.[17]

As in the past, the material quality of these new roads differed. A minority of them, such as the Akron, Canton & Youngstown, were built to demanding specifications and owned modern equipment. Others hardly possessed "Class 1" qualities, having at best branch line characteristics with well-worn rolling stock and track components. Evidence suggests that the traveling public might opt for the larger, older, and better roads whenever possible. Take the case of a Clarinda, Iowa, newspaper man, who in September 1913 journeyed to a meeting of the Western Iowa Editorial Association held in Atlantic. "On an Iowa map Atlantic is shown to be about forty-five miles north of Clarinda. There ought to be a way of getting between the two cities with a railroad ride of an hour and a half." Unfortunately that was not the case. This traveler decided to use a secondary main line train of the Burlington from Clarinda to Shenandoah and then a branch line local to Red Oak and still another

This badly constructed earthen fill near Blanchard, Iowa, known as Arnold's Cut, and the track structure outside College Springs, Iowa, belonged to the 17.5-mile Iowa & Southwestern Railway, a railroad proposed as an interurban but built as a steam road. These photographs attest to the poor quality standards often used by twilight short lines. The images date from early 1915; three years later the railroad called it quits. *Courtesy of John W. Barriger III, National Railroad Library.*

branch line train to Griswold where a transfer could be made to a Rock Island accommodation for Atlantic. This itinerary would consume most of a day. However, there was an obvious option; the recently opened Atlantic Northern & Southern Railroad from Villisca to Atlantic could be easily reached by using a Burlington branch line from Clarinda to Villisca. "Yet one hesitates to take the Villisca–Atlantic road for fear it will take longer to make the trip that way than by Red Oak."[18]

While similarities exist between the newly launched railroads and those carriers that appeared in earlier decades, an important difference stands out. Historian Albro Martin considered this twilight period as a time of "enterprise denied" for the railroad industry. The most troubling legislation for carriers involved the Hepburn Act of 1906 that empowered the Interstate Commerce Commission (ICC) to set rates upon complaints from shippers, and the still stronger Mann-Elkins Act of 1910 that required proposed rate increases to be approved by the ICC before going into effect. But Martin's carefully argued interpretation comes with qualifications. There is no question that progressive politicians, who sought to conduct a major house cleaning of the business world, significantly strengthened the ICC and most state railroad oversight bodies. If there was an epicenter for progressivism, it covered much of the Midwest, with Iowa, Minnesota, and Wisconsin being banner states. Builders of nearly all of these latter-day carriers studied, however, did not openly condemn the maturing regulatory process. More likely the opposite occurred. After all, at times there was no love affair between upstart and established carriers, and regulators might be asked by these twilight roads to address real grievances that carried important economic consequences. Commonly at issue were matters of freight rate divisions and reciprocal switching rights. Fortunately the ICC and state railroad commissions could offer a helping hand. Unhappiness with government officials more likely came about after Congress and President Woodrow Wilson agreed in late 1917 to "federalize" most steam railroads and strategic interurbans. Direct involvement by the national government was due to wartime problems of congestion, inefficiency, and carrier rivalries. Representatives of the United States Railroad Administration, who directed railroad policies until early 1920, could cause mischief, making decisions that especially hurt newer, less established roads.[19]

The regulatory climate before 1935 did not block a twilight road from becoming "intermodal." As with some much larger and wealthier railroads, a twilight carrier might take advantage of the growing utility of the intercity motor bus and truck. While it was not common for steam short lines of the 1920s and later to operate bus affiliates, the Minnesota Western—the reorganized Electric Short Line—acquired a small fleet of modern buses that management believed would enhance passenger revenues through connecting integrated highway operations. Similarly the company provided less-than-truckload pickup and delivery service. Since the railroad had stalled on the western Minnesota prairie, buses and trucks, it was thought, could conveniently and inexpensively tap nearby communities without laying rails.

What became a distinguishing and historically significant feature of twilight railroads was the economic development they spawned. Some writers have dismissed the least successful carriers as being silly, impractical endeavors, particularly critical of promoters who pushed for construction as the industry started to wane. Yet even the least successful road, whether the Creston, Winterset and Des Moines or the St. Joseph Valley, improved the economic health of the area that it served. Unmistakably, the actual construction phase pumped money into local economies, including the purchase of supplies and payment of wages. The excitement of the coming of the flanged wheel often caused residents to expand existing businesses or to launch new endeavors. Repeatedly, land values rose and the sale of town lots and houses increased. Even the unbuilt Ozark Short Line triggered a wave of real-estate speculation. "The railroad is coming" was often repeated in newspaper advertisements, and readers felt a sense of unbounded optimism when they contemplated this potentially powerful economic stimulant. Once a road opened, much happened. Bay City, Michigan, merchants and professionals, for example, increased their sphere of activity when passenger trains of the Handy Line brought customers from outlying areas of the Thumb Country. Similarly, farmers reaped the financial rewards of ready access to the best markets, whether it was shipments of cattle and hogs from Ettrick, Wisconsin, over the Ettrick & Northern, to slaughter houses in Chicago, or cans of milk and cream that the Electric Short Line picked up for delivery to dairies in Minneapolis. No wonder twilight railroads were honored and not vilified.

These twilight rails left positive marks. This cheery statement even fits roads that quit after only a few years. Even in a complete shutdown, viable pieces of trackage, if only short segments or sidings in places where there had been a competitor, likely remained active. If investors lost money, there had been those original gains for numerous communities. Fortunately, a majority of the eight roads in this study lasted for relatively long periods and one, the Akron, Canton & Youngstown, proved to be a moneymaking machine. A parallel story described the Port Huron & Detroit, a component of the failed Detroit, Bay City & Western. The viability of several twilight railroads was seen when major carriers took control: Chessie System with the Port Huron & Detroit; Milwaukee Road with the Chicago, Milwaukee & Gary; Minneapolis & St. Louis with the Minnesota Western; Norfolk & Western with the Akron, Canton & Youngstown.

Within the larger context of change, twilight rails appeared when another transportation revolution took hold. Just as progress occurred with road construction, vehicles improved. Until World War I, horse-drawn wagons and carts dominated the hauling of short-distance freight, but then motor trucks started to appear in sizable numbers. Owners benefited from better engines, transmissions, and tires. And a variety of manufacturers entered an expanding market. In 1918 the Ford Motor Company took out advertisements in the Midwest with this message: "Mr. Farmer! How Does This Look to You? A Ford 1 ton truck complete with body, cab, and wind shield." The copy continued, "This body will hold 80 bu. wheat. Very practical. IT'S JUST WHAT YOU NEED." But automobiles made more advances, rapidly replacing the horse and buggy and other conveyances. By this time these personal internal combustion vehicles were no longer playthings of the rich. The Model T, which Ford introduced in 1908, was a dependable car costing slightly more than $800, that enabled most middle-class purchasers to take to the road. By 1916 Model T production had soared, and prices had dropped to $360 for the touring car and only $345 for the runabout. By 1927, when the last of more than fifteen million Model Ts rolled off the assembly line, a new Ford car cost as little as $290. This iconic American product ushered in the age of "autobilism" and "automobility."[20]

While the nature of intercity transportation was changing dramatically, advocates of twilight-era railroad projects scurried to complete the railway map of the Midwest, doing so with determination and much success. The following pages explore the motivations, accomplishments, and failures of representative latter-day carriers in the sprawling expanse of the nation's midsection. Their stories have been largely untold and, when recorded, have usually not been treated in a scholarly fashion.

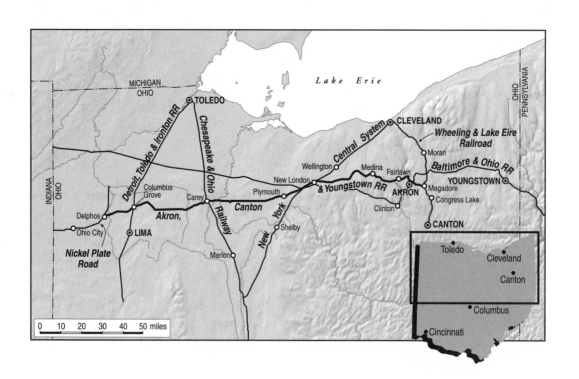

Chapter 1

A Road with a Bright Future: Akron, Canton & Youngstown Railroad

During the twilight years of railroad promotion and construction, projects emerged in the Midwest that were both urban- and rural-centered. The Akron, Canton & Youngstown Railroad (AC&Y), built in Ohio between 1911 and 1913, nicely represents the former category. Initially a seven-mile industrial road in Akron, with plans to reach the nearby cities of Canton and Youngstown, this company gained greater stature in 1920 when it took control of the 161-mile Northern Ohio Railway and became "a large factor in the movement of Akron's commerce." Until entering the orbit of the Norfolk & Western Railway (N&W) in 1964 as part of the "merger madness" that swept the railroad industry after 1960, the AC&Y became a profitable, customer-oriented freight hauler and an economic engine for the greater Akron community.[1]

Akron, the seat of Summit County, became the hub of the AC&Y, and for good reason. Dating from the mid-1820s, this dynamic city grew partly because of exceptional canal access. The 309-mile Ohio & Erie, or Ohio Canal, by 1832 connected Lake Erie at Cleveland with the Ohio River at West Portsmouth, and the eighty-two-mile Pennsylvania & Ohio, or Mahoning Canal, by 1840 extended from Akron through Youngstown to a tie in with the Pennsylvania canal network, the "State Works," at New Castle. The Akron economy likewise benefited from the two-mile Cascade Race, a hydraulic canal constructed in the early 1830s that powered mills in an era before the common use of stationary steam engines. By 1850 the two canal corridors supported an array of commercial enterprises that catered to the "ditch" trade, ranging from boat building and repair to hotels and dramshops. Without question, canal transport was a salient element in what historian George Rogers Taylor identified as the "transportation revolution" that swept much of the nation between 1815 and 1860. Akronites proclaimed their little metropolis to be the "Venice of the West," and relished the hum and clatter of their expanding industrial base. "[Akron] was a brisk young city of some 20,000 inhabitants," observed a Universalist minister who in 1873 made Akron his home, "enterprising in business, public spirited, large minded, up to date, and bound to win."[2]

Even though the iron horse reached Akron in 1851, the community continued to rely on the waterways, most of all the busy and more durable Ohio & Erie Canal. As late as the disastrous Easter weekend flood of 1913, boats laden with coal from mines in the Tuscarawas Valley to the south supplied fuel to Akron customers and also handled other bulk commodities economically. But canals were subject to freezing, which could cause closures during the coldest months, and they possessed other disadvantages: high maintenance costs, fluctuating water levels, and slow travel times.[3]

As a result, by 1890 three trunk roads dominated the transportation life of Akron and Summit County. The Cleveland, Akron & Columbus Railway (Pennsylvania System) connected the cities of its corporate name; Erie Lines (New York, Lake Erie & Western Railroad) with its main artery extending from Jersey City, New Jersey, to Chicago; and the Pittsburg & Western Railway (Baltimore & Ohio) that linked Pittsburgh with Akron. The latter had incorporated into its right-of-way portions of the abandoned Mahoning Canal. Within a year, the Baltimore & Ohio Railroad (B&O) enhanced its position when a subsidiary, the Akron & Chicago Junction Railroad, opened between Akron and Chicago Junction (later renamed Willard), Ohio, providing a better route between Baltimore, Pittsburgh, and Chicago.[4]

In that same year, a smaller road, the Pittsburg, Akron & Western Railroad (PA&W), entered Akron from the west. Sponsored by local capitalists, including farm machinery manufacturer Lewis Miller, the PA&W traversed some of Ohio's richest agricultural lands, but except for Akron, the road served no important community. Designed to connect the Pittsburg & Western and the Toledo, Delphos & Burlington (TD&B) railroads, the PA&W built slowly eastward from Delphos and on February 16, 1891, reached downtown Akron. Before the largely parallel Akron & Chicago Junction took shape, backers of the PA&W had contemplated a sale to the B&O, but they needed to reach

Chicago Junction, the eastern terminus of the B&O's Chicago Division. That did not happen and the west end remained at Delphos. Fortunately, rails to this community, which straddled the Allen and Van Wert county line, gave the PA&W a connection with the Toledo, St. Louis & Kansas City Railroad or "Clover Leaf Route" (née TD&B), and later the Nickel Plate Road, providing direct access to St. Louis. In 1895 the New York Central System gained control of the PA&W and reconstituted the property as the Northern Ohio Railway. Repeatedly announced plans to extend the road eastward to Youngstown and possibly beyond remained what an Akronite lamented as "that old, old statement."[5]

The decade of the 1890s also saw construction of a twenty-one-mile industrial road, the Barberton Belt Line Railroad (later Akron & Barberton Belt Railroad). Built by Ohio Columbus Barber, "the Diamond Match King," the Belt Line served his Barberton operations, immediately southwest of Akron, and tied in with area trunk routes. In 1901 the road opened a short extension to Belt Junction (Copley Junction), creating an interchange with the Northern Ohio, and a few years later the connecting roads bought out Barber.[6]

The electric interurban industry also made its presence known. Ohio

In the early 1890s an American standard-type steam locomotive of the Pittsburg, Akron & Western Railroad moves a "combine" across the high bridge over the Ohio & Erie Canal in downtown Akron. In time, the expansive Akron, Canton & Youngstown acquired this line, forging a strategic route across northern Ohio.

became the heartland for this alternative form of transportation, and by 1910 the northeast quadrant of the state featured a developed network of "juice" lines. In fact, the nation's first major intercity electric road, the Akron, Bedford & Cleveland Railroad, "The Alphabet Route," opened in 1895 between Akron and Cleveland and later became part of the Northern Ohio Traction & Light Company (NOT&L), one of the country's largest and most important interurbans. And throughout the formative years of the twentieth century, a wide range of traction lines were proposed but not built, including a heavy-duty interurban from Akron through Warren to Pittsburgh, and another from Canton to Youngstown "with a spur to Akron." Although this upstart transportation alternative concentrated on passenger service, considerable freight moved in specially designed rolling stock between Akron and points on the NOT&L and connecting roads.[7]

So seemingly complete was the transportation network that the *Akron Beacon Journal* bragged about what had taken place. "It is indeed doubtful if there is another city of less than 100,000 population in the entire country which can boast of transportation facilities as good," observed the newspaper in 1907. "The canal and railroads made Akron—the electric lines put the finishing touches to the job."[8]

The expansion of rail lines in greater Akron had made economic sense. Although the Panic of 1893 and the ensuing depression adversely affected this community of 27,000 residents, the city had developed a diverse industrial base, highlighted by cereal milling, clay products, farm machinery, iron foundries, publishing, and rubber. Once good times returned, Akron boomed. The population skyrocketed, reaching 69,067 in 1910 and an impressive 208,435 a decade later. "Akron's growth was almost magic," wrote a local historian in 1925. "It outgrew everything it owned, and in 1916 and 1917 some twenty to thirty thousand workmen came to the city."[9]

It would be the burgeoning rubber industry, which required substantial inbound cars of raw materials, generated high numbers of car loadings, and demanded a constant supply of coal for heat and power, that fueled excitement for railroad expansion. By 1905 several manufacturers, led by B. F. Goodrich Company, Diamond Rubber Company, Firestone Tire and Rubber Company, and Goodyear Tire and Rubber Company, made Akron their home. Collectively, these firms dominated the nation's production of tires and rubber products. "Of all the cities in the country Akron has shown the most rapid advancement in the rubber industry," crowed a local journalist in 1907. Between 1910 and 1915 tire manufacturers entered a period of dynamic growth, with the more than a dozen "gum mills" benefiting enormously. In 1910 a headline writer for the *Akron Beacon Journal* said it well: "Rubber

Industry the Bone and Sinew of Akron's Life," and the "Rubber City" became an appropriate nickname.[10]

Akron was not the only place in northeast Ohio that prospered. Cleveland, thirty-five miles to the north, served as the financial, commercial, and industrial capital. Between the 1860s and the 1920s, the "Forest City" swelled from 43,000 to nearly one million residents. Entrepreneurs took advantage of excellent water transport, followed by an expanding network of steam railroads and later a developing interurban system, to build a premier American metropolis. The presence of John D. Rockefeller's Standard Oil Company had a multiplier effect on the development of Cleveland, Cuyahoga County, and the region. By World War I the city's busy plants produced a myriad of products: automobiles, electrical equipment, machine tools, steel, and much more.[11]

Twenty miles south of Akron, Canton resembled its Summit County neighbor and during the early years of the twentieth century likewise flourished. Although the community, founded in 1805, missed being on the Ohio Canal and efforts to build a feeder canal failed, citizens profited from the fine rail service offered by the main line of the Pennsylvania (PRR). By 1910 this seat of Stark County, with a population of more than fifty thousand, also claimed the Wheeling & Lake Erie Railway (W&LE), providing direct access to Cleveland and Wheeling, West Virginia, and a branch of the B&O (former Valley Railway) that extended to Cleveland through Akron and served several small communities to the south. Cantonians had readily available interurban service with cars of the NOT&L and Stark Electric Railroad. The former juice road operated north to Akron and Cleveland, south to New Philadelphia and Uhrichsville, and west to Massillon; the latter ran east to Alliance and Salem with traction connections to East Liverpool and Youngstown.[12]

By 1910 Canton boasted a mixed industrial base. Important employers were the Dueber-Hampden Watch Company, Diebold Safe and Lock Company, Timken Roller Bearing Axle Company, and several large brick, tile, and stoneware works. Extensive deposits of high-quality clay and shale in the immediate vicinity allowed for expansion of an industry that required rail transport. The "Tip-Top City" proudly bragged of being the "Paving Brick Capital of the World."[13]

While Akron would become famous for tires and Canton for bricks, Youngstown, fifty miles east of Akron, became best known for iron and steel. Although settled at the end of the eighteenth century, Youngstown did not spring to life until the 1840s with the completion of the Mahoning Canal, and the construction of the first iron blast furnace. By the Civil War era Youngstown's iron industry, stimulated by adjacent coal fields and the coming of the rails, helped the Mahoning County seat to reach a population of about five thousand. But the great shot in the arm for the economy occurred toward the end of the century when the burgeoning steel industry took hold. By 1910 the Ohio Works of the United States Steel Corporation and Youngstown Sheet and Tube Company dominated metal production in the Mahoning Valley. Other manufacturing concerns also thrived in Youngstown and nearby East Youngstown, Girard, Niles, Struthers, and Warren. Within the first two decades of the twentieth century, the population of Youngstown soared from 44,805 (1900) to 79,066 (1910) and then to 132,358 (1920). It was a time of "luxuriant growth," but nevertheless, outsiders rightly called Youngstown the "Dirty City."[14]

Good transportation helped to drive Youngstown's expansion. By 1910 residents could patronize the main lines of the B&O, Erie and Pittsburgh & Lake Erie (New York Central System), the Cleveland lines of the Erie and PRR, and a branch of the Lake Shore & Michigan Southern (New York Central System). Interurban cars were also easily accessible. The Youngstown & Southern Railway, a sixteen-mile steam road that opened in 1904 between Youngstown and Columbiana and electrified three years later, was extended a few miles farther to Leetonia where it met the Youngstown & Ohio River Railroad, an interurban that ran between Salem (including a connection with the Stark Electric) and East Liverpool. Somewhat earlier Youngstown gained the services of the Mahoning and Shenango Railway and Light Company that operated a network of electric lines to surrounding communities in both Ohio and Pennsylvania.[15]

Understandably, railroad promoters, whether steam or electric, eyed the explosive growth of the Akron, Cleveland, Canton, and Youngstown areas. In their minds the railroad map could expand; profitable rail-building opportunities remained even in an environment of increasing regulation and emerging modal competition. The more smoke poured into the skies, the greater the need for railroads.

One individual who grasped the possibilities for enhanced rail service in northeast Ohio was Charles W. French. This ambitious farm boy from Huron County, Ohio, developed a knowledge of explosives and found employment blasting limestone in nearby quarries. In time he launched his own stone company in Richland County and made Mansfield the center of his business activities. Early on French displayed a remarkable ability to attract investors to his projects.[16]

This quarry operator entered the railroad business in a modest fashion. To serve his rock business, French organized the Northwestern & Monroe Railroad. This tiny (less than one mile) tap line had to rely on borrowed equipment from the PRR, its sole interchange partner. Conflict with the PRR, including French's alleged theft of a locomotive, and the onset of the depression of the 1890s caused financial reversals. Troubles followed, ending "in a mass of legal entanglements with most of French's investors losing thousands of dollars." Yet this indefatigable promoter turned to bigger schemes, although his railroad activities would remain mostly paper propositions.[17]

As the economy revived in 1897, French organized the Mansfield Short Line Railroad. Undeniably a man with a hunch, he realized that Mansfielders, who enjoyed main line service of the Erie and PRR, wanted improved passenger and freight connections to Cleveland and Columbus. A solution would be to build the dozen or so miles between Mansfield and Shelby, forging a connection with the Cleveland, Chicago, Cincinnati & St. Louis or "Big Four" Railroad, part of the Vanderbilt system or New York Central System. The smooth-talking French suggested that this little carrier would eventually become part of a much larger railroad. Although some grading occurred, investors expressed their unhappiness with the slow pace and sought unsuccessfully to oust French from control.[18]

French thought big in an attempt to save the Mansfield Short Line. In 1898 he announced creation of the Richland & Mahoning Railroad. If enough capital could be raised, he could attach the Shelby line to a route projected to extend eastward from Mansfield through Wooster and Canton to Youngstown, a distance of approximately 125 miles. For the next two years French toiled to make the R&M a reality. This beguiling entrepreneur suggested that he had the Vanderbilts' approval, implying that he was really their stalking horse. But the R&M project fizzled and so French returned to the Mansfield Short Line. In 1900 more grading took place between Mansfield and Shelby, yet not a rail was laid.[19]

Not to be defeated, French employed a new tactic. The Mansfield Short Line would be placed, along with another paper project, the Shelby & New Washington Railroad, into a holding company, grandiosely named the Chicago Short Line Railroad (CSL) and bonded for more than $2.6 million ($66 million in 2008 dollars). Yet he had not forgotten the stillborn Richland & Mahoning. That company would be reorganized and its building strategy altered: there would be the originally proposed route between Mansfield and Youngstown, the "Southern Division," and another line from Youngstown to Akron, the "Northern Division," that would extend westward from Youngstown through the Mahoning valley "on the company's own rails or those of leased lines . . . [following] the Mahoning river to Niles and passing through the manufacturing district, thence in an air line [direct route] to Akron."[20]

The Northern Division would not need to be built totally afresh in the Rubber City. The plan was to incorporate into the project the moribund

Akron & New Castle Railway (A&NC). In the early 1890s, capitalists, aligned with the PA&W, had sought to build from Akron to the industrial Mahoning and neighboring Shenango valleys, described at the time as "a region which for originating an immense volume of freight traffic is one of the first rank in the world." But the assets of the ill-fated A&NC were modest: a charter, less than two miles of track in Akron (then leased by the Akron Transfer Railway and operated by the Northern Ohio), and an assortment of right-of-way options in the Akron vicinity.[21]

French and his business associates continued to scheme, seek more investors, and keep reporters busy with pronouncements. "The Richmond & Mahoning company," observed an Akron newspaper, "is looming up on the railroad horizon as a giant that intends to seize its share of the business in its territory and as much more as it can get." The success of the Northern Division of the Richland & Mahoning, in the promoters' minds, depended on a belt line that could serve the lively manufacturing district along the Little Cuyahoga River on the east side of Akron.[22]

Yet the quest for Akron trackage and the greater Richland & Mahoning turned to dross. Since French appeared to be mostly talk and little substance—"improbable schemes" as an Akron editor put it—some potential shippers in Akron considered their own plans to enhance rail service. Frank A. Seiberling, being "a man of enormous energy," became a leading proponent. In 1898 Seiberling and his brother Charles had started Goodyear Tire and Rubber Company by converting an old strawboard factory on the industrial eastside into a rubber shop. Although the glory days for Seiberling, Goodyear, and Akron were in the future, the infant company grew rapidly, exploiting the market for tires that an expanding automobile industry provided.[23]

Apparently the future tire king did not trust the French people and rejected the plans of the Richland & Mahoning, or more specifically, the affiliated Akron South Side Belt Line Railway. In April 1901 a fight erupted between Seiberling and French over the real-estate assets of the ill-fated Akron & New Castle. Both men wanted this strategic property. "We will fight them to the last ditch for we mean to have the [David P.] Reighard right-of-way [Akron & New Castle] or know why," an agitated Seiberling told the press. "The R&M can enter Akron over some other [right-of-way] if they want to, that doesn't concern us, but we intend to have the Reighard Line. We have our surveys already made." The wrangling continued, even though Seiberling offered the Richland & Mahoning trackage rights. French refused. In the subsequent months Seiberling and other Akron associates organized the Akron Terminal Railroad, designed "to reach the manufacturing industries in the Old Forge and East Akron localities," but like French's company, the railroad remained a paper entity. Even though French announced additional plans for Summit County, he backed off temporarily and concentrated on the Southern Division of his stalled Richland & Mahoning.[24]

Still, Charlie French had not abandoned Akron, a city whose prosperity seemed unlimited. Surely he sensed that residents did not care for what a local businessmen's group called "the arrogance of the Central Traffic Association which has a stranglehold on area freight and passenger rates and services." And there were repeated complaints about freight delivery times, "as they are at present very slow, sometimes weeks behind." In 1902 French appeared intent on connecting local industries, dominated by clay and rubber, with the Wheeling & Lake Erie at Mogadore, located about seven miles east of Akron. The 430-mile W&LE ran between Toledo, Ohio, and Wheeling, West Virginia, and had several appendages, including secondary lines to Cleveland and Zanesville. Recently, the railroad had fallen into the hands of George Gould, son of the late railroad tycoon Jay Gould, and the property became an essential element in the plans for Gould's Wabash Railroad to reach Pittsburgh from the West. It seemed probable that the W&LE would become a link in Gould's efforts to forge the first-ever transcontinental system.[25]

Although French announced that railroad building between Akron and Mogadore would commence in early 1903, little happened, in part because of land acquisition and money problems. Instead he turned to restructuring his paper empire. Vital to his success, at least for raising investment capital, included his Chicago Short Line shell. French attracted some important backers, including Zebulon "Zeb" W. Davis, the well-to-do president of the Diamond Portland Cement Company, located near Canton, and Harry B. Stewart, a prominent Canton attorney. French seemed to be able to exploit the strong sentiment that favored another area network. In what railroad historian William S. Snyder has called "a maze of interconnected railroad companies," the CSL would be associated with still another scheme, the Lake & River Railway, a steam or electric road that would extend between the Ohio communities of Sandusky and Bellaire. French also planned to place the Northern Ohio, then in the hands of the Vanderbilts, into the CSL or what he immodestly called the "French Lines."[26]

Part of the strategy of the French group involved a small short line, the Ashland & Wooster Railroad (A&W). This twenty-mile pike ran between Ashland, seat of Ashland County, which only the Erie served, and Custaloga, a village in Wayne County. Originally chartered as the Millersburg, Jeromesville & Greenwich Railroad, the company soon changed its name and modified its objectives. Operations began in 1899 and the road contributed to "Ashland's boom and present prosperity." The investors, led by Horace (H. B.) Camp of Akron, wanted to switch Camp's clay products facility at Horace and to serve several "inland" communities. Then there was the feeling that the PRR, which the A&W met in Custaloga, might buy or lease the property.[27]

In 1903 the French group took control of the A&W. Although materially helped by Davis's resources, the A&W struggled, falling quickly into a receiver's hands. In June 1904 a reorganization occurred that changed the corporate name from the Ashland & Wooster Railroad to the Ashland & Western Railroad, and two years later another restructuring took place. While French claimed an association with the road, it would be Davis, Stewart, and other Cantonians who controlled the property. French subsequently left Ohio, going west to promote several ventures, most prominently the Pacific Steel Company. Then in 1908 he landed in jail for alleged business irregularities and later faced charges for mail fraud.[28]

By 1906 the Canton group, largely disassociated from French, wanted out of the Ashland & Western Railroad (which had become the Ashland & Western Railway). These investors realized that their road had to either expand or die and that a sale would be the prudent course of action. Although the PRR failed to make an offer, an acceptable proposal materialized. The buyers were led by Joseph Ramsey Jr., former chief executive of the Wabash, who had resigned in 1905 because of irreconcilable differences with George Gould. Attempting to regain momentum in his career, Ramsey took the presidency of the New York, Pittsburgh & Chicago Railroad, a high-density freight line projected to compete with the PRR between Gotham and the Windy City. Coinciding with that grandiose scheme, Ramsey pushed ahead with what would become another twilight venture, the Lorain, Ashland & Southern Railroad (LA&S), known as the "Ramsey Road." In late 1907 the Ashland & Western became a component of his LA&S. Ramsey planned to connect the burgeoning Lake Erie steel town of Lorain with either Bellaire on the Ohio River or a point in West Virginia to tap mostly outbound coal traffic. Ultimately the Ramsey Road reached Lorain, but Custaloga remained the southern terminus of this sixty-five-mile operation.[29]

Relieved of their A&W obligations, Davis and his Canton associates considered other railroad investment opportunities. Even though the French house of cards had collapsed, Akron remained a promising place for rail expansion. After the French assets were sold to Davis for $40,000 ($912,000 in 2008 dollars) in March 1907 by the U.S. Circuit Court in Cleveland, the Canton industrialist took charge of the remnants of the old Akron & New Castle, Akron Transfer, and Lake & River properties and hired a consulting firm to examine the area's transportation needs. The study made for good reading. "The increase of population and business and manufacturing importance of Akron has already reached a point where it is confidently believed this valuable property [A&NC], now lying idle, can, by the reasonable investment required to complete it, be made a factor in the further development of the city and suburbs and be converted into a successful business proposition."[30]

Notwithstanding the adverse impact of the Panic of 1907 that rocked the financial markets in March, Davis spearheaded the organization of the Akron, Canton & Youngstown Railroad, a company that on June 17, 1907, received a state charter. The provisions included an authorized capitalization of $15 million ($342 million in 2008 dollars) and authority to operate by either steam or electricity. The intent was more extensive than the final French plan for trackage only between Akron industries and the W&LE at Mogadore; the cities of the corporate name would be connected. But unlike what ultimately transpired, Davis called for an interurban, yet one capable of handling conventional freight equipment.[31]

Davis developed a financial plan designed to acquire the necessary land between downtown Akron and Mogadore which involved the sale of $200,000 ($4.5 million in 2008 dollars) of first mortgage bonds to the Cleveland Trust Company. Subsequently, surveying and engineering crews explored possible routes from Akron east to Youngstown via Mogadore, and from Mogadore and also Suffield south to Canton. Davis continued to seek an alternative to the W&LE at his Middlebranch cement works because he considered the road a "despicable monopoly" and "impossible to deal with fairly," and he firmly believed in the future of Canton. There was speculation that Davis would initially limit his AC&Y project to a line between Akron, Mogadore, and the eastern Portage County town of Deerfield. The reasoning went that Davis wanted to link the Northern Ohio, this Vanderbilt property, with a companion line at Deerfield "being built from Cleveland to Pittsburg, completing the system for which the Vanderbilt interests have been planning for years." The AC&Y might become a satellite in the Vanderbilt's galaxy of railroads.[32]

The prospect of a railroad to or through Mogadore excited residents. This community, which abutted the Portage–Summit county line and was initially settled in 1807, had, over the century, grown only to fewer than one thousand residents, with the Mogadore Stoneware Company being the principal employer. "To no town along the line will the advantage be so great as to Mogadore as it will enable the industries here to increase their capacities, and will attract other manufacturers," opined the *Akron Beacon Journal* in 1908. "It will also mean an increase in population, for the crying need of the village has been for transportation to Akron. It will mean a building boom, for there will be a demand for homes for the numbers of people who will work in Akron and live in Mogadore." More positive comments followed. "It will afford greater school privileges for the young men and women [of Mogadore] who desire to attend Buchtel college [in Akron] or the business colleges of Akron or Canton." And the writer made this statement: "Along the proposed route of the Akron, Canton & Youngstown Railroad are some of the finest and most desirable sites to be found in the state for tuberculosis sanitariums." Could a new railroad want for more?[33]

More cautious than French in his railroad pursuits, Davis commissioned another study. This document warned that construction of the Canton line, even with cement traffic, would be financially risky and recommended proceeding beyond Deerfield to Youngstown for a total distance of fifty miles. "Such a line would be seven miles shorter than either the Erie or the B&O and would have a much lower overall grade, not exceeding .3 or 1%." The feasibility report concluded that this piece of trackage "would likely be the last profitable steam line extension in Ohio." And at this time it was likely that Davis chose steam rather than electricity.[34]

Lengthy delays in implementing construction haunted the AC&Y. The difficulty of acquiring land parcels slowed the process, although there is no evidence that the Seiberlings or other Akronites interfered with the acquisitions process. Quite the opposite: potential customers desired the railroad; some were angered at the B&O "stranglehold" on the freight business in east Akron. While the AC&Y did not have trouble adding a right-of-way strip through much of Akron and most of Summit County, scattered parcels posed problems, forcing the company as late as July 1911 to institute several condemnation proceedings in probate court. While successful, a final victory had yet to be achieved. Somewhat later the railroad fought three property owners over the right to proceed through the Perkins Addition to the City of Akron. Again the AC&Y won, but this litigation underscored the difficulty of building in an urban area during the final wave of railroad construction. In every case land had to be purchased, different from the largely rural twilight roads that nearly always benefited from real-estate donations. Neither the AC&Y nor its predecessors received any "aids, gifts, grants, [or] donations."[35]

While right-of-way acquisitions took time and money, early on, the AC&Y faced a crisis with Akron city officials. As the population grew, citizens demanded the elimination of dangerous railroad grade crossings, especially involving those streets with the greatest vehicular traffic. The AC&Y expected that it could cross at grade Forge Street, a not particularly busy road that connected an assortment of businesses, residences, and the Summit County fairgrounds with the urban center, but the city demanded separation. The Akron solicitor surprisingly claimed, "A grade crossing Forge street would make it one of the most dangerous crossings in the city." If the company were to follow municipal wishes, two extremely unattractive options existed. The more expensive alternative involved erecting a nearly one-mile-long steel viaduct estimated to cost a whopping $571,000 ($13 million in 2008 dollars). The extensive length was necessitated by the need to elevate the line high over the nearby tracks of the Erie. The somewhat less costly recourse was to tunnel underneath Forge Street. The cost of that was estimated at $450,000 ($10.2 million in 2008 dollars) because of the presence of the adjoining hydraulic canal, requiring the excavation of a deep, rocky cut for almost a mile. "If the desired grade crossing is refused," editorialized a sympathetic *Akron Beacon Journal*, "the community will run a serious risk of losing a new railroad, since the only practicable way for the line to be built through the city is by crossing Forge street at grade."[36]

While Akronites had reason to be concerned about grade-crossing safety, there appears to be another explanation for the city's aggressive attack on the construction plans of the AC&Y. Speculation developed that the B&O was heavily involved, encouraging Old Forge residents to criticize the crossing and having local attorneys work quietly with these complainants. "At present the B. & O. has undisputed possession of the greater part of the freight business in East Akron. It is naturally a business proposition for the B. & O. to resent and oppose any intrusion into its territory and to prevent competition." The actions of the B&O were not new. "When the same railroad venture was projected in former years under a different name, obvious attempts are said to have been made by the B. & O. to block its progress."[37]

Extensive litigation followed. The Akron suit against the AC&Y went before the common pleas and circuit courts. In January 1909 the higher of these courts ordered a special master commissioner to review the arguments and recommend a solution. Then in April the commissioner concluded that the railroad should not cross Forge Street at grade. Additional meetings between railroad and city ensued, and in May both sides reached an accord. The street would be straightened and an underpass built with the AC&Y committing to pay any costs over the $25,000 ($571,000 in 2008 dollars) that the city earmarked for the project. And the railroad could temporarily cross the street at grade.[38]

Although not truly a roadblock, AC&Y promoters had to consider the possibility of direct competition from electric interurbans that desired to build eastward from Akron. For years, the traction trade press had reported rumors of such proposals. It's likely the activities of the Akron, Canton & Youngstown Electric Railway Company (AC&YE) were the most annoying. In December 1911 the *Electric Railway Journal* indicated that this Canton-based project had begun construction near the Rubber City and that "the line will be extended east to Youngstown via Mogadore." Presumably the AC&YE would be a traditional juice line, emphasizing passenger and package express rather than freight service, but the presence of another road could cause legal and other assorted problems. Fortunately, little came of the AC&YE.[39]

Another matter, which the embryonic AC&Y faced, involved resolving its routing strategy. Not until the June 1911 meeting of the board of directors, exactly four years after the charter was acquired, was the final decision made on the ultimate destination. The objective would be Sharon, Pennsylvania, and the traffic-rich Shenango Valley, with direct service also to Youngstown and the Mahoning Valley. Movement then commenced on realizing this goal. Directors voted to issue $13.5 million ($308 million in 2008 dollars) of capital stock and an equal amount of first mortgage, 5 percent bonds. But construction of the "Proposed Line of Railway" did not follow. As had happened in Akron, difficulties arose with securing the necessary right-of-way parcels between Mogadore and Sharon, especially in the Youngstown area, and the inability "to reach terms with the B&O and Erie on crossovers and interchange connections." Although these were not insurmountable obstacles, legal costs would be high and the issues might take years to resolve.[40]

While the feeling persisted that the Mahoning and Shenango valleys could be reached, perhaps with regulatory assistance, construction at last took place on the initial leg between Akron and Mogadore. Supervised by the Z. W. Davis Construction Company, designed to enhance profits for the promoters, laborers began work at both ends and also about midway. These toilers were aided at key points by the extensive use of the latest steam shovels. "The grading is heavy, averaging about 111,200 cubic yards per mile." Workers also placed a 206-foot concrete-lined tunnel under the tracks of the B&O, Erie, and PRR and installed several bridges, the largest being a 117-foot-long plate girder span over the B&O's Valley Line. Once a roadbed had been fashioned and the tunnel and bridges completed, crews laid new eighty-pound steel rails, installed several miles of sidings, built an 800-car-capacity yard and prepared interchange connections. An engine house, water tank, and other support equipment appeared in the central yards east of the Goodyear complex near Brittain Road. Two freight stations with wide loading platforms were also erected. Rolling stock arrived, including five 0-6-0 switchers from the Lima Locomotive Works and three hundred box, flat, and gondola cars. Even though management announced that the road would open on July 15, 1912, that long-anticipated event did not happen until October, when freight operations began without fanfare. There would be no special spike-driving ceremony. For several years, additional work continued on the 7.5-mile line and facilities.[41]

Customers like American Sewer Pipe, Buckeye Rubber, Goodyear Tire & Rubber, Great Western Cereal, and Robinson Clay Products offered real hope for permanent profitability. Early revenue reports were encouraging. For the year that ended June 30, 1914, the AC&Y generated freight earnings of $101,457 and claimed net earnings of $38,921. Two years later the annual figures reached $276,104 and $166,084, respectively. "The road was almost immediately successful, covering its bond interest in increasing amounts," remarked an industry expert in the 1930s. "Gross revenues displayed a remarkable growth. Tonnage handled increased at a rapid rate but revenue per ton showed an even more rapid increase." If Charles French read these financials, he surely took a degree of satisfaction in them, having early on grasped the potential of that Akron-to-Mogadore rail link.[42]

But it was not always easy for the upstart railroad. Most of its troubles involved conflicts with Akron's "Big Three." Complaints varied: the B&O, which had earlier been involved in the Forge Street controversy, charged fifty cents per car more for switching the AC&Y than it did the Erie; the Erie failed to expedite AC&Y merchandise to Mansfield, Youngstown, and other destinations; the PRR refused repeatedly to grant the AC&Y a physical connection. And the Akron & Barberton Belt Railway, which the "Big Three" owned, dragged its feet in allowing the establishment of an interchange. Appeals to regulators brought satisfaction, but often after extensive delays. Yet the W&LE aided the AC&Y whenever possible, for the new road happily provided entry into traffic-rich Akron.[43]

AC&Y leaders subsequently experienced more headaches. In December 1917 the U.S. Railroad Administration (USRA), because of wartime necessities, assumed control of most steam carriers, including the Davis road. "Confusion and mismanagement" were the words F. A. Seiberling used to describe the situation, being especially annoyed by the shortage of freight cars. Zeb Davis expressed the same sentiment. "The confusion and bother of the United States Railroad Administration made me long for the quiet and happiness of my home." And so Davis decided to exit the road, selling most of his holdings to his longtime legal advisor and business associate, H. B. Stewart, and the Seiberling family.[44]

While not then an officer of the AC&Y, Frank Seiberling applauded what was happening; after all, Goodyear continued to be the road's largest customer. "The AC&Y from its beginning established the standard of service to and from Akron, reducing the time and cost of transit." And for decades he took a keen interest in the property. The AC&Y, however, was not his sole foray into railroading. In 1912 he had become heavily invested in what might be a contender for the poster child of lunatic-fringe railroad projects during the twilight years, the Midland Continental Railroad (Midland).[45]

Early in the twentieth century the Midland came into being when a group of midwestern entrepreneurs formulated a daring plan. Spearheaded by Herbert Duncombe, a corporate lawyer from Chicago, and Frank K. Bull, president of the J. I. Case Threshing Machine Company of Racine, Wisconsin, these men proposed a north–south transcontinental rail system, a "second Illinois Central." But unlike the Illinois Central, which traversed a populous region, the Midland would be built hundreds of miles to the west in the much less developed Great Plains. Rails would link Winnipeg, Manitoba, with the Texas ports of Galveston and Corpus Christi. The 1,800-mile line would provide a direct outlet for Great Plains shippers, especially wheat growers. It was believed that the Panama Canal, then under construction, would make Gulf ports more important as the waterway revolutionized patterns of global trade.[46]

In August 1909 the Midland began to take shape. Construction commenced near Edgeley, North Dakota; the initial object was to span the forty miles between Edgeley and Jamestown. But, like the AC&Y, progress was painfully slow. Not until November 1912 did the company complete the Edgeley to Jamestown segment.[47]

It was while construction crews approached Jamestown that Seiberling entered the picture. "In the fall of 1912 while in New York City about to board a passenger liner for Europe, Mr. Seiberling met an old friend of his, F. K. Bull," wrote a historian of the Midland. "Bull told Mr. Seiberling that he was in need of funds for a project of his out west and after explaining the project briefly, he asked Mr. Seiberling if he would be willing to make the needed loan. [B]eing in a jubilant mood over his coming trip and being a man of considerable wealth and large business affairs, [Seiberling] signed the [$400,000] notes without giving the matter too much thought and without the slightest notion that the loan would ultimately make him a railroad career." By 1916, though, Seiberling had misgivings about his hasty investment. "I came into the property through the solicitation of Mr. Frank Bull," Seiberling told an officer of the First National Bank of St. Paul, "and find myself in the unhappy position of owner of the entire property through my interest in Mr. Bull and my effort to protect his investment and mine." What Seiberling had was a sixty-eight-mile grain-carrying prairie pike that included a short extension, completed in 1913, between Jamestown and Wimbledon. Efforts to expand the road never succeeded. Yet Seiberling did not lose his shirt financially, and in 1966, eleven years after his death, the Seiberling family received a generous buyout from interchange partners Northern Pacific and Soo Line when these two companies jointly acquired the Midland.[48]

Frank Seiberling learned something from his association with the Midland that had a direct, positive impact on the AC&Y. He realized the attractiveness of an affiliated land development company. Herbert Duncombe prompted Seiberling to consider railroad-sponsored land promotion, a common response by carriers throughout the trans-Chicago West, even during the final thrust of railroad building. Duncombe urged Seiberling to support a subsidiary Midland townsite company. "The Land Company does not require very much capital," argued Duncombe. "[It] costs very little money for platting, surveying, examination of abstracts, etc. about $1100 or $1200 for a town consisting of forty acres. Profits can be considerable and this could make the Midland a realization." Soon Seiberling and fellow investors formed townsite affiliates.[49]

In March 1913, several months after the exchange with Duncombe, Seiberling commented on railroad land development. "I see that it is absolutely imperative," he wrote Zeb Davis, "that the AC&Y, or any railroad operation for that matter, have a land department that aggressively attempts to add shippers along its route and that further seeks to acquire inexpensive land parcels which can be developed for the profit of the stockholders." Specifically noting the Duncombe argument (which he underscored in red ink), Seiberling said, "A Chicago acquaintance of mine is dead right about land sales. Creation of a land company is a simple financial matter. Unless you are forced to buy land at inflated prices, there is virtually no risk at all." Seiberling made a final point: "It is clear from my knowledge of railroading in Dakota that such corporations should legally split their operating and land activities. That way the professional talents are best utilized and harmony reigns between the true railroaders and the land people."[50]

Shortly thereafter Seiberling expressed these sentiments to fellow AC&Y investors. Apparently there was no disagreement about the desirability of land promotion, and on April 21, 1913, formation of the East Akron Land Company (EALC) took place. A separate corporate structure with a modest capitalization, the infant concern came about for the stated purpose "of buying, acquiring, owning, improving, holding, selling, disposing of and of dealing in and with real estate, and of doing any and all things incident to or convenient in the proper management of such property and business." At the organizational meeting, the EALC selected Seiberling as its head and also approved a small staff, but there were no sales representatives, rather, "Mr. Seiberling will solicit business."[51]

At first the EALC acquired real estate slowly. In 1919, however, the company purchased about 800 acres of mostly undeveloped land located east of the AC&Y shops. The price, however, was high, a reflection of the continuing boom in area real estate. Yet the land was situated in the best direction for Akron to expand industrially and where several businesses already operated.[52]

The tardiness of the EALC in buying large tracts of property for development is understandable. It is explained partially by the company's conviction that it must first develop its original purchase of approximately thirty-five acres near the Goodyear complex. Moreover, Seiberling, the force behind the company, had become heavily involved with the construction and furnishing of his family's Tudor Revival–style mansion, Stan Hywet, that overlooked three thousand acres of rolling fields and woodlands in northwest Akron. And two local residential land schemes also competed with this labor of love. The city's acute housing shortage led Seiberling to launch the Goodyear Heights Allotment Company for his blue-collar employees near the factory. And he spearheaded the Fairlawn Heights Company, an executive white-collar development in west Akron—"On the Watershed West of the Smoke"—that became synonymous locally with power and privilege. As a result of the recent purchase of nine miles of Northern Ohio trackage between downtown Akron and Belt Junction, the AC&Y touched Fairlawn Heights; in fact, the AC&Y initiated commuter service, supplied by a General Electric–built gas-electric car, to link this upscale residential district with Goodyear. White-collar employees could ride conveniently to their offices, and domestics and other wage earners could board outbound runs in their working-class neighborhoods to reach their places of employment.[53]

During this period the AC&Y became increasingly vital to Goodyear Tire & Rubber; the railroad had become the "Road to Goodyear." Tons of raw materials, including chemicals, fabrics, and raw and scrap rubber, arrived at the Akron plants on the AC&Y, as did copious quantities of soft coal. In fact, these black diamonds came from Goodyear-owned mines near Adena, Ohio, and were moved over W&LE and AC&Y rails in solid coal trains with Goodyear-owned hoppers. Tires and tubes filled innumerable boxcars, and these finished goods regularly traveled to the automobile assembly lines in Detroit via an AC&Y–Northern Ohio–Detroit, Toledo & Ironton (DT&I) route. To the surprise of no one, Goodyear took control of the AC&Y in 1919.[54]

Although there had been grumbling about USRA policies, the experiences of federal involvement between 1917 and 1920 did not produce disastrous financial results. The AC&Y was no Colorado Midland or Georgia & Florida, railroads crippled by the USRA. The balance sheet continued to reflect strong returns. Gross earnings stood at $477,703 in 1917, rose to $527,648 in 1918, jumped to $721,204 in 1919, and reached $977,372 in 1920. Net earnings generally mirrored these robust figures: $261,669 in 1917, $252,951 in 1918, $316,850 in 1919, and $235,801 in 1920.[55]

Business from Goodyear might ensure the financial well-being of the AC&Y, but Seiberling, taking a somewhat unorthodox point of view, saw the

EALC as an effective organization to combat negative forces. "If the owners of the AC&Y are to protect their financial interests and if there is to be profit in the future, then land promotion is absolutely essential," he observed in February 1919. "With restrictive statutes, the profitable sale or lease of industrial lands and the revenue generated by new shippers will likely mean the difference between financial success and failure for the railroad."[56]

Just as every twilight railroad project enhanced local economies, the AC&Y and EALC had a similar impact. The attraction of new or expanded businesses bolstered tax revenues, expanded employment, and increased carloadings. Parcels were either leased or sold to several important customers, including Standard Oil Company of Ohio (Sohio) and Akron Domestic Coke Company. Unfortunately, the nasty postwar recession damaged development and distracted Seiberling. By the end of 1921 the New York investment house of Dillon, Read had forced the Seiberlings out of Goodyear, although the family continued to hold a sizable block of stock in the company, as well as in both the AC&Y and EALC (reconstituted as the AC&Y Terminal Properties Company). By the end of the 1920s the Seiberlings had regrouped with the establishment of the Seiberling Rubber Company in Barberton.[57]

Before the business recession of the early 1920s, the AC&Y took control of the 152-mile Northern Ohio, a property that had been leased by a New York Central affiliate, Lake Erie & Western Railway. For years speculation about the future of the Northern Ohio had been widespread. A report in 1916 suggested that the recently formed Akron Belt Line Railroad, which planned to construct an electric line on a strip of state canal land extending from Market Street to Bartges Street, would buy the Northern Ohio. The belt road would initially place under wire the line as far west as New London, a distance of fifty-eight miles, and later the remaining section to Delphos. Although this prediction was nonsense, the AC&Y did assume a long-term lease arrangement on March 1, 1920, the day the U.S. government relinquished control. With that action, any serious talk of pushing the AC&Y beyond Mogadore toward Youngstown or Sharon disappeared. "Last year [1920] we were simply a progressive, profitable terminal operation and now we have acquired a railroad nobody really wanted," observed H. B. Stewart, AC&Y president, "but a line that is of tremendous potential to our unique traffic [rubber products] situation. We'll never go to Youngstown, Sharon or Canton unless it's a trackage rights agreement." And he asked pointedly, "Why go there at all?"[58]

The orientation of the AC&Y–Northern Ohio was freight. While the combined carrier served scores of on-line customers, including lumber dealers, grain elevator operators, and clay products and quarry owners, it would be those shipments of manufacturing materials destined for the Akron rubber shops, mostly to Goodyear, and of tires and tubes bound for Detroit and distributors throughout the nation that generated profits. "The road carries and originates more freight tonnage in and out of the rubber center than any other steam road operating into the city," observed the *Wall Street Journal* in November 1922. Freight revenues gave the company the envious distinction of being a Class 1 railroad (revenue driven), albeit one of the smallest in the country, and the operating ratio for 1922 stood at an astounding 60.8 percent, lowest of all Class 1 roads. Even though Ohio was in the throes of a crusade to upgrade public roads, and truck usage increased, the railroad was somewhat immune from this highway competition. Surely the AC&Y was "a road with a bright future."[59]

In the mid-1920s the stunning performance of the AC&Y–Northern Ohio caught the eye of financial writer H. P. Faxon. He saw the road as occupying a virtually unique position among American railroads. "While other and larger carriers are deploring the vexatious delays occurring in their freight yards and the uneven loads of their business, at the same time regarding any diminution below 80 per cent of their incomes for operating costs as an accomplishment, this line has a twelve-hour service over its 150 miles of

The Akron, Canton & Youngstown maintained a large stable of iron horses to handle extensive switching chores and, after 1920, over-the-road assignments. The company owned a number of 2-8-0 Consolidation switchers. No. 353, built by the American Locomotive Company in 1928, pauses at the Brittain Road engine house. *Courtesy of Archives of Michigan.*

The Service Code

OF

The Akron, Canton & Youngstown Railway Co.

THIS RAILWAY SYSTEM is founded on the belief that "He Who Serves Best Profits Most." The gain, ofttimes, far exceeds monetary value; for frequently it comes in the form of satisfaction gleaned from the knowledge of work well done.

THIS RAILWAY SYSTEM entertains no selfish ideas regarding the privacy of its business There is no secrecy! The company sees itself as being the servant of the public which it serves. The trustees, as it were, of the public's interests. Its priceless legacy, its most cherished possession, is the faith of every individual with whom it comes in contact. This commission of confidence is indeed one of which even a railway system may be proud.

THIS RAILWAY SYSTEM has a policy, that should not be regarded as uncommon or unusual in these enlightened days; every inquiry for service, in any form, must always have the most careful attention of the proper person; then that service, if extended, must be delivered with such care that it will be satisfactory to every party concerned.

THIS RAILWAY SYSTEM strives to be a constructive force in each community throughout its territory. It is proud to be aligned with forces working for industrial development and economic betterment.

THIS RAILWAY SYSTEM believes that honorable competition gives life to business and makes it better. Its own business, constantly competitive, leads to this conviction. Yet it submits that each man should profit commensurately with service as rendered by himself.

THIS RAILWAY SYSTEM, believing in progress and growth, puts its resources a-work encouraging industries to locate and expand along its lines; thus is created more business, with competition. More posts for workers result. and this leads logically to satisfying their needs in the way of home-sites, with advantages in goodly number. that there may be contentment and stalwart. upstanding citizenry.

THIS RAILWAY SYSTEM knows that in serving others as it would be served it will achieve success—and satisfaction. That its policies are human and simple makes them only the easier to observe!

THE AKRON, CANTON & YOUNGSTOWN RAILWAY COMPANY
NORTHERN OHIO RAILWAY
GENERAL OFFICES
12 E. EXCHANGE ST., AKRON, OHIO

GENERAL AGENCY	GENERAL AGENCY	GENERAL AGENCY	GENERAL AGENCY
601 HERBERICH BLDG.	520 MARQUETTE BLDG.	536 PIERCE BLDG.	941 OLIVER BLDG.
AKRON, OHIO	CHICAGO, ILL.	ST. LOUIS, MO.	PITTSBURGH, PA.

Independent railroads that opened in the twilight period were characterized by personal service for shippers. Circa 1930 the Akron, Canton & Youngstown distributed this circular that extolled its commitment to the public.

track and maintains an operating ratio of 48 per cent or less." Faxon argued that geography contributed to profitability. "Main truck lines passing through [Akron] have to follow the channel of a small river and are located far below the level of the city itself. To reach the rubber factories, therefore, a huge belt line [Akron & Barberton Belt] was built, traveling twelve miles out in the country and returning by a gradual climb. Shunting freight about therefore requires haulage of twenty-four miles to travel a direct distance of less than one, and the making up of freight trains, which, if destined to St. Louis, Chicago or Detroit, must be broken up again in the congested termini of Cincinnati, Columbus or Cleveland, occasioning delays of several days at least." But the AC&Y satisfied customers by taking outbound freight directly from Akron and using twenty-three junction points to interchange these shipments, and dispatching those solid trains of rubber products to Detroit through the interchange at Columbus Grove with Henry Ford's DT&I that took "not more than ten minutes." Noted Faxon, "So efficiently is the system worked out that Ford alone has been able to cut his tire inventories to less than half the number carried before the A.C.& Y." Here was an early example of just-in-time delivery.[60]

Even though it was a fast freight operation, for a few years the AC&Y had considerable passenger train movements. The railroad's large motor car made fourteen daily-except-Sunday round-trips between Copley and Akron, with most runs terminating at Goodyear Avenue, providing a convenient walking distance to Goodyear destinations. But widespread use of the automobile soon led to drastic cutbacks. By the mid-1920s Akron claimed the second-highest per capita ownership of cars, behind Los Angeles, California. Service then became daily-except-Sunday passenger trains Nos. 90 and 93 between Mogadore and Delphos, and eventually a mixed train that, until 1951, carried mail, express, and an occasional rider.[61]

Notwithstanding the downgrading of passenger service, the AC&Y, which employees called simply "ACY," remained a busy property. But like the industry, the company mirrored the ups and downs of the national economy. The Great Depression had its negative effects. As H. B. Stewart observed in February 1932, "Gross operating revenues for the year showed a decrease of 29.6% as compared to the previous year. Statistics show that the industrial area of southern Michigan and northeastern Ohio has been more affected than possibly any other industrial section, due primarily to the sharp curtailment in the automotive industry, which naturally caused a severe reduction in the business of the rubber industry in the Akron District." Then several major Akron banks failed, making "certain current assets more or less frozen" and forcing the AC&Y into the hands of the federal court on April 7, 1933. This financial misfortune prevented the company from meeting a payment of $161,000 due

THE AKRON, CANTON & YOUNGSTOWN RY.
Schedule of Trains—WESTWARD
READ DOWN

Stations	7 Daily Ex. Mon.	1 Daily Ex. Sun.	9 Daily Ex. Sun.	11 Daily	13 Daily	15 Daily	17 Daily	19 Daily
	AM	AM	AM	AM	PM	PM	PM	PM
MOGADORE				9:35	12:40		5:40	8:55
Forest Hill				f9:36	f12:41		f5:41	f8:56
Greenwood				f9:37	f12:42		f5:42	f8:57
Upson				f9:38	f12:43		f5:43	f8:58
Brittain Yard				s9:41	s12:46		s5:46	s9:01
Goodyear Ave.	s12:22		s7:30	f9:44	f12:49	s3:45	f5:49	f9:04
								Arr.9:15
AKRON	s12:30	Lv.7:15	s7:38	s9:55	s1:00	s3:57	s6:00	Lv.10:15
Merriman Road	f12:36		f7:44	f10:01	f1:06	f4:03	f6:06	f10:21
Portage Path	f12:37		f7:45	f10:02	f1:07	f4:04	f6:07	f10:22
Hawkins Ave.	f12:40		f7:48	f10:05	f1:10	f4:07	f6:10	f10:25
Fairlawn	f12:44		f7:52	f10:09	f1:14	f4:11	f6:14	f10:29
Schocalog Road	f12:46		f7:54	f10:11	f1:16	f4:13	f6:16	f10:31
Copley	s12:57	s7:50	s8:05	s10:20	1:25	4:23	6:27	10:42
f—Flag stop.	AM	AM	AM	AM	PM	PM	PM	PM

For information, write or call   S. J. WITT, General Freight and Passenger Agent.
Akron, Ohio.   (Over)

Although designed as an industrial switching road, the Akron, Canton & Youngstown, for a brief period during the era of World War I, provided commuter service between Copley and Mogadore, Ohio. This time card, effective on August 29, 1920, shows how the single motor car gave access from downtown Akron and the east side office and manufacturing complex of the Goodyear Tire & Rubber Company.

on three series of Northern Ohio bonds. Federal Judge John Paul Jones of Cleveland named Stewart the temporary trustee and a month later he became the permanent trustee. Then after his death in 1938, his son, "Bart" Jr., a company executive, took his place, the same year that the Interstate Commerce Commission (ICC) approved a reorganization plan. But complications caused by the bond structure delayed freedom from court supervision, and the AC&Y–Northern Ohio merger until early 1944.[62]

As with other Class 1 roads, the war years resulted in substantial operating revenues. Never had Akron factories been busier. Freight income soared from $13.4 million in 1940 to an all-time high of $26.9 million in 1944. While the AC&Y continued to add and replace its fleet of switch engines, by the late 1920s over-the-road freights were no longer operated with inherited Northern Ohio power, which included an assortment of elderly 2-6-0s and 4-6-0s. The company acquired, beginning in 1926, several mighty 2-8-2s. Commented locomotive expert William D. Edson, "The road's biggest and best-remembered steam engines were the 400-series Mikes [Mikados] bought new from Lima, one of them as late as 1944."[63]

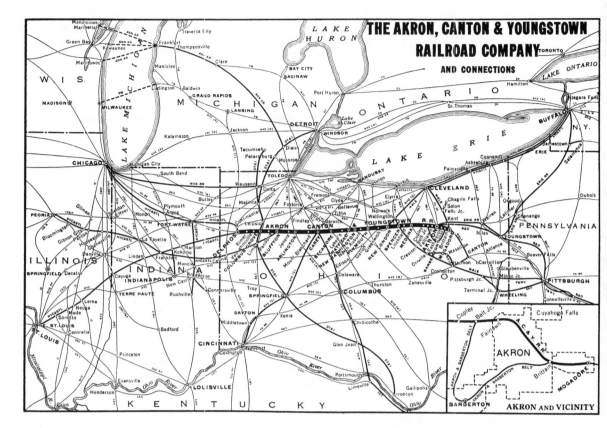

Following World War II the always-progressive Akron, Canton & Youngstown issued a promotional brochure that lauded its freight service and convenient connections. In 1920 this industrial carrier gained control of the Northern Ohio Railway and later merged this much longer road into its corporate structure, making the AC&Y a strategic midwestern artery.

The AC&Y continued to prosper. Akron businesses thrived and the number of shippers increased along the line to Delphos, especially in Medina, the growing seat of Medina County. The company, too, did a brisk interchange business with the Erie and "there were days when it delivered 200 cars to the Erie, principally for Eastern destinations." Dieselization also improved profitability. This process began in 1942 with a single 1,000-horsepower switch engine and then more diesel switchers arrived. Starting in 1948 the AC&Y made an unusual choice in its selection of diesel road units, rejecting the largest manufacturers and choosing the smaller Fairbanks-Morse Company. By 1957 the railroad owned fifteen of these locomotives, pleasing train crews because of their dependability and safety features. The AC&Y also benefited from being a nearly freight-only road with its numerous connections. "We

The Akron, Canton & Youngstown Railroad extends 170 miles across Northern Ohio from Mogadore west through Akron — the rubber capital of the world — to Delphos, Ohio. An integral part of the Nation's rail system, the A. C. & Y. makes direct and prompt connections with nine other railroads at twenty-one junctions. Schedules, coordinated with connecting railroads, combine with modern equipment to give the fastest service possible to and from all points in the Nation.

2000 H.P.
DIESEL-ELECTRIC
LOCOMOTIVE

1000 H.P.
DIESEL-ELECTRIC
LOCOMOTIVE

CLASS R-2
MIKADO STEAM
LOCOMOTIVE

70-TON COVERED HOPPER CAR

30-FOOT ALL-STEEL CABOOSE

didn't have that awful passenger money drain," remarked a company executive.[64]

Surprisingly, the dream of a more direct Akron-to-Youngstown rail link, which had been so much a part of early twentieth-century thinking, reappeared. In 1947 the AC&Y studied such an extension, designed to tap traffic generated by the steel industry and "to serve as a route around the congestion of Cleveland." But, alas, nothing happened.[65]

Failure to reach Youngstown and the Mahoning Valley did not prevent AC&Y officials from keeping that area in mind. In 1949 the Riverlake Belt Conveyor Lines, Inc., headed by Bart Stewart, proposed a two-way, 130-mile Ohio River-to-Lake Erie conveyor belt that would transport coal and iron ore to the "Steel Valley." Opposition from other railroads and their allies, however, prevented the Ohio General Assembly from granting the rights of eminent domain for what some experts considered to be a "sound engineering plan."[66]

Being a small Class 1 carrier caused managers and owners to reconsider the company's independent status in wake of the "urge to merge" trend in the early 1960s. When plans by the Norfolk & Western to purchase the Nickel Plate Road and lease the Wabash Railroad became known at Akron headquarters in 1961, the Stewart administration and heirs of Frank Seiberling feared a drastic loss of bridge traffic at Delphos with the Nickel Plate Road and asked the N&W to include the AC&Y in the unification process. The N&W agreed, for two reasons. The AC&Y continued to have a good business and N&W management "didn't want to anger the Akron rubber people." On January 10, 1962, the N&W filed an application with the ICC for control and, after the proscribed procedures, regulators granted approval. "We were lucky," remembered J. Penfield Seiberling, son of Frank Seiberling. "We found someone to buy us out at a very good price." On October 16, 1964, the AC&Y, whose stock the N&W acquired for $6.5 million ($44.6 million in 2008 dollars), became a wholly owned subsidiary of the greatly expanded Roanoke-based railroad, and remained so until January 1, 1982, when the N&W, in a restructuring, dissolved the corporation. Yet during this time, the AC&Y proudly claimed, "100% locally managed" and painted that slogan in large letters on the side of its eight-story downtown Akron office building.[67]

Even though the AC&Y disappeared as a corporate entity, a substantial amount of the former railroad remains active, namely 114 miles between Mogadore and Carey. Owned since 1990 by the recently formed regional carrier Wheeling & Lake Erie Railway, fifty-five miles of the West End (Delphos to Carey) have been retired, but stone quarries near Carey and a large grain facility at New Washington contribute significantly to the road's on-line traffic, as do an assortment of businesses on the East End. Today, sections of track sport heavy welded rail and deep rock ballast, including a portion of the original line west of Mogadore. Although tire production has ended in Akron, firms that occupy sites developed by the EALC and AC&Y Terminal Properties still generate revenue along the old core. The AC&Y was a twilight railroad that succeeded; the foremost illustration of such a carrier in the Midwest.[68]

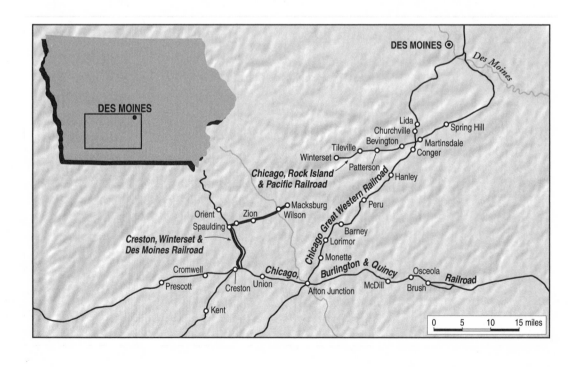

Chapter 2

Crazy Willie & Dandy Molly: Creston, Winterset & Des Moines Railroad

Although the map of steam railroads in Iowa had seemingly jelled by 1900, additional railroad schemes periodically appeared. By the eve of World War I, some projects had become more than paper proposals. The successful undertakings consisted of several main line relocations, a few trunk line extensions, and more than a half dozen short lines. As for the latter, these pikes developed in places where residents believed that new or additional steam car service was vital for their economic well-being. Yet enthusiasts failed to recognize the potential impact of internal combustion vehicles and better roads. That lack of foresight resulted in these companies failing financially, and in a majority of cases becoming so much junk not long after their opening. Sadly for their backers, the age of the automobile and truck was at hand. Nevertheless, roads like the Creston, Winterset & Des Moines (CW&DM) initially had a profound and positive impact on their service territory and cannot be easily dismissed as total economic disasters.[1]

By 1900 few states could rival Iowa in the density of railroad mileage or, for that matter, of total mileage. "Iowa's railroads cover the state like a heavy morning dew," said one wag, and no Hawkeye State location was more than thirteen miles from a depot. Mileage stood at 9,353, but continued to grow until it peaked in 1914 at 10,018 miles. This figure did not include trackage operated by electric interurbans that increased from a negligible amount at the turn of the century to a high of 507 miles in 1917. Several Hawkeye State interurbans, though, had earlier been steam operated and then had been converted to electricity. In 1914 the Centerville, Albia & Southern Railway, for one, electrified after having previously been the Albia & Centerville Railway, a steam short line that the Iowa Central Railway had controlled for some years.[2]

Several of the steam railroads that appeared in Iowa during the twilight years initially had been projected as interurbans. Such planning was hardly shocking. Juice enthusiasts in Iowa, with few exceptions, had in mind more than a rural trolley reminiscent of the cheaply built lines commonly found in New England and parts of the Midwest. Instead backers wanted a property constructed to the more demanding steam road specifications. The idea, as expressed by one Hawkeye State editor, was for promoters not to build "a line that follows the contour of the country, up hill and down hill, but a line as straight as the crow flies, and at a grade that might as well do for a trunk line where the heaviest engines and the longest trains are to be pulled." This building strategy would permit heavyweight passenger cars and "motors" to handle standard freight equipment that could be interchanged with steam carriers. In this way grain and livestock could be sent outbound and coal and lumber received.[3]

Shortly before the Panic of 1907, interurban enthusiasts in Des Moines and Creston and the intermediate territory in between began to consider construction of a sixty-five-mile electric road. Des Moines, the state capital and seat of Polk County, enjoyed excellent steam road service in most directions, and after 1902 had the electric cars of the Inter-Urban Railway to Colfax and, in 1906, to Perry and Woodward. Then a year later, Des Moines benefited from the electrified Fort Dodge, Des Moines & Southern Railway (FtDDM&S) to Ames, Boone, and Fort Dodge. But connections to the southwest from Des Moines were less attractive. Although a predecessor of the Chicago Great Western Railroad (Great Western) had sliced through this region in the late 1880s, the company served no county-seat community. Its principal stations were the villages of East Peru (Peru), Lorimor, Talmage, Shannon City, Diagonal, and Blockton. Even though the Great Western missed Creston by about a dozen miles, the 6,924 residents of this thriving Union County seat had access to the busy Chicago–Denver main line of the Chicago, Burlington & Quincy Railroad (Burlington) and two branches, lines northwest to Greenfield and Cumberland and southwest to Bedford and St. Joseph. If the new interurban were built, Winterset would also benefit. This seat of Madison County suffered from mediocre rail service, being at the end of a forty-two-mile branch of the Chicago, Rock Island & Pacific Railroad (Rock Island) that ran east to

Carlisle and then north to Des Moines. And Macksburg, a village in Madison County southwest of Winterset and on the projected route, had never seen the iron horse.[4]

Long before reports speculated on interurban construction between Creston and Des Moines via Macksburg and Winterset, efforts had been made to bring rail service to portions of the projected path. In the early 1870s residents of Creston, Winterset, and intermediate points had unsuccessfully promoted the St. Paul & Southwestern Railroad that would connect the Union and Madison county seats. A few years later citizens supported in vain the Bedford, Winterset & Des Moines Railroad, designed to link the towns in the company's corporate name. Additional schemes popped up intermittently, again with the objective of a direct route between Creston and Des Moines and to communities not served by the Great Western. Shortly after the turn of the century, new hope for this "air line" emerged, and some sporadic grading took place between Creston and Spaulding, a hamlet several miles north of Creston.[5]

While the preliminary construction in northern Union County failed to yield anything of significance, advocates of a Creston-to-Des Moines railroad soon felt encouraged. More planning suggested that an electric interurban was within their reach. "The line is fifty-eight miles of construction and sixty-four miles of operation, the understanding being that we use five and seven-tenths miles of the Des Moines City Railway's tracks for passenger terminals in Des Moines," a backer told the *Creston Advertiser-Gazette* in August 1907. "We have deeds and contracts over eighty per cent of the right of way already secured; also franchises in Creston, Macksburg and Winterset." Although the Creston, Winterset & Des Moines Electric Railway (CW&DMER) was estimated to cost a hefty $1.8 million ($41 million in 2008 dollars), supporters considered the project a winning proposition. "Our total tributary population, as estimated, is about one hundred and sixteen thousand people. The total tonnage produced in the territory tributary to our line is three hundred and seventy-six thousand tons, of which approximately two hundred and fifty thousand tons is [*sic*] available for haul, either long or short." Unlike some interurbans, the CW&DMER would transport steam road rolling stock, freight equipment that the electrics, Inter-Urban and FtDDM&S, could also accommodate. These enthusiasts did not miss the point that both of these interurbans generated strong revenues, and Des Moines showed all the signs of being "a good interurban city."[6]

Excitement spread, being particularly strong in and about Macksburg, an inland community that physician-founder Dr. J. H. Mack Jr. had laid out in 1873. "Some of the people around Macksburg are very much elated over the prospects of the interurban railroad," noted the Macksburg reporter for the *Winterset Madisonian* in January 1908. "They know personally of the benefits the people have in sections where there are trolley lines. Liberal subscriptions are being offered [because] a railroad through this section will benefit every farmer within five miles of the line, to the extent of one dollar per acre every year for the next twenty years."[7]

While farmers and villagers might express excitement for the CW&DMER, meaningful financial support was mandatory if the road was ever to be more than hot air. In February 1908 supporters took heart when the press revealed that F. M. Hubbell, a prominent Polk County businessman who controlled the Des Moines Union Railway, a profitable terminal property, indicated that he would subscribe $5,000 ($118,000 in 2008 dollars), and members of the Des Moines Commercial Club announced their approval, expecting to raise $250,000 ($5.9 million in 2008 dollars). News soon followed that Winterset interests agreed to buy $30,000 ($710,000 in 2008 dollars) worth of securities, and commitments would also be "substantial" in Creston. "PROGRESS, ADVANCEMENT, MODERNISM" became the slogan for the ongoing crusade.[8]

More good news followed. In late September the *Des Moines Register and Leader* revealed that Leslie M. Shaw, former Iowa governor and U.S. Secretary of the Treasury in the Theodore Roosevelt administration, endorsed the project and C. C. Wolf, described as a Parkersburg, Iowa, "capitalist," planned to commit $60,000 ($1.4 million in 2008 dollars). Newspaper readers may have expected dirt to fly at any moment, but that did not happen.[9]

Early in 1909 unwelcome reports came from a Des Moines meeting of interurban backers. Apparently efforts to arrange for the sale of construction bonds of the still unincorporated enterprise had failed. A recent state law, the Peterson Act, designed to tighten the sale of securities, had deterred investors. Moreover, fallout from the Panic of 1907 had made bonding houses more cautious. Creston attorney Richard Brown believed that these two events "will necessitate a much larger amount of money being subscribed by the people locally than was previously asked for."[10]

The financial situation prompted backers of the CW&DMER to rethink their goals. "[T]he company is seriously considering the road in sections, either building from Des Moines to Winterset, or from Creston to Macksburg," observed the *Creston Semi-Weekly Advertiser*, "the plan being to complete the road in two or three years." If that were to happen, individuals who had already subscribed to stock needed to agree to this new arrangement since the original proposition called for building the entire road at one time.[11]

The news then worsened considerably. "The Creston Road Is Abandoned" proclaimed the *Des Moines Capital* in March 1909. Even though "the project was practicable," backers concluded that the financial obstacles were too great. Subscriptions had lagged, and franchises awarded by local governments in Creston, Macksburg, and Winterset were about to expire and some doubt existed about whether they could be quickly renewed.[12]

Yet reports of the demise of the CW&DMER proved to have been premature. In April 1909 supporters circulated an open letter that offered promise. "This road is owned and controlled by your own neighbors and fellow citizens who are determined to build the road. All they need is the continued loyal support of those who have befriended the undertaking in the past. We have not been talking much noise, but we have been quietly and persistently at work." And they were. By July these interurban enthusiasts revealed that Engineering, Construction & Securities Company, a small Chicago-based firm led by C. A. Ross, president, and C. B. Judd, chief engineer, had agreed to participate. The company had successfully financed and built several electric and steam short lines in Iowa, including the recently opened ten-mile Albia Interurban Railway between Albia and the coal-mining camps of Hiteman and Hocking. Indeed, Ross and Judd encouraged rail-hungry communities to build interurbans or steam short lines, and went from place to place offering their services, including financing and construction. "A survey gang will be put to work soon to complete the survey commenced and well progressed about a year ago and as the facilities of the Judd & Ross Company will permit construction work."[13]

The interest of an out-of-state construction firm did not mean the interurban would quickly take shape. Soon plans changed dramatically. The Des Moines interests had retreated, showing greater excitement for building the Red Oak & Des Moines Railway, a 104-mile electric road between Des Moines and Red Oak, via Winterset and Greenfield. This left backers of the CW&DMER who were mostly from Creston, Macksburg, and Winterset and the surrounding countryside. In an exaggerated way, *Railway World* reported, "The incorporators are wealthy farmers living along the right-of-way." Now leading the project were Robert Brown of Creston, president, Jerry M. Wilson of Macksburg, first vice president, M. F. Harris of Winterset, second vice president, A. S. Lynn of Orient, secretary, and W. W. Walker of Macksburg, treasurer. "The new organization has nothing to do with the old organization, which has been wholly abandoned." Newsworthy, too, was the announcement that the railroad would be a conventional steam road, and that construction would begin initially between Creston and Macksburg and later between Macksburg and Winterset; a Des Moines destination would not be an immediate goal. Even if constructed to the cheapest standards, an interurban involved more than rails on a graded right-of-way or alongside a public road, requiring also a pole line and overhead, electrical substations, and a source of electricity, supplied by existing power companies or from the railroad's own generating plant. A steam road, though, could be built inexpensively, perhaps for as little as $10,000–$12,000 per mile, and used locomotives and other pieces of rolling stock were readily available on the equipment market at reasonable prices. Or the railroad might become a "wireless interurban" of sorts, using gasoline motor cars for passenger service and steam for freight operations. Indeed, in early 1911 the *Electric Railway Journal* reported such a strategy.[14]

The new approach appeared practical. In October 1909 a Winterset journalist wrote, "Between Creston and Macksburg nearly every farmer benefited by the road has agreed to subscribe to stock and it is thought that the financing of the proposition will not be difficult." The backers must have been encouraged by happenings not far to their west. In late 1907 the northern division of the steam (although proposed as an interurban) Atlantic Northern & Southern Railroad (AN&S) had opened between Atlantic and Kimballton, a distance of seventeen miles, and three years later the company had completed the thirty-eight-mile southern division between Atlantic, Grant, and Villisca. It seemed probable that an extension of the AN&S would be pushed south through Clarinda, College Springs, and Blanchard to Tarkio, Savannah, or St. Joseph, Missouri, and likely the original line would be extended northward to Manning, a Carroll County town already served by three steam railroads, and eventually to Sioux City. However, only the seventeen-mile Clarinda-to-Blanchard portion appeared, opening in January 1912 as a steam road under the corporate banner of the independent Iowa & Southwestern Railway ("Ikey"). The press was impressed that the AN&S "has been entirely paid for by farmers and business men in towns and country along the route." Moreover, the Engineering, Construction & Securities Company had been involved in the AN&S and Ikey projects. It also appeared that a portion of another road was about to open nearby, the fourteen-mile Red Oak & North Eastern Railway (née Red Oak & North Eastern Interurban Promotion Company) between Imogene, Iowa, on the Wabash, and Red Oak, a county seat community like Creston monopolized by the Burlington main line and two Burlington branch lines. Although this project had sputtered for some time, Red Oak voters in August 1912 overwhelmingly approved a 5 percent tax for two years to complete the initial construction. Altogether, these events encouraged residents of Macksburg and the surrounding countryside.[15]

Support in Creston grew. Some civic-minded residents continued to express remorse that the Union County metropolis had earlier missed a chance for a competitor to the Burlington. "May she never again let slip the opportunity that was hers when the Great Western was permitted to go right past her door, without so much as passing the time of day," wrote a visiting reporter from the *Council Bluffs Nonpareil* in November 1909. And by this time a new spirit of community pride and purpose had developed in Creston. "A booster movement is on foot that bears the aspect of determination and success in its every line. The booster club is to be incorporated. The thousand dollars is to be placed in the treasury by popular subscription, and, thus armed the boosters are going up to look for factories and things for their town—thus instead of waiting for the good thing to come along and then try to raise the needed funds in a haphazard way."[16]

Then during 1910 the Creston-to-Winterset project made some behind-the-scenes progress. Stock solicitations dominated the activities. "Work is progressing very satisfactorily," opined *The Madisonian*, "though little has been said or done to attract newspaper attention." By September, Creston newspaperman Paul Junkin revealed "that all subscriptions necessary to finance the road as far as Macksburg had been secured and that the contract for that portion of the road would probably be let this winter."[17]

The following year, on September 16, 1911, backers of what was now the Creston, Winterset & Des Moines Railroad, paid $518 to file articles of incorporation with the Iowa secretary of state. The document authorized capital stock of $500,000 ($11.4 million in 2008 dollars) and gave the company the right to operate "in whole or in part by steam, electricity, gasoline, or other such motive power as shall be adopted by the Board of Directors." Reports speculated that by summer 1911 construction would begin between Creston and Macksburg. Even though the area press had earlier announced that stock subscriptions had been finished, with approximately four hundred investors, financial matters still remained to be finalized. In July a Creston journalist wrote, "The sale of stock at Macksburg was completed this week, [and] the solicitors will go into Union township [Adair County], where there is $1,500 yet to raise." He added, "It is expected that two weeks will be required in that territory, and after bringing the subscriptions up to the required amount there, the solicitors will move into Spaulding township [Union County]." Yet stock subscriptions would not be the sole source of financing. In October special elections were held in Grand River township [Macksburg] and Union township that resulted in voters overwhelmingly approving a two-year, 5 percent property tax subsidy. Supporters expected that a combination of stock subscriptions and tax money would make bonds attractive to investment houses, thus completing the financing.[18]

The slow advance of the CW&DM continued. Local funding was in place, at least for the Creston to Macksburg leg, and C. B. Judd of the Engineering, Construction & Securities Company unequivocally announced that construction would begin in the foreseeable future. "Macksburg is about to get a railroad—a hope deferred from time to time during the past forty years," proclaimed *The Madisonian* in January 1912. In the time-honored spirit of civic boosterism the newspaper added, "If the road is built to Macksburg, it is certain to be built on to Winterset and Des Moines."[19]

Management of the CW&DM still needed to juggle financial matters. It had to sell bonds, since subscriptions to stock were payable only when the bonds had been placed. This became a challenge, in part because neither the Burlington nor the Rock Island wanted the road built. Not wishing "to lose a valuable slice of territory," these powerful corporations pressured bonding houses in Chicago and New York to avoid these offerings. Forced to be resourceful, the CW&DM, likely at the suggestion of Ross and Judd, formed a subsidiary firm, the Iowa Bond and Security Company, which marketed the 6 percent gold first mortgage notes, targeting mostly Iowans. Although some prospective investors became skeptical when the AN&S entered bankruptcy and other recently opened Iowa short lines encountered financial reversals, success followed.[20]

Finally, in August 1912, the CW&DM let the construction contract. Following the announcement, "residents of Macksburg held a jollification meeting," reported the *Page County Democrat*. "Enthusiasm is manifested by every one there over the prospect of securing a road." The company had raised $135,000 ($2.9 million in 2008 dollars) from stock and taxes, and generated $144,000 ($3.1 million in 2008 dollars) from bonds. Now the pressing concern was that the track had to be completed by the stroke of midnight on December 31, 1912, to receive the township tax money.[21]

Under the supervision of C. B. Judd, the twenty-one-mile route between Creston and Macksburg became a construction zone. Employees of the St. Joseph, Missouri, contractor used hefty steam traction engines to pull earthmoving equipment to shape the right-of-way and were assisted by fifty mule teams; carpenters built three wooden deck bridges, including a substantial span over the meandering (and occasionally treacherous) Grand River; and laborers unloaded rails, ties, and other materials at Burlington sidings in Creston, Orient, and Spaulding. Tracklaying began on the east side of Creston near the fairgrounds, a location that became "Creston Transfer," and proceeded northward on the west side of the Cumberland or "North" branch of the Burlington through the village of Spaulding (1910 population of 100). Then a mile north of the Adair–Union county line at "Burlington Crossing," the rails turned eastward through the Zion settlement (earlier called Leith City) and shortly entered Madison County. But before tracks could reach Macksburg, graders faced a steep ascent coming out of the Grand River valley and a massive clay ridge immediately west of Macksburg. This route through Iowa's "Blue Grass Country" was hardly flat as a floor.[22]

Judd also traveled to Chicago to acquire secondhand rolling stock. He found two 4-4-0 American Standard steam locomotives that could be used in the building process and later as the motive power for the completed road. In the nineteenth century this engine type, which had been introduced in 1836, was extremely popular, and by the 1870s more than 80 percent of the country's steam engines were 4-4-0 locomotives. The universal utility of the American Standard provided what the CW&DM needed: decent speed and high operating reliability over a cheaply built and roughly laid track. A large steam ditcher and two center and two side-dump cars were likewise purchased, essential for work on the difficult terrain near Macksburg.

Like most steam short lines, old and new, secondhand equipment provided the motive power. When the Creston, Winterset & Des Moines was under construction, and then during the first several years of operation, the company used an elderly 4-4-0 American Standard locomotive, No. 6. Apparently the engine was nearly worn out and by 1916 had left the property. Somehow the name of the previous owner, Illinois Terminal, was not completely removed when the C. W. & D. M. R. R. lettering was painted on the tender. This photograph from 1913 catches the No. 6 coupled to one of the road's side-dump cars at Macksburg.

Public Auction Sale!

Of Lots at Macksburg, Iowa.

I will sell at Public Sale

Wednesday, November 13th, 1912

Sale Begins at 10:00 a. m.

150 Lots in the Town of Macksburg, Iowa

Macksburg is in the southwest part of Madison county.   It is the terminus of the railway now being built from Creston.   It is the farthest from competition of any town in the state, being thirteen miles from Lorimor, seventeen miles from Winterset, twenty miles from Creston, and twenty-two miles from Greenfield.

In consequence of this large territory, and being located in the richest farming district in Iowa, it is safe to say that it will be a town of several thousand within the next two years.

Now is the time for those looking for locations for business of any kind to get in on the ground floor. The railway will be completed January 1st.

The lots to be sold are divided into business, resident lots and acreage.   The business lots are conveniently located to the depot; the resident lots and acreage are further back on high, sightly land.

Also, an EIGHT ROOM HOUSE, conveniently located to business center, with good Barn, Wells and Outbuildings.

I am the sole owner of this property, which is unencumbered and in consequence will be sold without reserve at bidders' prices; also, the 160 acres on which these lots are located, and in consequence can satisfy anyone wishing a location.

We have arranged for a suitable tent in which sale will be held in case of bad weather.

Take the C. G. W. to Lorimor; C. R. I. & P. to Winterset; or C. B. & Q. to Creston or Orient.

TERMS---This property will be sold on contract; One-fourth cash on day of sale; balance in three annual payments at six per cent.

For further information, apply to GUY BARKER, Des Moines, Iowa, or ADAM BUSCH, Macksburg, Ia.

S. K. NOLAND, AUCT., 401 Clapp Blk. Des Moines, Iowa.   **Capt. E. G. BARKER, Owner**

W. W. WALKER, Clerk, Cashier National Bank, Macksburg.

The approaching rails of the Creston, Winterset & Des Moines caused considerable excitement in the inland town of Macksburg, Iowa. A land speculator took advantage of the anticipated transportation benefits when he sponsored a town-lot auction on November 13, 1912. The sale went well and soon Macksburg blossomed into a thriving trade center. From *Winterset Madisonian*, November 6, 1912.

A passenger coach and several freight cars were also part of the equipment acquisitions.[23]

As the CW&DM took shape, excitement grew along the route, being greatest in Macksburg. Even before residents heard the shrill whistle of a steam locomotive, economic activities accelerated. Taking advantage of the approaching rails, Captain E. G. Barker, who owned 160 acres of raw land that adjoined the townsite, vigorously promoted the sale of 150 lots at a public auction scheduled for November 13, 1912. Handbills and newspaper advertisements told of the exciting possibilities of Macksburg: "It is the farthest from competition of any town in the state, being thirteen miles from Lorimor, seventeen miles from Winterset, twenty miles from Creston, and twenty-two miles from Greenfield." The copy continued, "In consequence of this large territory, and being located in the richest farming district in Iowa, it is safe to say that it will be a town of several thousand within the next two years." Apparently the auction went well. The Fullerton Lumber Company, which operated a chain of yards in western Iowa, for one, became involved in the local land transactions, prompting a Macksburg resident to comment, "With three lumber yards, it looks as if one could certainly get lumber at the right price."[24]

The red-letter day for the CW&DM came on December 31, 1912. In order to meet the deadline imposed by township voters, construction workers, numbering at times about two hundred men toiling in day and night shifts, pushed the steel rails toward Macksburg. "Splendid weather" aided their heroic efforts. By December 20, the tracklaying gang had come within five miles of West Macksburg, the site of ongoing earth-removal work, but technically within the town's corporate limits. In order to win the race with the calendar, the last several miles were built to the barest standards. "The latter part of the road is not graded at all, only the surface dirt taken off so the track could be laid and the train pass over it," related a local writer. Helped by this drastic shortcut, the first train arrived at the hastily installed West Macksburg siding at 4:30 p.m. on that closing day of 1912. There was no driving of a special spike amid a frenzied crowd, or any other celebration, only relief that rails had finally reached Macksburg.[25]

Much remained to be done, however. Track, especially the final section, had to be reworked; the cut near Macksburg needed to be completed; and depots in Creston and Macksburg had to be finished. Yet on Friday, January 4, 1913, "the first passenger train" took directors and perhaps additional riders from Macksburg to Creston. After more work and a favorable inspection by an examiner from the Iowa Board of Railroad Commissioners, the CW&DM became a bona fide common carrier. By June 30, 1913, the company had spent more than $235,000 ($5 million in 2008 dollars) on its physical plant and rolling stock, or approximately $11,000 per mile, somewhat less than the average for a contemporary short line in the Midwest.[26]

Another red-letter day occurred on February 4, 1913. The CW&DM offi-

Using a small steam shovel, workers deepen a drainage ditch along the recently installed track of the Creston, Winterset & Des Moines west of Macksburg. The grade leading to this location was extremely steep by railroad standards, estimated at nearly 5 percent.

cially issued its first public timetable, listing the schedule between Creston and West Macksburg (the mile of track into Macksburg, a few blocks north of the public square, remained unfinished, as did the depot, engine house, and turntable). If patrons expected frequent, fast trips on the two daily-except-Sunday mixed trains (a freight with an attached coach for express, mail, and passengers) between the two end points, they were sorely disappointed. The morning "accommodation" left Creston Transfer at 7:00, but did not reach the end of the line until 9:05 a.m., having to struggle up the West Macksburg hill. There were intermediate stops at Spaulding, CB&Q Crossing, Rams-bottom, Zion, and Wilson. The afternoon mixed from Creston operated on a slightly faster schedule, leaving at 3:00 and arriving in West Macksburg at 4:50 p.m. The morning run from West Macksburg departed at 9:30 and steamed into Creston Transfer at 11:00 a.m. and the afternoon train left at 5:00 and reached its destination at 6:20 p.m. Ballast-scorching it was not; speeds averaged about ten miles per hour. What a Creston journalist had proclaimed as "Iowa's brightest railway project" was hardly a showcase for modern railroad technology.[27]

To add to these unimpressive train operations, the CW&DM experienced an early setback. On the evening of September 27, 1913, flames reduced the depot in Creston to ashes. "The building was used as a depot and store house and several barrels of oil was [*sic*] consumed," reported the *Creston Morning American*. "The depot was of wood and burned very rapidly."[28]

If there was a grand opening of the CW&DM, it took place a few weeks after the disastrous Creston fire. That October, at the invitation of commercial interests in Macksburg, the Boosters Club and the Business Men's Club of Creston made a special trip over the road. Representatives from the Creston business and professional community and members of the Creston Concert Band packed the coaches borrowed from the Burlington. The train also included a car reserved for "ladies"; perhaps the sponsors anticipated a raucous group of males. Likely, Creston residents considered the railroad as a way to attract business, and their counterparts in Macksburg undoubtedly wished to show that their community was full of live wires, energized by their new rail link.[29]

Almost immediately the CW&DM became the transportation artery for Macksburg and the surrounding countryside. Newspapers reported that considerable livestock moved over the somewhat rickety track structure, including cattle and hogs destined for Swift & Company in Creston and packing plants elsewhere. But the little road hauled more than agricultural products. Inbound shipments ranged from lumber and cement to hardware and farm machinery. The figures for total volume are not known, but the railroad probably handled about three hundred to four hundred revenue cars during its first year of operation.[30]

The railroad business was not easy. It took time to finish the line into Macksburg and for the track corridor there to have active businesses, but eventually several grain elevators and lumberyards appeared. Livestock pens were also built in Macksburg, Zion, and other designated stations en route to Creston. While the company's ditcher scoured out the big cut at West Macksburg, crews tamped the mostly dirt ballast and attended to other maintenance chores associated with a freshly finished track structure. Not only was the railroad burdened with an enormous grade east of the Grand River, reported to be a 5 percent incline, making this possibly the steepest piece of trackage in Iowa, but the company had to deal with the not-so-friendly Burlington. This sole interchange partner forced the CW&DM to maintain an expensive crossover near Spaulding, but more troubling were rate divisions on freight traffic. The short line lacked any real bargaining power, and the only recourse was to file complaints with the Iowa Board of Railroad Commissioners and the Interstate Commerce Commission. Residents came to blame the Burlington for the short line's growing financial woes. "The lack of good will has been a serious handicap." A true understatement.[31]

Not long after the first trains chugged over the line, discussion resumed about building to Winterset. A route was possible but the hilly terrain and the need to bridge the meandering Middle River would make the seventeen-mile extension expensive and time-consuming. Still, backers thought that the commercial rock traffic outside Winterset alone, which the Rock Island monopolized, justified expansion. Even though the Rock Island would resist competition, rate divisions with the Burlington and Rock Island might become more attractive if a second outlet could be established. This had been the case for several other recently opened short lines in the state.[32]

But the balance sheet damped down any immediate efforts for expansion. The income statement for the period from January 21, 1913, to June 30, 1913, revealed net operating revenues of a paltry $513.11. Although figures for the second half of 1913 are unavailable, the year 1914 had a staggering net deficit of $16,124.79 ($342,000 in 2008 dollars). As red ink spilled, the railroad decided that its only course of action was to seek court protection from creditors. On June 25, 1914, Clarence Wilson, a resident of Macksburg and longtime backer, became the receiver and general manager and the individual who hopefully would lead the company through a successful reorganization. The contributor to the Macksburg section of the *History of Madison County and Its People*, published in 1915, duly observed that "the line has been in operation under many vicissitudes practically all its life, and it is said that unless the property is placed under different management, Macksburg will be bereft of an improvement in which she took a great deal of pride."[33]

With additional funds raised from stockholders and from the sale of several pieces of equipment, the receiver made essential improvements. Trackmen attended to "soft spots" that continually plagued the line during wet weather, and replaced rotting, untreated ties with more durable creosoted ties. In a creative move, the company acquired a motor car for mail and passenger service. Although this piece of equipment is a mystery, the car may have been a small gasoline-powered chain-drive vehicle, a type that a few short lines, such as the St. Joseph Valley Railway of Indiana, were using. Time Table No. 4, which became effective on August 18, 1914, showed that, at least on paper, the motor car offered superior service to the mixed trains. The car departed Creston Transfer at 7:15 a.m. and 3:30 p.m. and Macksburg at 8:45 a.m. and 4:55 p.m. and averaged speeds that were about twice as fast as earlier scheduled runs. Yet the railroad dispatched this car only on Tuesdays, Thursdays, and Fridays, a decision based on traffic needs. On Mondays, Wednesdays, and Saturdays, the slower mixed train, which handled the more lucrative shipments of carload freight, made a single round-trip between Macksburg and Creston.[34]

Even though the receivership improved the CW&DM, in 1915 the company failed to generate black ink. While railroad-operating revenues stood at $14,840.46 ($312,000 in 2008 dollars), operating expenses reached a disappointing $17,683.62 ($372,000 in 2008 dollars). The road, though, hardly squandered money. Approximately $10,500 of these expenditures involved payroll, but the yearly compensation for the thirty-one employees was low. The twenty trackmen, most of whom worked part-time, averaged $166 each, and the three section foremen earned somewhat more, $220. The two highest-paid employees, the receiver/general manager and the locomotive engineer, got $1,800 and $1,200, respectively. Although the workforce was subsequently trimmed, overall conditions the following year failed to improve. Then on July 1, 1916, the railroad shut down.[35]

Patrons were not about to quit the CW&DM. The spirit of boosterism remained strong, reinforced by the launching in July 1916 of the *Macksburg Independent*. The editor, Charles Saiser, pushed hard for the resurrection of the CW&DM and kept the community informed on happenings. Although an area entrepreneur established an "Auto Passenger and Freight Service to and from Macksburg and All Neighboring Points," this alternative form of transportation, in the minds of the local citizenry, was not an appropriate substitute for a freight-carrying, all-weather railroad.[36]

In the wake of the closing, a series of meetings followed. In early September at a gathering held at the home of the receiver, the approximately fifty men in attendance voted unanimously to push for solicitations to reopen the road. The feeling existed that the line must be extended to either Lorimor (Great Western) or Winterset (Rock Island). "It is highly desirable that more mileage be added eastward or northward to some connecting road that would give us the advantage of eastern markets and better freight rates."[37]

In order to return the CW&DM to life, management believed a minimum of $18,000 ($351,000 in 2008 dollars) was required, and by September 28, 1916, all but $1,600 ($31,000 in 2008 dollars) had been raised. At last, prospects looked promising for renewed service. Supporters, though, expressed annoyance that some citizens failed to contribute. "There are men, men of ample means who ought to be interested in this project to take care of all that is yet needed," observed the *Independent*. "But there are some folks who are always willing to go coasting if some one else will pull the sled to the top of the hill. Yes, they are even willing to ride up the hill."[38]

On October 12, 1916, the *Independent*, in a front-page headline, announced good news. "STOP—LOOK OUT FOR THE CARS!" The necessary funds had been secured and "train service will be established just as rapidly as the track and equipment will warrant." And editor Saiser continued to agitate for a connection with either the Great Western or Rock Island and to have within at least

Like many twilight short lines, the Creston, Winterset & Des Moines struggled with its track structure. The poorly ballasted roadbed and badly aligned rail attest to the physical limitations of the road.

three years "a line of railroad through Macksburg that will be worthy of the name and a credit to all."[39]

Restoring the CW&DM remained largely a community affair. "Last Friday morning a hurry call was sent out for help to get the C. W. & D. M. track repaired some so that the old 7 spot [locomotive] might be taken to Creston for some repairs," reported the *Independent*. "A number of our town folks responded and by night the track was in shape so that early Saturday morning the engine was started out. Owing to dirt covered crossings and pasture fences across the track, it was not until about five o'clock that Creston was reached."[40]

On December 1, 1916, the rebirth officially occurred, although the CW&DM remained in receivership. Unlike in the past, the railroad handled only freight. Yet this second attempt at profitability turned out no better than before. The backers must have been saddened by the financials for 1917: operating revenues, $4,596.91 ($76,500 in 2008 dollars); operating expenses, $10,323.10 ($172,000 in 2008 dollars). Even with increased demand for railroad service because of America's entry into World War I, the future seemed hopeless for an operation that continued to hemorrhage red ink.[41]

Underscoring the dire financial situation, the district judge, who oversaw the bankruptcy, expressed alarm, telling the receiver in June 1917 that "the road must not cause any more indebtedness" and that "the road had better sell to the highest bidder." Yet the court failed to follow through with its death sentence; the judge bowed to the receiver's commitment of additional money that would make possible the repairs to No. 7, the remaining locomotive (somewhat earlier the No. 6 had been sold), and the replacement of three thousand bad ties. "Courageous loyalty" had saved the day.[42]

Still, the CW&DM limped along, providing service only as needed. Train operations became so intermittent that the Macksburg newspaper often reported these activities. In the March 18, 1918, issue the local column noted, "A joyful sound was heard here this morning. It was the simple toot, toot of the old 7 spot pulling out for Creston." Less joyful were accounts of derailments. "The C. W. & D. M. experienced a delay in traffic this week due to a derailment last Wednesday, which tied up the services until Wednesday of this week," reported the *Independent.* "After working until night to get the cars back on the rails, the crew started for Creston and after a few miles travel the tender became derailed. Altogether the track repairs and putting the rolling stock on track again used up the major portion of the week." The railroad struggled on, occasionally with borrowed motive power from the Burlington, hauling coal, which was much-needed due to wartime fuel shortages and rationing by the U.S. Fuel Administration, and other necessities, to the several stations, and taking grain and livestock to Creston.[43]

As the CW&DM deteriorated, rumors spread about the railroad's fate. Would the line be rehabilitated? Would the Great Western buy the road and extend it to Lorimor or East Peru? Would a scrapper dismantle the property?[44]

In November 1918 the entangled saga of the final demise of the CW&DM began. On November 9 the receiver, with court approval, sold the mortgage to Ralph Beaton and Sigmund Ornstine, junk dealers from Columbus, Ohio, for $30,000 ($425,000 in 2008 dollars). These men quickly peddled the steel and rolling stock to Harris and Greenberg of Chicago, a firm also engaged in the salvage business, and in early December junkers began lifting the rails in Macksburg.[45]

Response among railroad supporters was swift. Robert Brown, the Creston attorney who had been active in the affairs of the company from the start, brought suit in district court to restrain Harris and Greenberg from dismantling the line, arguing that the CW&DM had not been legally abandoned. The contention was also made that the railroad could be operated at a profit and that stockholders and taxpayers had not been fairly compensated for their investments. By the time the judge issued a restraining order, about six miles of track had been removed. Soon the heavier sixty-five-pound steel rails went to Japan, and the used ties were offered cheaply to area residents.[46]

The legal battle raged on. In May 1920 the *Des Moines Sunday Register* succinctly summarized events. "The state of Iowa then [1919] started mandamus proceedings on complaint of various parties. Later the attorney general of the state joined the plaintiffs. Various applications to various judges were made. Some were granted; others were denied. Finally the attorney general secured a restraining order and a trial was held. The state was beaten, but on Jan. 20, 1920, it appealed the case." By summer, however, the legal wrangling stopped; the Iowa Supreme Court allowed the process of dismantling to proceed. And on June 26, 1920, the Iowa secretary of state cancelled the company charter for failure to file the mandatory annual report for 1919.[47]

Through this time of legal maneuvering, hope for resumption of rail service had amazingly not ended. "We are not ready to give up," editorialized the *Independent* on December 12, 1918. "Cheer Up! Every cloud has a rainbow." This sentiment remained strong. A series of meetings had taken place in Creston and Macksburg about how to restart operations. Toward the end of 1919 there was a glimmer of hope. The salvage company seemed willing to sell the railroad, less the rolling stock and track materials already removed, for $50,000 ($617,000 in 2008 dollars), which "is a fair price for the property in its present condition." But efforts to raise that amount failed. Then there were other plans. One called for operating a stub road from Burlington Crossing near Spaulding to Macksburg. Yet more talk centered on regaining ownership and extending the line to a Great Western connection, "preferably to Peru."[48]

Then there were rumors that bordered on the absurd. A story circulated that unnamed promoters expected to build an interurban between Des Moines and Kansas City and the defunct CW&DM would be part of that route. Another told of area men who owned a section of the old grade of the unfinished Rock Island extension between Winterset and Greenfield that passed about four miles north of Macksburg, and this never-railed right-of-way might save the day. With new construction and the completion of the old Rock Island line, entry into the Madison County seat could be achieved, giving the Macksburg railroad that long-coveted outlet.[49]

A decade or two earlier, such speculation about railroad building might have had some credibility. After the war, however, the use of motor vehicles on better roads increased substantially. Local newspapers regularly carried advertisements for the sale of new and used automobiles; frequently told of commercial trucking operations; and spotlighted road improvements. Vehicles were better mechanically and more affordable and the viscous mud and gumbo were becoming less of a hindrance to travel. As early as 1911, Ed Smith, who edited *The Madisonian*, sensed the impending transportation revolution. "Will the motor car replace the passenger coach as a means of travel?" he asked. "If one had put this question ten years ago, his sanity might have been questioned. Today there is enough of an argument in favor of the motor car to make the question a live one and there is no doubt but that the automobile has already cut deeply into the passenger receipts of the railroad companies." Added Smith, "Dirt auto roads are being built and kept in good condition between the principal cities of Iowa and surrounding states. With the auto perfected and the highways further improved, the use of motor cars may soon become the ordinary mode of travel."[50]

Those individuals who wanted to save the CW&DM lacked a grasp of economic realities. The railroad had always been a troubled operation, and neither rebuilding the line nor an extension made much sense. If there had been enough business in Macksburg and Zion, the Burlington would have acquired the several miles from near Spaulding to maintain service. The Great Western had no reason to get involved. The company focused on main stems and hardly wanted to build and buy what would never become more than a minor appendage, even if this extension siphoned some freight traffic away from the Burlington in Creston and tapped the hamlets of McPherson and Orda in Madison County. It also made no sense for the Rock Island to buy the remains of the CW&DM and build connecting trackage. These trunk carriers faced their own challenges, highlighted by adjustments to the end of federal wartime controls.[51]

Boosterism and sentimentality had driven the proponents of a CW&DM resurrection. Many villagers and farmers expressed a genuine love of *their* railroad. "Do Your Best to Get Our Little Willie Home Again," editorialized the *Independent* in January 1920. Residents affectionately referred to the company as the "Crazy Willie & Dandy Molly" (CW&DM), an unexplainable, albeit memorable, nickname, but pet names were not an uncommon practice during the Railway Age.[52]

Macksburg survived the loss of the CW&DM. Although about the time of the railroad's dismemberment, the *Independent* folded, and a lumberyard and the oldest mercantile store closed. Still, other businesses continued, attesting to the positive economic benefits that the railroad had brought. And for decades the population remained rather stable. Even today the village claims approximately one hundred residents, but in recent years the community has lost most retail and service activities to businesses in Creston and Winterset. Although the railroad has been abandoned for nearly ninety years, physical remains exist, including the cement sidewalk to the site of the long-dismantled Macksburg depot, portions of the grade that cross farm pastures, some rotting bridge timbers, and the old brick-lined well at Wilson near the Grand River that provided water for the iron horse. Sprawl has not disturbed much of what was once considered "Iowa's brightest railway project."[53]

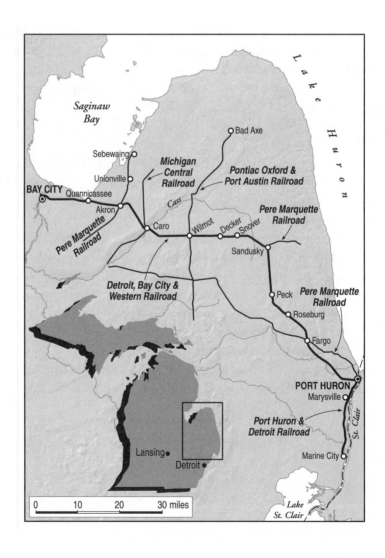

Chapter 3

The Handy Lines: Detroit, Bay City & Western Railroad and Port Huron & Detroit Railroad

B y 1900 Michigan, like other states in the Midwest, claimed impressive steam railroad mileage. At the start of the century the Wolverine State had a 7,946-mile web of steel rails, the fourth-greatest density in the eight-state region. A decade later Michigan mileage reached 9,021 miles, and when the predictable decline set in, it dropped to 8,734 miles in 1920 and 8,072 miles by 1930. This well-developed grid included track owned by lumber carriers, both common and private, that expanded and contracted as timber operations changed. Similar pikes flourished in the forests of northern Minnesota and Wisconsin and the Ozarks of Missouri, and frequently altered their route structures, helping to explain the fluctuations in state mileage statistics during the twilight era.[1]

Neither did the interurban era bypass Michigan. Although the state never had the density of intercity electric lines that covered Illinois, Indiana, and Ohio, mileage grew rapidly before 1910, ultimately reaching about one thousand miles. Two giants, Detroit United Railway and Michigan United Railway, dominated traction operations, and together served every major city in the Lower Peninsula and scores of smaller communities.[2]

The Detroit, Bay City & Western Railroad (DBC&W) impacted the twentieth-century mileage figures for Michigan. By World War I this well-constructed steam road completed its core, but then faltered, forcing within a decade the abandonment of much of its trackage. As with the much smaller and less successful Creston, Winterset & Des Moines, the DBC&W provides further testimony to the positive impact twilight carriers had on their surroundings, and also shows what could have been a better, more integrated regional rail network.

Even when a midwestern state reached railroad maturity, some businessmen believed that opportunities remained for building more lines. Four entrepreneurial brothers from Bay City, Michigan, Charles W., Frank S., George W., and Thomas L. Handy, concluded that the territory to the east of their hometown, the "Thumb Country" on the state's geographical mitten, required better service. If properly executed, such a steel artery could become more than a needed local road, emerging as a strategic link in a larger transportation system.[3]

The Handy brothers, the men behind the Detroit, Bay City & Western Railroad and the companion Port Huron & Detroit Railroad (PH&D), possessed a diverse business background. It would be the resourceful and "always energetic" Thomas Lincoln Handy (1866–1922), known as Tom, who led these twilight railroads as president. His three brothers also held key positions: Charles served as vice president, Frank acted as corporate secretary, and George functioned as treasurer.[4]

The Handy brothers were not native Bay Citians or even Michiganders, but hailed from Illinois. The life of Thomas tells of family and business activities before the brothers' involvement with the DBC&W and PH&D. Born on February 4, 1866, in the central Illinois city of Decatur, a developing manufacturing and railroad center, Thomas was a middle child, the third of Thomas and Mary Housworth Handy's four surviving sons. He also had an older sister, but his younger twin brothers had died in infancy. Thomas's father, an immigrant from England, worked as a machinist, and his mother, a Virginian by birth, managed the household. Like so many men of his generation, Thomas received only a basic education, attending public schools until the age of sixteen. Believing that better opportunities could be found in Chicago, he left Decatur to work in a machine shop. Somewhat later he departed the Windy City to join forces with Frank McClung, whom he had recently met, to take over a lumber-planing mill in the western Michigan town of Hart, located north of Muskegon. But water and boiler problems prompted the men to sell the facility and relocate in West Bay City. Thomas was barely in his twenties, "too young to legally transact business in this state so he grew sideburns to give him the appearance of being an older man." Soon the partnership dissolved when McClung decided to become a preacher, although Thomas found a new associate, a Mr. Cramer. Soon they launched

Handy and Cramer, a box-making enterprise at the corner of South Henry and Main streets, that exploited the vast quantities of mill waste left by the fading lumber industry. Within a few years Thomas's older brother Charles bought out Cramer and later brothers Frank and George joined the company, with Thomas as president and Charles, Frank, and George in positions identical to those they would later hold on their railroads. Their widowed mother and several other family members also moved to West Bay City. The brothers married and raised families. In the early 1890s Thomas wed Harriet Emery, a member of a wealthy lumber family, and they and their three sons and a daughter occupied the "Handy Mansion" that stood on fashionable North Euclid Street in West Bay City.[5]

The move by Thomas and the rest of the Handy clan to West Bay City was a smart decision. (In 1905 Bay City and West Bay City merged to become a single municipality.) An excellent location and natural resources blessed this bustling Bay County seat of more than forty thousand residents situated about one hundred miles northwest of Detroit. Bay City straddled the Saginaw River, a navigable stream that connected to nearby Saginaw Bay on Lake Huron of the expansive Great Lakes. Commercially important stands of white pine, "green gold," had grown nearby, although by the 1890s these trees had been heavily depleted. Fortunately, other valuable extractive resources were available, including deposits of salt, coal, limestone, and gravel. And rich "muck" soil fostered a diversified agriculture that produced beans, corn, hay, oats, sugar beets, and garden truck. Livestock also flourished.[6]

Greater Bay City developed into an important manufacturing, trade, and transportation center. Taking advantage of the forests, by the early 1860s Bay City and West Bay City had become the site of sawmills and related wood product companies. In fact, lumbermen often floated logs down the Saginaw River directly to processors. The community gained fame for the W. D. Young Company, producers of hardwood floors and wooden pails, and the North American Construction Company that sold "redi-cut" Aladdin houses. Other businesses bolstered the local economy, including the North American Chemical Company; National Cycle Company, a maker of bicycles and predecessor of the Louis Chevrolet automobile plant; and the Bay City Industrial Works and the Bay City Dredge Works, manufacturers of steam shovels and other heavy machinery. There were also shipbuilding and repair companies, which included the Defoe Shipyard that opened in 1905. Bay City and West Bay City boasted of being a distribution center for the Thumb Country. "There are many villages in northeastern Michigan that look to us to supply the many needs of their citizens and neighboring farmers," observed a Bay City writer. "Our wholesale merchants, of whom there are said to be more than in any other city in Michigan north of Detroit, include the wholesale grocers, the fruit and vegetable commission merchants, wholesale hardware dealers, tobacco dealers, millers, bakers and others." Bay City and West Bay City took advantage of water transport, and by the end of the nineteenth century the place possessed a good railroad network. Lines of the Detroit & Mackinac, Grand Trunk, Michigan Central, and Pere Marquette fanned out in most directions. Moreover, this environment attracted traction builders. By the early years of the twentieth century, the Saginaw–Bay City Railway and the Michigan United Railway served the area, the latter providing easy access to other electric roads in Michigan and adjoining states. "Bay City is one of the most progressive cities of its size in the country," wrote Thomas Handy in 1916. "It has active, growing industrial interests and a large per capita wealth."[7]

The Handy brothers prospered in the dynamic economy of Greater Bay City. Their venture into box making was lucrative, growing to "immense proportions." Although they remained in the business through World War I, after which a fire destroyed the facility, another enterprise struck their fancy, coal mining. By 1900, soft coal deposits in the area were being mined profitably, so Thomas and his siblings entered the field, launching Handy Brothers Mining Company, with Thomas, the senior partner, as president. Their initial mine, a shallow-shaft operation, was located near Wenona Beach in Bangor Township in Bay County. Somewhat later the brothers acquired Wolverine Mine No. 2 west of Bay City and developed the nearby Wolverine Mine No. 3. In order to serve these diggings, they embarked on their first railroad venture, building the Huron & Western Railroad. This little pike, incorporated on May 26, 1902, served only their coal facilities. "Through the building of the Huron & Western, the Handys were the first to give the local railroads, other than the Michigan Central, direct access to the coal mines of Bay County." Within a short time the brothers sold their mines to the Consolidated Coal Company and the railway to the Pere Marquette Railroad, likely making good profits. These actions did not end their coal-mining ventures, but rather they speculated in area coal lands and opened other mines, driving shafts near Akron and then Unionville, situated in Tuscola County east of Bay City. And they continued to operate a wholesale coal yard near their box factory.[8]

Being knowledgeable about business happenings in their hometown and its vicinity, Thomas and his brothers decided to take a flyer with an established railroad, the Pontiac, Oxford & Northern Railroad, popularly known as the "Polly Ann." Built in the 1880s as the Pontiac, Oxford & Port Austin Railroad, this road operated a one-hundred-mile line from Pontiac northward to Caseville on Lake Huron, and served the intermediate Thumb Country towns of Oxford, Imlay City, and Pigeon. Never a stellar property, this lightly constructed road had been reorganized in the early 1890s and had entered a receivership in 1905. But in the reorganization process a battle had erupted for control, and Thomas worked successfully with the warring factions. In late 1908 at a courthouse-step sale he took charge of the contested property with a bid of $400,000 ($9.4 million in 2008 dollars). It is unclear, but Thomas may have been a stalking horse for officials of the Grand Trunk Railway of Canada who wished to protect their monopoly on Pontiac traffic from rival Michigan Central. Irrespective of the role played by the Canadians, the Grand Trunk took over the Polly Ann on November 2, 1909, and again the Handys fared well. A former employee speculated (probably incorrectly) that the brothers' profit amounted to $2 million.[9]

The experiences gained from the Huron & Western and the Polly Ann seemingly whetted the appetites of the Handy brothers for more railroad ventures. These triumphs were a rehearsal of sorts for their greater involvement in the railroads of Michigan through both construction and acquisition.

The Handy brothers, of course, wished to succeed in their business endeavors. Yet it is evident that Thomas, the titular family leader and spokesman, had also become an enthusiastic booster of his adopted community. At the time of his death, the *Bay City Times-Tribune* editorialized that "in the passing of Thomas L. Handy Bay City has lost a man who never lost faith in his home city, and who lived up to that faith in his business as well as his private life."[10]

Thomas and his siblings concluded that they and Bay City could profit together from another railroad. Plans for building the Detroit, Bay City & Western took tangible form on May 8, 1907, when the Handys signed articles of association to form the company. And five days later they received a charter from the Michigan secretary of state to span the approximately one hundred miles from Bay City to Port Huron, and authorization to issue $400,000 ($9.1 million in 2008 dollars) of capital stock and $350,000 ($7.9 million in 2008 dollars) of first mortgage, 5 percent bonds.[11]

The Handys had not formulated this scheme out of thin air, but reacted to several factors. For years Bay Citians had sought another line into the Thumb Country, the "Garden Spot of Michigan." Commented a local historian, "It is peculiar that a railroad so much desired by the residents of Bay County should be the last steam road to be built into the country, yet such was the case." Residents also wanted a better connection to Port Huron. With the October 24, 1891, opening of the 6,025-foot St. Clair Tunnel under the St. Clair River between Port Huron and Sarnia, Ontario, Port Huron had become a strategic railroad center, providing convenient links to Toronto, Buffalo, and the Atlantic East. In 1908 this "International Main Line" became upgraded with the electrification of tunnel motive power. Furthermore, marine traffic through Port Huron was growing rapidly because of congestion at Detroit. And this metropolis of nearly twenty thousand residents benefited from a more diversified economy, no longer dependent on a lumber base. "After numerous groups of promoters and near-financiers had talked for a generation of building a railroad from Bay City to Port Huron and other Bay City businessmen on two or three occasions had subscribed for stock and bonuses in futile endeavors to build such a road," commented a Bay City editor, "'Tom' Handy built it without asking a dollar of aid from Bay City." The tease had ended.[12]

But the drive by the Handys to build the DBC&W involved more than a commitment to their hometown. The brothers wanted to enhance their coal-mining operations near Akron, and they sensed that places between Bay City and Port Huron, and even Detroit, could benefit from a railroad connection or improved service. "The vast amount of sugar beets shipped annually and the bright prospects of the coal industry of the valley offer splendid inducements for additional transportation projects," opined a Bay City writer in 1905. By this time strong domestic demand for sugar, and stable prices aided by federal tariff policies made beet production a rewarding agricultural pursuit. Profitable "bridge" traffic was also expected. Proclaimed Thomas Handy, "Our entire mileage will have a low grade line which, comparatively, should give our railroad considerable advantage in handling through freight en route East, or via Straits of Mackinac to Duluth and the Northwest."[13]

The Handy brothers understood that a railroad between Bay City and Port Huron would face competition from the Pere Marquette. In fact, their anticipated projection would run between two lines operated by that company, a northern route that at times hugged the shore of Lake Huron and a more southerly inland line. Yet the presence of the Pere Marquette did not frighten or discourage the Handys. Both pieces of Pere Marquette trackage had been poorly engineered and cheaply constructed by narrow-gauge predecessors in the late 1870s and early 1880s. Neither the Port Huron & Northwestern Railway nor the Saginaw, Tuscola & Huron Railroad employed quality construction standards; their lines contained sharp curvatures and heavy grades. Furthermore, at this time the Pere Marquette limped along and lacked competitive qualities. "In the next four years [1908–1912]," noted a historian of the company, "[the Pere Marquette] was to reach the lowest depths of physical inefficiency that it is possible for a road to reach and still operate."[14]

The process of building the Handy road took longer than casual observers or even the brothers may have expected. Although the first dirt was turned in

1907, rails did not reach Port Huron for nearly a decade. But throughout this era such slow progress was more often the norm rather than the exception. Initial construction took place between Bay City and Akron, a distance of nineteen miles, as the Handys wanted to reach their mine about a mile west of "Tuscola's enterprising coal town." This community would also provide an interchange with that circuitous northern line of the Pere Marquette that ran between Port Huron, Bad Axe, and Bay City, and entry of the DBC&W to the Akron area would surely provide better service than what the Pere Marquette offered. Except for a few streams, most notably the Cass River east of Caro, the DBC&W would face a terrain that was relatively flat, a favorable feature of much of the topography of the Thumb Country. But once again it took time to acquire a right-of-way strip. Fortunately, farmers made land donations, realizing that their acres had "already greatly increased in value by the expectation of easy loading of beets, potatoes and other farm products and also easy means of communication with Bay City."[15]

While the Handy brothers knew that their railroad would connect Bay City with Akron and serve Quanicassee and a few other intermediate settlements, for some time the routing beyond Akron remained undetermined. In the latter part of 1909 Thomas Handy, speaking for the company, flirted about the projection with representatives from Cass City, located on the Polly Ann, and Caro, southwest of Cass City and poorly served by the thirty-three mile "Caro Branch" of the Michigan Central. Caro won out. Residents offered a bonus of $3,000 ($71,000 in 2008 dollars), "nearly every citizen had a share in the good work." This seat of Tuscola County offered more local traffic, and the town would be on a more direct path to Port Huron. It did not take long for surveyors and land agents to work their magic and to cause much anticipation and excitement in Caro. As an advertisement for the Commercial & Savings Bank proclaimed, "The New Railroad Will Mean More Business for Caro," and confidently announced that it "is fully prepared to do all business instructed to its care."[16]

The Handy brothers grasped the ins-and-outs of railroad-making. In order to maximize their personal profits, they organized the Bay City Construction Company to oversee the actual building of the DBC&W, and later they would use this firm to construct the PH&D. Creating such a subsidiary had become a standard ploy used by twilight railroad builders, and was really a timeless practice. In their construction endeavors, the Grand Trunk gave the Handys assistance, providing them with motive power and rolling stock and a modern tracklaying machine. Not until late summer 1910 did Handy road rails reach Caro, twenty-nine miles from Bay City, and that October the railroad began to dispatch freight trains between these end points. Somewhat earlier, crews switched what timetables called Akron Coal Mine, and the road provided limited freight service between Bay City and Akron.[17]

Construction standards for the first major component of the DBC&W were reasonably high. Although the company laid acceptable sixty-seven-pound used steel rail for the nineteen miles between Bay City and Akron, it opted for heavier eighty-pound relay rail between Akron and Caro, and the line was well-ballasted and tied. Following a favorable inspection in November 1911 by the Michigan Railroad Commission, the official report indicated that "the right of way is well ditched, new woven wire fence the entire length of the line; crossing signs and whistling posts were being installed." In the wake of the first passenger runs between Bay City and Caro, the Caro newspaper mentioned that "surprise was expressed at the good condition of the road-bed, the car running smoothly, with little side motion or jolting, accounted for largely perhaps by the fact that the steel rails are much heavier than is commonly used on new roads."[18]

Trackside structures, however, were not out of the ordinary. The DBC&W economized on depots in Akron and Caro, yet the results were wholly practical. In Akron, workers remodeled a two-story house and in Caro they modified a former horse stable. In time the company erected a small masonry depot in Bay City on Madison Street "one block nearer the business section than the station of the Michigan Central [and] street cars run within 200 feet of the station." And the road constructed a utilitarian frame engine house and repair facility near the corner of Sherman and North streets that unfortunately burned on January 8, 1913, but $20,000 of insurance money allowed for a rapid rebuilding.[19]

Once laborers had placed most of the finishing touches on the Bay City-to-Caro line, the company announced that passenger service would begin in early 1911. The first public timetable of the self-proclaimed "Thumb Country Short Line," which took effect on March 18, 1911, listed three daily round-trip trains, leaving Bay City at seven and eleven in the morning and 3:45 in the

In February 1911, officials of the Detroit, Bay City & Western Railroad (President Thomas L. Handy stands farthest right) posed alongside their newly acquired passenger train set in Bay City. This was fancy equipment for the "Thumb Country Short Line," at the time less than thirty miles long. *Courtesy of Bay County Historical Society.*

afternoon, and taking one hour and ten minutes to make the twenty-nine mile run. After a brief layover in Caro, the trains returned to their home terminal. These runs handled the shipments for the American Express Company and, somewhat later, "closed pouched" U.S. Mail.[20]

Even before the debut of train service, management proudly displayed the newly acquired passenger rolling stock. Unlike typical short lines of the day, the DBC&W offered travelers truly remarkable accommodations. Although selecting secondhand equipment (probably from the friendly Grand Trunk), the road provided beautifully refurbished cars that were "strictly up to the minute in every particular." In February 1911 reporters and the curious toured the train-set that was placed on display near the Sherman Street crossing in Bay City. "There are three full vestibuled coaches finished in the most modern and attractive style, fully equal to any other coaches now entering Bay City. The train is composed of a combination smoker and baggage car, a day coach and parlor car." Added this reporter, "They are right out of the shops and sparkle in their coat of maroon paint, varnish and gilt letters." Glamorous indeed, but perhaps too much for only a twenty-nine-mile railroad. Yet the Handys held high hopes for expansion. By World War I the greatly lengthened road possessed five additional baggage cars and coaches. Rumors of acquiring gasoline-powered motor cars were mere speculation. In this regard the DBC&W would differ from many contemporary short lines.[21]

Motive power, though, was far less impressive. Again the DBC&W selected secondhand equipment with at least four locomotives coming from the Grand Trunk. A Bay Citian commented in 1910, "Did you observe these engines have been repainted and striped in the same style as Grand Trunk locomotives?" Neither the first nor the later steamers possessed stellar qualities. When the Bureau of Valuation of the Interstate Commerce Commission (ICC) inventoried DBC&W rolling stock in 1919, it listed eight relatively small steam locomotives; three 4-4-0 American standards, one of which Baldwin had built in 1875; two 2-6-0 Moguls; one 2-8-0 switcher; and two 4-6-0 ten-wheelers. The newest engine, No. 10, a ten-wheeler that came from the Nickel Plate Road, dated from 1892, and surely saw frequent assignments on freight runs. But on a trackage that lacked substantial grades, these light pieces of motive power, "all of the old hand-fired variety," probably performed satisfactorily. If needed, double-headers could be assigned to high-tonnage trains. The company, though, painted and lettered its locomotives attractively and provided good maintenance.[22]

The number of pieces of freight rolling stock was adequate, and greater than many comparable roads, old and new. In March 1913 the DBC&W reported a fleet of twenty-five gondolas, used primarily to haul coal and sugar beets, and three boxcars. At this time the company also possessed two cabooses and some miscellaneous maintenance equipment, including a 7.5-ton crane that had been built in 1911 by the Bay City Industrial Works. In subsequent years the size of the freight fleet increased. By 1921 the railroad owned 105 gondolas, eight maintenance of way units, and five cabooses.[23]

Characteristic of twilight carriers in the Midwest, the DBC&W immediately bolstered on-line economies. While the financial impact the railroad had on Bay City is difficult to assess, the company, which maintained a general office on Johnson Street and nearby maintenance facilities, enhanced local spending by employing a score or two of workers. And Bay City extended its sphere of commercial influence, at times altering trade patterns. In an era of dreadful public roads and unreliable or exceedingly slow vehicles, the railroad gave residents of Akron and Caro and the adjoining locale direct, convenient access to the advantages of the city. Significantly, the first organized passenger movement over the road to Caro, which took place on March 16, 1911, carried about three hundred members of the Bay City Merchants' Trade Association and the Bay City Board of Commerce. The groups extended "a personal invitation" to Caro residents to visit their metropolis the following day. Many accepted this opportunity to become better acquainted with the businesses and services in their hosts' community, and the Handys provided these trains at their own expense. Participants wore badges that said, "A Handy Day for Caro, Akron, Bay City, DBC&W Railroad." Civic leaders saw the developing Handy Line as an engine for growth; "rapid development of the Thumb seems assured."[24]

It is somewhat easier to ascertain the positive economic effects that occurred in Caro, particularly in 1911 and 1912. Residents rightly expected that the coming of the Handy road "will tend to increase the lead it already enjoys over all other towns of the Thumb." In late 1911 Caro got a new lumberyard, a partnership between William Fitzgerald and the Cummins brothers; a year later the Peoples State Bank, which was capitalized at $40,000, opened its doors and an ensuing "building boom," involving mostly residences, took place. After Caro businessmen entertained visitors in October 1913, the editor of the *Tuscola County Advertiser* crowed that these out-of-towners "marveled at the transformation," being impressed not only by new and expanded businesses but also by the concrete pavement and "attractive boulevard lighting system" that graced the commercial section.[25]

Just as the several communities served by the DBC&W reaped the benefits of the new service, the company itself looked to be a winning proposition. The earnings statement compiled for the first half of 1911 listed freight revenues at $15,990, passenger revenues at $7,139 and net income at $2,069. And for the following year a stronger balance sheet resulted, due in part to the November 1912 opening of the extension to Wilmot, eleven miles east of Caro, and a tie-in with the old Polly Ann. A striking feature of the financial picture involved the volume of riders, nearly 200,000 for the period, which even surprised the general passenger agent. The company's eagerness to promote travel and to operate specials at the drop of a hat explains this impressive number. In early September 1911, for example, the Handy road offered a one-dollar round-trip ticket between Caro and Bay City on regularly scheduled trains and special runs that allowed riders to attend the annual fair and horse races sponsored by the Bay County Agricultural Society. The fare also included admission to the fairground that adjoined DBC&W tracks just east of town.[26]

What precisely did the Handy brothers have in mind for their road? Evidence suggests that, early on, they expected to push toward Port Huron, possibly reaching Detroit, and to remain independent. "I have been greatly impressed by the wealth of the country east of Wilmot and in Sanilac County, which is sadly in need of better transportation facilities," Thomas Handy told the press in June 1911. "I should say the prospects of a road running east from Wilmot were never as bright as at the present moment." He added, "We have huge coal fields lying along the line and if the road proves as good a property as it now promises to be, we shall hold and operate it ourselves."[27]

Yet this desire for corporate independence may have been fleeting or untrue. As early as 1910, area newspapers thought that the Grand Trunk would take charge, seeing the DBC&W as "eventually being owned and operated by the Grand Trunk, making a new through line from north central Michigan to the east." Surely these journalists were on the right track; the Grand Trunk likely had entered the Hardys' business equation, offering the possibility of another profitable sale. This Montreal-based carrier, which operated extensively in Ontario and Michigan, had embarked upon an expansive phase. Under the leadership of Charles Melville Hays, an experienced American railroad executive who had joined the Grand Trunk as general manager in 1896 and became president in 1909, the Canadian carrier embarked on big, even grandiose endeavors. Under Hays, the company responded to keen competition from the Canadian Pacific Railway and several American roads by gaining control of the Central Vermont Railway, joint control of the Detroit & Toledo Short Line Railroad, and absorption of the Canada Atlantic Railway. "The most important undertaking has been the building, under Mr. Hays's direction, of the Grand Trunk Pacific," noted the *Railway Age Gazette* in 1912. "[It] is being built from Moncton, N.B., west to Prince Rupert, B.C., and is to have 3,550 miles of main line." Although Hays had misgivings about the costs and objectives of a rapidly growing Grand Trunk, he went along with demands for expansion from politicians and other believers in a greater Canada. "Hays and Grand Trunk," observed historian Don L. Hofsommer, "were swept up in it."[28]

In a small way, Hays had already demonstrated Grand Trunk thinking when the Polly Ann entered the orbit of his company. Just as this short line had a role to play in the Michigan network of the Grand Trunk, the DBC&W, finished or not, promised a direct route from Port Huron to Bay City, and then possibly to Mackinaw City (via the Detroit & Mackinac Railway) and Sault Ste. Marie, and ultimately to Chapleau or Porcupine Lake, Ontario, for connection with the Grand Trunk Pacific. Enhancing this routing strategy were rumors that the Grand Trunk would take control of the 200-mile Detroit & Mackinac. Already, a tie-in between the Handy Line and the Grand Trunk's Polly Ann was being forged, and the two roads interchanged in Bay City.[29]

The reminiscences of a former employee, Irl Baguley, support a Hays and Grand Trunk interest in the DBC&W. In the 1970s Baguley, who joined the Handy Lines as station agent at Caro in 1920, wrote an account of the alleged relationship between the Handy brothers and Hays. Baguley suggested that a sales agreement had been finalized, awaiting only the proper signatures, but then tragedy struck. When Thomas Handy and his attorney arrived in Montreal to complete the transaction, word reached the city of the *RMS Titanic* disaster of April 14, 1912. Hays and his wife were among the 2,200 passengers, and only Mrs. Hays was counted as one of the seven hundred survivors. There would be no sale, for the new leadership of the Grand Trunk "would have nothing to do with the purchase of an unknown road."[30]

The inability to sell the developing DBC&W to the Grand Trunk may have prompted the Handys to push ahead with construction as quickly as possible. Perhaps a completed artery might appeal to the Grand Trunk or another road. Indeed, the mighty Pennsylvania Railroad (PRR) at this time contemplated a route from Toledo to Detroit, and a finished DBC&W could provide the PRR easy access to the traffic of the Sagninaw River valley. Business boomed in Detroit, largely because of accelerating automobile production, and the population reflected this economic surge: 285,000 in 1900, 466,000 in 1910, and almost a million in 1920. The PRR did not appreciate that New York Central affiliate Michigan Central dominated the lucrative Detroit market. This desire to penetrate eastern Michigan, encouraged by industrialist Henry Ford, propelled the PRR in 1917 to organize the Pennsylvania-Detroit Railroad and proceed with land acquisition and construction. Yet PRR trains would not reach the Motor City for another decade.[31]

Before the PRR arranged financing for its entry into Detroit, Thomas Handy and his brothers, with approval from the Michigan Railroad Commission, floated a major bond issue through the First Trust and Savings Bank of Chicago. The Handys expected that the $1.2 million ($26.4 million in 2008 dollars) of first mortgage, 5 percent twenty-year bonds would permit completion of their road and cover the necessary support facilities. Taking advantage of a robust regional and national economy, the debt found buyers, and the future looked rosy for the Thumb Country Short Line.[32]

Even prior to the bond sale, Handy crews prepared the right-of-way east from Wilmot to Sandusky, a town of nearly one thousand and the seat of Sanilac County. And this community eagerly anticipated enhanced railroad service. The nineteen-mile extension would traverse a thriving agricultural area where sugar beet production was expanding. "The territory is already developed and the land is of unexcelled richness and is dotted with large barns and fine houses, conditions seldom found along a new line of railroad," opined the *Tuscola County Advertiser*. The DBC&W would also serve several inland settlements, with Snover being the most important. Sandusky itself would provide a connection with an eight-mile stub of the Pere Marquette from Carsonville, a station on its north–south Bad Axe to Port Huron line, and Sandusky would likely generate immediate traffic, especially passengers and freight destined for Bay City and points beyond to the north and west.[33]

In autumn 1913 the eighty-pound rails reached Snover and, several months later, Sandusky. As with the previously completed sections, arrival of the DBC&W sparked heightened economic activities. While there were no new towns, except for several way stations that each contained a combination freight and passenger shelter, livestock pens, and a sugar beet weighing "shack," the railroad brought about real growth to existing towns. Decker, a formerly rail-starved community in western Sanilac County, was one such place, and the village experienced much excitement. Shortly after operations began, residents took pride in the opening of their first financial institution, the Decker State Bank, and then applauded construction of a large bean elevator. The community happily regained its post office, which had been closed since 1906. In Snover, four miles east of Decker, a similar spurt occurred. "Two cream buying stations have already been established and the outlook for the town is bright," was the assessment of an area journalist in November 1913. Sales of town lots were also brisk, so much so that some unhappiness followed. "Some complaint has been heard of the prices asked for building lots in Snover, but the owner of a large number of lots offers them at prices ranging from $35 to $150, but naturally wants them to go to persons who will build upon them and not hold them for speculative purposes." There was no outlandishly wild speculation in Snover, but the coming of the iron horse energized the local real estate market.[34]

While the DBC&W crept toward Port Huron, the Handy brothers contemplated other construction. In late 1912 and early 1913, discussions took place about building the half-dozen miles north from Akron to Unionville and perhaps somewhat farther to Sebewaing, a small port town on Saginaw Bay. "Citizens of Unionville and Sebewaing as well as farmers between Akron and Unionville are greatly interested in the extension." Although Unionville and Sebewaing had access to the rather rickety Pere Marquette, the Handy road would be built a few miles to the east and would also serve the brothers' coal mine and an anticipated second shaft. Thomas Handy made it clear to residents along the proposed route that they must provide financial assistance and the right-of-way, requirements that were neither surprising nor unreasonable. Although the needed support was not forthcoming, for years maps of the DBC&W showed the never-to-be-built branch as a broken line between Akron and Unionville. Still, this was not map fakery; the railroad obtained trackage rights over 5.5 miles of the Pere Marquette to reach the Handy mine.[35]

Less discussed than the Unionville spur was building beyond Bay City, making the "& Western" a meaningful part of the corporate name. In 1910 and again in 1913, reports circulated that the Handy brothers contemplated expanding northeastward from Bay City for approximately seventy-five miles, through Harrison in Clare County to Marion in Osceola County. At Marion, the DBC&W would met the Manistee & Grand Rapids Railroad (later the Michigan East and West Railroad), a sixty-five-mile short line headed by Halleck Seaman, an active participant in twilight-era railroad projects, and first president of the Illinois, Iowa & Minnesota Railroad. This connection would give the Handys a friendly outlet to Manistee on the shores of Lake Michigan, and would provide a useful interchange at Marion with the Ann Arbor Railroad, whose main line stretched from Toledo, Ohio, through Ann Arbor and Cadillac, to Frankfort, a busy Lake Michigan port. Along portions of this talked-about route, the DBC&W would again be in competition with the Pere Marquette.[36]

Even before the DBC&W reached Sandusky, the business community of Bay City once more sought to extend its influence. On the eve of scheduled passenger service beyond Wilmot to Decker and Snover, which occurred shortly before Christmas 1913, the Bay City Board of Commerce invited residents to ride a special train, compliments of the Handys, as part of a "get acquainted" program. A large number of people took advantage of the invitation and soon likely became regular patrons of commercial and professional services in Bay City and, of course, bought tickets "via the Handy Line."[37]

With the arrival of the DBC&W in Sandusky, which was met with great

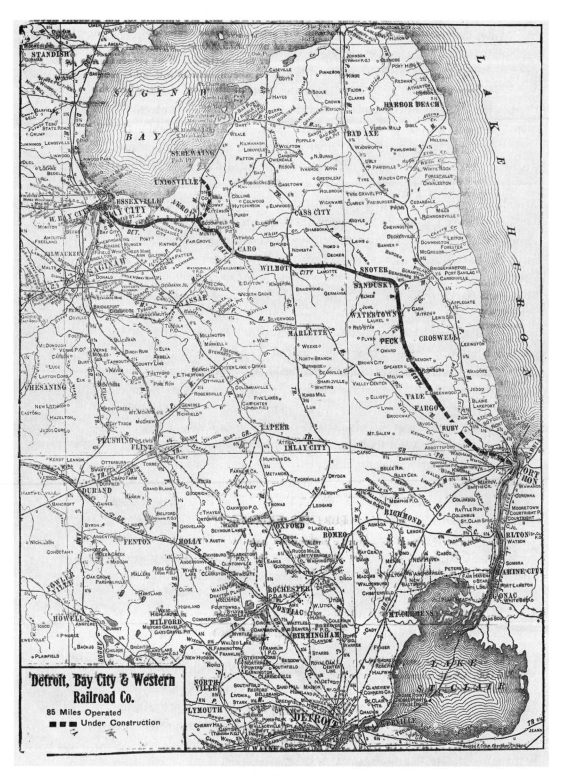

The reverse cover of a Lawrence Mills and Company flyer promoting the sale of first mortgage bonds of the Handy Line shows a map of the portion in operation as of 1916. The proposed construction between Akron and Unionville and Fargo and Port Huron, together with other railroads in the Thumb Country, are indicated.

jubilation, the Handy brothers operated a fifty-eight-mile railroad. Increased length meant more train miles and operating revenues. The figures for the fiscal year that ended June 30, 1914, revealed income of $146,712 ($3.1 million in 2008 dollars) and net earnings of $76,021 ($1.6 million in 2008 dollars). The surplus for the period stood at a respectable $47,151 ($1 million in 2008 dollars), and the company listed a surplus carryover of $46,137. The Handys had hardly created a third-rate short line reminiscent of the then-struggling Creston, Winterset & Des Moines, but rather a carrier that offered prospects for greater earnings, especially if it could tap profitable bridge traffic on the east end.[38]

For some time, Sandusky remained the end-of-track. The town, not unexpectedly, became more lively economically; businesses opened or expanded and the population rose by several hundred. Likely the outbreak of the European war made placing the remaining bond issue of 1912 more difficult. By the end of 1914, however, the Handy brothers had their financial house in order. Confidence among Sanduskyians for sustained growth surely received a boost when at last construction resumed toward Port Huron.[39]

Yet building occurred at a slow pace. It would not be until July 1, 1915, that the DBC&W established freight and passenger service for an additional eleven miles to Peck, an inland village in southern Sanilac County. Later, rails were extended the thirty-one miles through the Sanilac and St. Clair county villages of Roseburg, Fargo, and Ruby, and on October 27, 1916, they at last reached Port Huron. Trackage rights for approximately three miles between Westover Junction and Port Huron over the Pere Marquette, a not-so-kind host, gave a linkage to connecting lines, most importantly the Grand Trunk. Unlike much of the previous portions of the route, workers needed to erect more piled bridges, including a high trestle over Mill Creek near Fargo, about fifteen miles southeast of Peck. And the physical terrain presented challenges, much of it being of a boggy consistency. Occasionally this peat-like soil caught fire and burned, or smoldered for months, even years.[40]

As with previous segments, the general condition of the physical plant was good. On June 13, 1916, representatives of the Michigan Railroad Commission inspected the road and they liked what they saw. "The track is ballasted with a good grade of ballast and the surface and alignment is [sic] satisfactory for the traffic presented. A large number of sidings have been constructed for the accommodation of shippers." Added the examiners, "The openings in the track where bridges and culverts are maintained are generally constructed with concrete and steel. The company expects to renew about two thousand ties this year. The ties are generally in good condition." Commission inspectors also endorsed the railroad's operations in the Bay City area: "This road

Detroit, Bay City and Western R. R. Company

SCHEDULE OF TRAINS

Effective February 5, 1917

ALL TRAINS DAILY
EXCEPT SUNDAY

C. S. RUTTLE,
G. P. A.

THOS. L. HANDY,
President and Gen'l Mgr.

The Handy Line issued typical public timetables, including this one that became effective at the time the road at last reached Port Huron. Passenger train service was not extensive, but double daily-except-Sunday service was common for short lines and secondary main and branch lines of Class 1 roads. *Courtesy of A. B. Magary Collection.*

DETROIT, BAY CITY & WESTERN R. R.

THE ONLY LINE BETWEEN BAY CITY AND PORT HURON
Without changing cars.

TRAINS EAST BOUND **TRAINS WEST BOUND**

EFFECTIVE MONDAY FEBRUARY 5, 1917

Miles from Bay City	STATIONS	2	4	6	STATIONS	1	3	5
		A.M		P M.	(Tunnel Sta.)	A.M.		P.M.
0	BAY CITY ......Leave	7.15		4.15	PORT HURON..Leave	6.00		4.15
2	Center Avenue..........	7.21		4 21	Wadham....	6 12		4.27
4	Raby	7.26		4.26	Ruby....	6.23		4.38
7	Farleigh..............	7.31		4.31	Fargo.................	6.34		4.49
11	Quanicassee..........	7.43		4.43	Roseburg............ ...	6.49		5.06
13	Gardendale........	7.48		4.48	Peck	7.05		5.20
15	Sharpville......	7.53		4.53	Watertown............	7.18		5.33
16	Downing..............	7.56		4.56	Sandusky	7.28		5.43
18	Akron Coal Mine........	8.01		5.01	Hazelwood....	7.34		5. .9
19	Akron..	8.04		5 03	Elmer	7.44		5.59
22	Mitchells......... ...	8.09		5.09	Snover..	7.49		6.04
23	Montei	8.12		5.12	Decker.................	7.56		6.11
24	Gravel Pit.............	8.16		5.16	Hemans................	8.01		6.18
29	Caro	8.28		5.28	Wilmot................	8.15		6.34
33	Seeley	8 37		5.37	Wellsford............	8.23		6.41
35	Daytona	8.42		5.42	Daytona	8.28		6.46
37	Wellsford.	8.46		5.46	Seeley..............	8.37		6.51
40	Wilmot	8.52		5.52	Caro..................	8.45		7.03
45	Hemans..	9.05		6.05	Gravel pit.............	8.55		7.13
47	Decker	9.11		6.11	Montei.................	8.59		7.18
52	Snover	9.19		6.19	Mitchells	9.02		7.20
54	Elmer.	9.24		6.24	Akron....	*a* 9.07 *d* 9.20		7.25
57	Hazelwood	9.34		6.34	Akron Coal Mine........	9.23		7.28
60	Sandusky.............	9.40		6.40	Downing....	9.28		7.32
65	Watertown.	9.50		6 50	Sharpville..............	9.31		7.35
71	Peck	10 03		7.03	Gardendale.	9.35		7.40
78	Roseburg..............	10.18		7.18	Quanicassee........ ...	9.40		7.45
85	Fargo	10 35		7.35	Farleigh	9.53		7.57
90	Ruby	10 49		7.49	Raby	9.57		8.02
96	Wadham	11.00		8.00	Center Avenue..........	10.02		8.07
102	PORT HURON...Arrive (Tunnel Sta.)	11.15		8.15	BAY CITY.......Arrive	10.10		8.15
		A. M		P M.		A. M.		P.M.

Note: Column 4 (Train No. 4) and Column 3 (Train No. 3) are marked "DISCONTINUED TEMPORARILY".

ALL TRAINS DAILY EXCEPT SUNDAY

Connections at Bay City with Michigan Central, Pere Marquette, Detroit and Mackinac, Grand Trunk Ry. System and electric lines for all points.
At Akron with P. M R. R.
At Caro with M. C. R. R.
At Wilmot with P. O & N. R. R.
At Sandusky with P. M. R. R.
At Port Huron with G. T. Ry., P. M. R. R., and electric lines.

Have your freight consigned in care of

D. B. C. & W. R. R.

We Solicit Your Patronage.

C. S. RUTTLE,

Gen'l Pass Agt.

During the early stages, construction personnel encountered mostly easy grading and bridge-building work, but as the Handy Line progressed toward Port Huron, conditions became more challenging, including the spanning of Mill Creek near Ruby. This trestle proved expensive to maintain and was one reason the successor, Detroit, Caro & Sandusky Railway, retired the line between Fargo and Port Huron in the mid-1920s. *Courtesy of T. J. Gaffney Collection.*

crosses six spur tracks of the Michigan Central Railroad at Bay City. The crossings are protected by gates, normally against the traffic of the said spurs. They also cross the Pere Marquette Belt Line at Bay City, the same being protected by the full-interlocking system; and they also cross the Pere Marquette main line at Akron, which crossing is protected by a half-interlocking system, normally clear for the Pere Marquette Railroad." These comments closed the report: "This property is found to be in a satisfactory condition and much improved since the last inspection."[41]

Differing from most railroads that served farming communities, the DBC&W owned depots that were not frame structures, except for the recycled buildings in Akron and Caro. The Handy brothers creatively opted for modern cement construction. Such building materials were readily available, and these depots were judged to be "neat and convenient and ample for the traffic presented." Since these structures were unlikely to be engulfed by flames, the company benefited from reduced fire insurance premiums.[42]

By April 1917 the DBC&W served the string of cement block depots with double daily passenger service. Train No. 2 left Bay City at 7:15 a.m. and traveled the 102 miles to Port Huron, reaching its destination at 11:15 a.m. No. 6 departed Bay City at 4:15 p.m. and arrived in Port Huron at 8:15 p.m. Train No. 1 steamed out of Port Huron at 6:00 a.m. and pulled into Bay City at 10:10 a.m. No. 5 left Port Huron at 4:15 p.m. and terminated in Bay City at 8:15 p.m. These schedules allowed residents of Caro, Wilmot, Peck, and other communities ample time to shop, conduct business or engage in additional activities in Bay City and, to a somewhat lesser extent, in Port Huron. Passenger trains used the company's downtown station in Bay City (which it wanted to replace with a larger structure, costing $75,000) and shared the Tunnel Station with the Grand Trunk and Pere Marquette in Port Huron.[43]

This passenger service was not only important to patrons, but to the railroad as well. Even before the line reached Port Huron, a growing ridership contributed significantly to company coffers. "The entire section contains numerous small settlements from which a passenger traffic has developed to the extent of accounting for about forty per cent of our revenue," revealed Thomas Handy in September 1916. Yet a combination of increased public road building and expanded automobile ownership were beginning to threaten the financial health of passenger trains. Indeed, it would be in May 1916 that the Huron Shore Pike Association was formed, a civic organization that agitated for a hard-surface road for the 125 miles between Port Huron and Bay City.[44]

As with most steam railroads, the DBC&W fell under the control of the U.S. Railroad Administration (USRA) after December 1917, and remained in government hands for the next twenty-six months. While federalization caused disruptions for the Handy road and led to sizable deficits in net earnings, the brothers were able to expand their rail operations and increase gross revenues.

About the time DBC&W rails advanced toward Port Huron, the Handys purchased the pint-size Port Huron Southern Railroad (PHS) from Joy Morton, president of the Morton Salt Company, for an undisclosed price. The 4.9-mile industrial road, incorporated in 1900 and opened the following year, stretched southward from Tappan Junction in Port Huron to the Morton plant. With access to a steam road, the adjoining village of Marysville (née Vicksburgh) boomed as new industries and businesses appeared, and in the early 1920s the growing community achieved "city" status. The road, though, was nothing extraordinary. The line consisted of old, sixty-seven-pound rails, tamarack ties, and cinder ballast, and it contained at least one nasty curve. "The curve entering 32nd Street [in Port Huron] was so sharp," wrote the chief engineer for the PH&D, tongue in cheek, "it was necessary to unhitch one suspender, when walking around it." The frame engine house and office were part of the salt works complex and the sole railroad structure was an old boxcar fashioned into a section shanty.[45]

With the Port Huron Southern in tow, the brothers organized the Port Huron & Detroit Railroad on September 1, 1917, and filed the required paperwork on the 28th of that month to extend southward from Marysville. Survey work began immediately, and through the winter months of 1917–18 the right-of-way was acquired. Grading began in April 1918 at the PHS railhead and continued south along the St. Clair River to Marine City. The actual tracklaying started in June and would be completed in October.[46]

Although the Handys' construction company did not face any daunting challenges shaping the grade and bridging the Pine and Belle rivers, wartime labor shortages plagued the building process. "The limited crew consisted of men from skid row in Detroit, old men, boys, and cripples," recalled the chief engineer. "One man, a good worker at that, had only one arm, with a steel hook replacing the missing member." And the builders showed creativity. "Due to lack of men to handle rail, a long wooden boom was built on a derrick car extending 70 feet beyond the front of the car. In front of this was a carload of rail and behind a car of ties. The ties were hauled ahead by team and wagon and distributed on the grade. The crane of the derrick car would pick up a rail, move it forward and lower it on the ties where sufficient spikes would be driven to hold the track to gauge. The full spiking was done by air-operated spike drivers following behind the derrick car on which the air compressor was mounted." The approach worked well, allowing for about a quarter mile of track to be laid in a day.[47]

When the PH&D opened to Marine City, the USRA took charge, just as it had done earlier with the DBC&W and PHS. Although stymied by federal intervention, the Handys wanted to continue beyond the new end-of-track. Plans called for the forty-mile extension to veer west to Chesterfield and then south toward Detroit, following the west side of the Grand Trunk's heavy-duty Detroit-to-Port Huron line, and make a connection with the Detroit Terminal Railroad at Seven Mile Road, north of Motor City. Soon after the USRA relinquished control, the Handys commissioned a survey. In the early 1920s the route chosen was mostly farmland and posed no construction problems. The PH&D also selected some right-of-way parcels. These were "optioned where options could be secured at a top price of $500 per acre and secured with a $1.00 down payment." But the final push to Detroit never moved much beyond the preliminary stage.[48]

By 1918 the Handy brothers operated what they immodestly called the Detroit, Bay City & Western Railroad System, or the "Handy Lines," a 120-mile network of railroads. The total length included approximately twenty miles of the Port Huron Southern and the Port Huron & Detroit. (And to streamline their corporate books, in June 1920 the Handys transferred the PHS to the PH&D.) During the war, the always entrepreneurial Handys launched the Independent Sugar Company and opened a sugar beet processing plant in Marine City. Since the war effort demanded increased sugar production, the U.S. War Industries Board, backed by the Sugar Division of the U.S. Food Administration, allowed the Handys to acquire the steel to build between Marysville and Marine City. Federal officials diverted a shipment of rails destined for Russia for what they considered essential construction.

The Handy Lines never owned large motive power. No. 8, a 2-6-0 switcher formerly owned by the Michigan Central, waits at the engine facility in Port Huron in August 1921. *Courtesy of Railway and Locomotive Historical Society Archives Collection.*

Certainly part of the Handys' business plan involved hauling beets from stations along the DBC&W to the sugar facility.[49]

By the early 1920s the Independent Sugar Company was one of several major users of the PH&D along what was becoming a busy industrial zone. Its rails had made a difference. Train crews switched several large facilities, including Diamond Salt, Detroit Edison, St. Clair Rubber Company, and C. H. Wills & Company (soon the Wills Sainte Claire Company), the latter an important maker of automobiles.[50]

Unlike the remainder of the Handys' railroad, the busy appendage south of Port Huron offered only carload freight. Workers who were employed in these various plants either used their own transport or rode the electric cars of the Detroit United Railway between Mt. Clemens and Port Huron. This "Port Huron Route" was popularly known as the Rapid Railway, the company that in 1900 had built this interurban line.[51]

The decisions by the Handys to acquire the Port Huron Southern and build the Port Huron & Detroit smacked of real brilliance. While traffic sputtered along the core route, business thrived south of Port Huron. In August 1921 the *Wall Street Journal* reviewed economic conditions in greater Detroit and noted activities along the Handys' property. "Due principally to increased production at the plant of C. H. Wills & Co., the Detroit, Bay City & Western Railroad reports an increase of 2,500 tons in freight carried during July. August will make July's increase look small, it is said." In this optimistic milieu, rumors circulated that Handy rails would finally reach Detroit by the end of 1921.[52]

But what happened turned out much differently for the Handys and their railroad system than they or others expected. The nasty postwar recession hurt customers in the Thumb Country, especially sugar beet farmers who saw commodity prices plummet from a wartime high of twenty cents per pound to less than four cents per pound. Soaring automobile and truck competition also had a negative impact, reducing passenger and less-than-carload freight revenues. Then there would be two unexpected deaths. On January 5, 1922, fifty-four-year-old Frank Handy, who did bookkeeping for the various Handy enterprises, committed suicide in his Bay City office by firing a bullet into his head. Perhaps the youngest of the brothers had become distraught by mounting financial concerns in the Handy empire. The press reported, "Despondency following a nervous breakdown three months ago is given as the probable cause for the act." This tragedy was followed ten months later by the death of Thomas Handy. The captain of the family businesses suffered a paralyzing stroke in early October 1922, shortly after the DBC&W entered receivership, and at a time when severe financial losses plagued the Independent Sugar Company. Several weeks later, on October 22, 1922, "with only the slightest hopes of his recovering," Thomas died peacefully at his home.[53]

The financial difficulties that the DBC&W found itself in seemed solvable through court intervention. It was hoped that Judge Arthur Tuttle of the Federal Court in Detroit could straighten out the suits filed jointly by the Millikin National Bank of Decatur, Illinois, and the Valley Coal Company of Ohio. The former alleged that it held unpaid notes against the railroad that amounted to $12,500 ($159,000 in 2008 dollars), and the latter charged claims of $41,683.68 ($531,000 in 2008 dollars) against the sugar company. In both cases the parties argued that the firms had sizable liabilities, $715,000 ($9.1 million in 2008 dollars) for the DBC&W and $725,000 ($9.2 million in 2008 dollars) for Independent Sugar. The bank and the coal company believed that this level of indebtedness had greatly impaired the credit of the Handys' operations. Judge Tuttle appointed H. L. Stevens, vice-president of the Detroit Trust Company, as receiver for the two companies. Yet all was not gloom and doom. "The receiverships are part of a plan to conserve the property to the best advantages for the benefit of the owners as well as the creditors." Maybe the Handys and their financial backers could resolve the crisis. After all, court involvement was designed to protect the property while the problems with long-term debt were reconciled.[54]

Even with the deaths of Thomas and Frank Handy and the actions taken by the federal court, trains continued to run. Concern, however, grew for the future of the Handy Lines, especially the much longer Bay City–Port Huron core. Rumors circulated that this track might be sold to another railroad or possibly junked. About the time of the receivership, a major financial setback occurred when the Grand Trunk won regulatory approval for revised freight rates that severely damaged DBC&W earnings. The company previously had benefited from charges that were about 20 percent greater for shipments that moved through the Caro Gateway with the Michigan Central, and "overnight the traffic on the Handy Brothers line declined." Also, the troubled operations of the brothers' coal mines caused severe losses, and production ended.[55]

While failure of the Hardy coal operations created little public reaction, the possible demise of the Bay City-to-Port Huron road caused alarm. As a result, communities along the line labored mightily to retain freight service. "As much traffic as possible has been directed to this road by local shippers," related the *Tuscola County Advertiser* in January 1924, "and receipts at Caro have been the best of any station, yet the railroad has steadily been losing money." Still, the editor was not discouraged. "With four or five years of careful management, [the DBC&W] can be placed on a paying basis." These advocates of maintaining the property also expressed hope that another trunk road might acquire the property, or even that the faltering Detroit United interurban would assume control.[56]

In the interim between the bankruptcy and the Caro newspaper report, principal investors of the DBC&W had organized a Bondholders' Protective Committee, with A. Lawrence Mills of Chicago serving as chair. It was Mills's brokerage house, reconstituted as Mills & Gray, that had acquired a sizable amount of the bond issue of 1912, and committee members strategized on how best to protect their position. The group agreed with the receiver that losses must be minimized, and endorsed the decision to end all passenger service. In fact, at the start of the bankruptcy, the receiver, with court approval, reduced passenger runs to a single daily-except-Sunday train that left Bay City at 7:00 a.m. and arrived in Port Huron at 1:00 p.m. The train then departed Port Huron at 2:30 p.m. and reached Bay City at 8:10 p.m. And to achieve additional savings, the DBC&W closed its depot in Bay City and rented space in the nearby Michigan Central facility.[57]

By summer 1923 the receiver and the Bondholders' Protective Committee agreed to petition the ICC to close down the DBC&W. Judge Tuttle concurred, making it clear that he believed that the railroad was useless and opined (wrongly) that it should never have been built. The consensus was that this draconian act had become financially mandatory. Since alternate rail access was available in Akron, Caro, Wilmot, Sandusky, and Fargo, closure also would not cause grave harm to customers. So the DBC&W moved toward its end when the last through freight train rumbled between Bay City and Port Huron on January 17, 1925. (Passenger service had already stopped.) "Regret over the present condition of the road is universal along the entire line," editorialized the *Tuscola County Advertiser*, "and especially in towns served by no other steam road." What would Thomas Handy have thought?[58]

Yet an obituary for the Detroit, Bay City & Western was really premature. The bright spot involved the nineteen-mile industrial segment between Port Huron and Marine City, namely the Port Huron & Detroit Railroad. After a legal dispute, instigated by the Handy family, James E. Duffy, who had been the Handys' counsel and also represented the receiver, and other investors achieved control of what turned out to be a profitable switching operation. The road was repeatedly improved with heavier rail, treated ties, and gravel ballast. Over time, piled trestles were replaced with concrete bridges. And the Duffy family continued to run the line under the PH&D moniker until the Chessie System acquired the property in 1984. This trackage has survived to the present day, attesting to the good business sense of the Handys.[59]

On March 28, 1925, the assets of the DBC&W were offered for sale by the federal court, and the firm of Mills & Gray took charge. Its successful bid

of $200,000 ($2.4 million in 2008 dollars), which substantially exceeded a shipper's offer of $85,000 ($1 million in 2008 dollars), allowed the road to be reorganized by Lawrence Mills and John R. Gray. The articles of incorporation were signed on May 1, 1925, and filed several weeks later, and the new company, the Detroit, Caro & Sandusky Railway (DC&S), came into being. Immediately, the management dispatched a daily round-trip freight. (Between the shutdown of the DBC&W and the start-up of the DC&S, Michigan Central crews operated a daily freight between Caro and Fargo "to relieve local shippers who otherwise would have been without rail service.") Because of the expense of terminal costs in Port Huron and rehabilitation of the Mill Creek trestle, the DC&S decided to retreat to Fargo and to reduce service between Bay City and Caro. Only trains that carried sugar beets to processors in Bay City during the fall rush continued, and these movements ended after the 1928 shipping season. About this time, flood waters of the Quanicassee River severely damaged bridges and the roadbed of this historic section. By 1929 wreckers had unbolted the rails, torn out the ties, and removed the salvageable materials from both ends of the line. Income derived from the abandonments, including the sale of real estate, helped to retire the bonds that Mills and Gray had issued a few years earlier.[60]

The forty-eight-mile DC&S performed well and produced a profit, except for modest losses during the depression years of the 1930s. At times the operating ratio was a healthy 75 percent or less. Based in the former DBC&W

In the 1940s locomotive No. 15, a 4-6-0 ten-wheeler belonging to the Detroit, Caro & Sandusky, steams along a section of the former Handy Line between Sandusky and Caro. This train of sugar beets is bound for a processing plant in Caro.

depot in Caro, the road handled much the same freight that had been carried since the tracks were laid. Sugar beets, coal, gravel, lumber, and petroleum products became the company's bread and butter. This successor road retained some DBC&W equipment and employees.[61]

In time the DC&S retrenched. During the Great Depression the company retired the line between Roseburg and Fargo, and then the mileage between Peck and Roseburg. The explanation was simple: "due to the scarcity of business over that portion." In 1948 the trackage was shortened further by the abandonment of the portion from Sandusky to Peck. The remaining segment between Caro and Sandusky amounted to slightly more than thirty-one miles.[62]

In 1953 the end came to the last portion of the former DBC&W. While the road could haul sugar beets, the most important crop in the Thumb District, to a processing plant in Caro, the Michigan Central took advantage of its position to move the more profitable end product. Dwindling financial resources and a several-years-old muck fire that weakened the roadbed near Sandusky prompted owner John Gray, who in the early 1940s had bought out Lawrence Mills, to seek authorization in June 1952 to suspend operations. With approval from the ICC in hand, the company announced an embargo, and at several places nailed this sign:

> All cars for OUTBOUND shipments must be loaded or unloading can be completed and cars moved out by 12:01 A.M. January 15, 1953.
>
> This embargo has been placed due to insufficient funds to continue operation and to the physical condition of the property making for unsafe transportation.
>
> It is with deepest regret we are compelled to take this action and we are giving you this information in order that you may plan accordingly. We wish to express our sincere appreciation for your past patronage and cooperation.[63]

Liquidation went smoothly. A Saginaw junk dealer acquired the scrap metal, including the rails and the three steam locomotives (the road never dieselized). The real estate that did not revert back to adjoining property holders was sold, including most of the right-of-way from the eastern limits of Caro to the western limits of Sandusky to the Detroit Edition Company for a pole line. (Earlier, the power company had acquired portions of the right-of-way on the east end of the former DBC&W.) The DC&S had not become a bankrupt carrier, and money on hand and income generated from the sale of assets allowed the company to redeem the remaining bonds and pay all outstanding bills. In an unusual happening, Gray gave the employees severance pay, based on position and length of tenure. "The railroad ceased operation with honor and financial integrity," remarked the company auditor.[64]

The general consensus of those who have commented on the Handy Lines, whether contemporarily or later, is negative. The feeling is that the DBC&W had been a colossal mistake; the Handy brothers had erred badly in their collective business judgment. But at the time, there were sound reasons to build through the Thumb Country. The quality of competing railroad service was poor—the Pere Marquette hardly offered first-class service—and there were communities that lacked convenient, economical access to the rails. This thinking, in fact, led to the creation in 1910 of a "paper" interurban project, Detroit, Bay City & Northwestern Railway, that planned an electric road from Detroit to Bay City via Romeo, Imlay City, North Branch, and Caro. Moreover, existing public roads remained dreadful and would not be widely improved until the 1920s and later. And for the Handy brothers there was that real possibility of a profitable sale of their railroad, completed or not, to the Grand Trunk and later perhaps to the Pennsylvania. Without a doubt, the coming of the DBC&W advanced the sphere of commercial interests that Bay City had in the region, and trackside towns and villages reached by its rails flourished, at least initially. The penetration of the Handys south of Port Huron was a smart decision, attested by the continued financial success of the Port Huron & Detroit. Even portions of the original core made money after the dismemberment of the Handy Lines.[65]

Unforeseen external events and bad luck do much to account for the reversals. Damaging were the steep downswing in the postwar economy and the sudden deaths of Frank and especially Thomas Handy. As with nearly all carriers, expanding competition from automobiles and trucks that traveled over improving roads ultimately took its toll, and was not wholly anticipated by the brothers, or most everybody else, prior to World War I. The Handy Lines were no unmitigated business disaster, but instead these carriers were relatively durable and profitable, at least with the PH&D and the dismembered DBC&W. And similar to the experiences of other twilight carriers, on-line development again stood as a hallmark and lasting legacy of these rails through the Thumb Country.

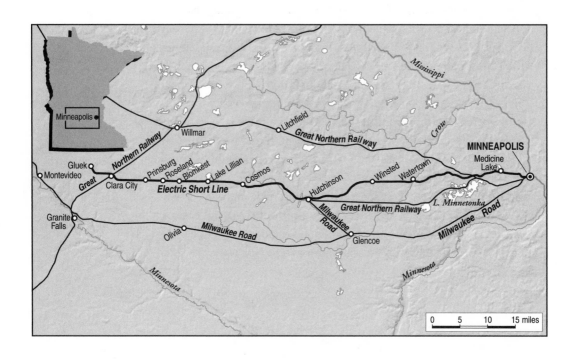

Chapter 4

Luce Line: Electric Short Line Railway and Minnesota Western Railroad

The last major independent railroad to be built in the Midwest was the Electric Short Line Railway, whose corporate existence began in 1908 and whose track started to appear five years later. By 1916 the company operated a fifty-eight-mile line west from Minneapolis to Hutchinson, Minnesota, and further expansion followed. Notwithstanding the national progression from trains and tracks to cars and roads, construction into South Dakota appeared likely, but finally, in 1927, the rails of what had become the Minnesota Western Railroad reached Gluek, Minnesota, which became the permanent end-of-track. In the building process, this Minnesota railroad, more than any other contemporary carrier in the region, spawned new towns, attesting again to the tangible economic progress that a twilight-era road could bring. In the 1910s and 1920s Minnesotans mostly knew this upstart railroad with its unusual motive power and passenger equipment not by its official name, but rather as the "Luce Line," a reference to founders William L. Luce (1857–1948) and his son Colonel (later General) Erle D. Luce (1882–1946).[1]

Father and son Luce participated in assorted businesses before becoming railroaders. The senior Luce was born in Lawrence, Massachusetts, but relocated to the Midwest. As a young man he lived in Burlington, Iowa, later moved to Red Wing, Minnesota, and then in 1889 settled in Minneapolis.

While in Red Wing, he prospered in the grain trade, owning "a number of well-equipped elevators along the line of the Chicago Great Western Railroad." The subsequent sale of these assets at the end of the 1890s provided capital to invest in real estate, including the Phoenix building (the future location of the general offices of the Luce Line) and the Hampshire Arms Apartments (later hotel) in Minneapolis. Son Erle, born in Red Wing in 1882, graduated from high school in Minneapolis in 1903, and four years later earned a law degree from the University of Minnesota. At the time of the Spanish-American War, the junior Luce interrupted his schooling to rally to the colors, joining a Minnesota militia unit and rising to the rank of colonel in the reconstituted Minnesota National Guard. In 1916 the younger Luce suspended his developing railroad career to command the First Minnesota Infantry during the troubles with Pancho Villa and Mexico. Not long afterwards he prepared to leave for the fighting in Europe, but on September 18, 1918, he contracted influenza and for the next six months required medical care. For the remainder of his life, Erle Luce would be associated with the military. Throughout the Luces' business careers the public thought highly of them. "These men have lived in Minneapolis for a number of years, owned

The Luces visited the end-of-track as the Electric Short Line took shape. Erle Luce is at right, wearing a bowler hat with his hand on his knee. His father, William, is likely the man standing between two ties immediately in front. *Courtesy of Pete Bonesteel.*

a very large amount of valuable property and have an excellent reputation in every way," concluded a group of businessmen. The observation, made in 1923, rang true that "the worth and value of the service of William L. Luce in connection with the development and up building of Minnesota can scarcely be over estimated."[2]

On August 7, 1908, as the nation and the region recovered from the Panic of 1907, the Luces entered the railroad business in a modest fashion. Their firm, the Electric Short Line Railroad Company, incorporated by the State of Minnesota, began to acquire land and a right-of-way strip for a terminal at 7th Street North and 2nd Avenue North in downtown Minneapolis, and for a three-mile line to Boagan Green, near the western city limits. Although this venture was designed principally to enhance their real-estate projects and was controlled initially by their Glenwood Real Estate and Improvement Company and later by the Phoenix Loan and Investment Company, father and son had greater ambitions. Early on they indicated that they would construct an electric interurban across Minnesota, enhanced by feeder branches, and ultimately reach Watertown, South Dakota, a growing trade center. The entity, though, that would build beyond Boagan Green would be the Electric

The past and the present in construction techniques can be readily seen in this undated view of the Luce Line taking shape near the Osseo line of the Great Northern Railway west of downtown Minneapolis. The Marion shovel is hardly the largest or latest piece of excavating equipment made by this prominent Ohio manufacturer; the worker with his team of horses represents an age-old way of fashioning railroad rights-of-way. *Courtesy of Pete Bonesteel.*

Short Line Railway, which the Luces incorporated on December 1, 1908, in the Territory of Arizona, probably for tax purposes and because of business interests in Phoenix.[3]

Construction crept forward. Resembling what had happened during the gestation period of the Akron, Canton & Youngstown Railroad, financing and acquisitions of land took longer than expected. Although the road began to shape a right-of-way in downtown Minneapolis in 1909, four years passed before workers had installed eight miles of track for the railway between Minneapolis and Medicine Lake and construction gangs had fashioned the grade another five miles west to Watertown, Minnesota. Passenger service began in January 1914 when the company reached Parker's Lake, ten miles from Minneapolis. By fall, the railway unit had in operation fifteen miles of line between Boagan Green (later Luce Line Junction) and Stubbs Bay on Lake Minnetonka, making the Luce Line an eighteen-mile property. The slow progress resulted partly from the need to complete a 120-foot steel truss span over the main line of the Great Northern Railway (GN) near Wayzata. What the Luces had achieved was a small road that was built to acceptable standards with "comparatively heavy" grading and sporting seventy-five- and eighty-pound rail, and operated with first-generation gas-electric motor cars and conventional steam power. Their property would serve, perhaps profitably, the popular lake region immediately west of Minneapolis. The company expected to capitalize on its urban terminal in the heart of Minneapolis that was "nearer to the retail district of the city than the Union Station."[4]

Unlike some contemporary railroad builders, father and son Luce understood that there was no place for dreamers in creating a successful railroad enterprise. Being practical men they considered their options and showed flexibility in their building strategies. Watertown, South Dakota, was presumed to be the western terminus, yet over time, the Luces pondered other destinations, including Brookings and Madison, South Dakota, and even distant Denver, Colorado. If the Electric Short Line were to become a real moneymaker and more than a suburban operation, it would need to exploit what was truly an agricultural cornucopia; the rich, productive wheat lands of south-central and western Minnesota and eastern South Dakota, and the developing sugar beet industry in Minnesota. "This black loam is over two feet deep in most places. [Farmers] hardly ever hit clay closer than a foot and a half." Or, as the A. G. Krans Company of Hutchinson observed, "Gently rolling black loam soil—clay subsoil—no stones—no swamps—natural drainage." And this land firm remarked, "Don't go to a wilderness unless you want to fish and hunt!" Dairying and livestock raising also flourished. The senior Luce understood the grain trade and the role railroads played in the business. He and his son agreed that an additional rail artery to capture the golden stream of wheat from western Minnesota and eastern South Dakota to the Twin Cities, the greatest center of flour milling, made sense.[5]

A cursory glance at the railroad map of Minnesota in 1910 revealed a maze of lines in the middle and southern sections; in fact, the state's total railroad network stood at an impressive 8,484 miles. Yet there was a largely empty railroad corridor west of Minneapolis that measured about forty miles wide. Two major trunk roads bordered what would become the path of the Luce Line. To the north, the GN operated a primary artery from the Twin Cities through Willmar and Breckenridge, Minnesota, to Fargo, North Dakota. To the south, the Chicago, Milwaukee & St. Paul Railway (Milwaukee Road) had its recently completed main line to the Pacific Northwest from the Twin Cities, and served the communities of Montevideo and Ortonville, Minnesota. Yet both the GN and Milwaukee Road sensed the commercial value of the intermediate country, the former (then the St. Paul, Minneapolis & Manitoba Railway) constructing a forty-four-mile branch line from Minneapolis to Hutchinson in 1886, and the latter racing that same year to complete a fourteen-mile appendage from Glencoe to Hutchinson. But the territory west of Hutchinson remained devoid of rails for nearly sixty miles until the Willmar-to-Sioux Falls, South Dakota, secondary line of the GN sliced through the countryside on a northeast to southwest axis, and the main line of the Milwaukee Road turned to the northwest. Beyond the Clara City and Montevideo area the "West End" of the Minneapolis & St. Louis Railway (M&StL) served several lively farming communities on its somewhat circuitous route between Minneapolis and Watertown, South Dakota, and points beyond to the Missouri River. And by 1916 improved automobile roads generally followed the routes of the GN and Milwaukee Road and only paralleled the proposed Luce Line from Minneapolis as far as Watertown, Minnesota.[6]

The Luces pored over maps, attempting to locate the most favorable route. Long before construction crews entered the field, these promoters and their business associates made repeated visits to the region beyond the suburban lake country. In August 1912 the *Hutchinson Leader* reported the presence of "railway magnates," namely the Luces, a civil engineer, and an expert on interurban construction and operation. "The purpose of their coming being to familiarize themselves with the extent of the county's population, the prospects for business for a new line crossing it and, most important of all, to select the most feasible route for the line westward from Winsted, [twenty-three miles from Stubbs Bay] into which town they assert they will be running cars before January next." It would, however, take time to determine the exact route or routes through McLeod County.[7]

train on Luce line crossing over bridge Winsted Lake

In the winter of 1914–15 construction of the Electric Short Line advanced westward from Minneapolis. Work involved the crossing of the south bay of Winsted Lake, and crews braved cold and snow to accomplish their assignments. *Courtesy of Gary Lenz Collection.*

Although by 1915 the Luce Line had acquired the right-of-way as far west as Hutchinson, completion of the line segments took time. Construction between Stubbs Bay and Winsted did not begin until October 1914 and was finished the following February. Then in August 1915 crews turned to the seventeen miles between Winsted and Hutchinson, much to the unhappiness of the GN and Milwaukee Road, who did not wish to share business in the busy economic capital of McLeod County. In February 1916 the rails reached Hutchinson, and for some time the town remained the end-of-track. For that reason the company put in about 2.5 miles of side tracks and a turning wye. The final twenty-five miles or so of line had been easier to build, having a slightly undulating roadbed with few curves. The first part of the route, though, had been more challenging, being "rather rough with many curves and heavy grades." Workers also installed a mile-long spur to serve an ice company on Medicine Lake.[8]

But a widely distributed prospectus suggested much more trackage. This document, prepared in late 1912, revealed four branches diverging from the main line: Wayzata south to Mound; Winsted south through Gaylord and Brighton to New Ulm; Hutchinson north to Litchfield, and from a point in Kandiyohi County south and west through Redwood Falls to Marshall. The proposed map further showed a short "cut off" between Winsted and what the company called Hutchinson Junction. Yet these projected appendages and an alternate main line came to naught, although several mass meetings took place in the prospective communities, and discussions continued until the early 1920s. Also, some stock was sold to residents along these paper extensions with the promise to build within a five-year period.[9]

The modest nature of the Luce Line by 1916 can be attributed to a desire to control debt and to the badly damaged capital market caused by the European war. The Luces did not press hard for monetary support from public coffers, a demand that promoters often made; instead they relied more on their own resources; friends, including Charles Gluek, who headed the Gluek Brewing Company; and farmers and businessmen along the line, both built and projected. The press indicated that individual investments in Electric Short Line securities would be prudent. The commentary in a published letter dated January 27, 1913, from W. F. Roche of Lakeville, Minnesota, to J. E. Ziska, a Silver Lake resident who wanted to know about the developing Minneapolis, St. Paul, Rochester & Dubuque Electric Traction Company, better known as the Dan Patch Lines, and another "wireless interurban," must have been reassuring: "As to the stock of the company, will say that I am a stockholder as are a great many more in this vicinity. No dividends have been paid yet because none have been earned. You will understand that this road is being built on

For an unknown reason, a crowd gathers around a Luce Line passenger-mail-express unit on an apparently chilly Minnesota day. The plow fixed to the pilot may not have been needed, but frequently this attachment was essential for operations. *Courtesy of Gary Lenz Collection.*

A freight train of the Luce Line, a pioneer in the use of internal combustion motive power, poses at an undisclosed location circa 1915. *Courtesy of Gary Lenz Collection.*

the proceeds from the sale of stock, and that so far the company does not owe a dollar." Added Roche, "While the company could have borrowed money and built their line into Faribault and Owatonna, the officers have been content to wait until the stock was sold. None of the stockholders here expected any dividends until the road got running into the large cities. We believe it will pay as soon as it reaches those cities and I haven't seen anyone around here who was anxious to dispose of his stock." This optimistic theme was repeated frequently. "People are beginning to realize that this [stock] is not a donation but an investment," observed the *Watertown News* in July 1913, "and it looks to most of them as a first class investment."[10]

The Electric Short Line was a strategically placed passenger and freight carrier, but a property that could be expanded if the opportunities appeared. Yet it would be another seven years before service extended beyond Hutchinson. In the interim, the company served patrons well. The timetable that took effect on May 19, 1918, for example, indicated three passenger round-trips between Minneapolis and Hutchinson: one daily, one daily-except-Sunday, and one Sunday only. Additional passenger runs were made between Minneapolis and Stubbs Bay: one Saturday and Sunday only, and one Sunday only. And the company dispatched special trains, usually on weekends for such events as fraternal lodge gatherings and the Minnesota State Fair. As with typical electric interurbans and some steam short lines, passengers could expect to board virtually anywhere. "To flag train passenger should stand near track and wave hand or handkerchief by day, and a match or lantern by night while train is at least 1,000 feet [away]. Keep flagging until motorman answers with short blasts of the whistle." There existed widespread endorsement for the road's fleet of gasoline-electric passenger motor cars; they were clean, comfortable, and relatively fast, and more attractive than the steam-powered GN and Milwaukee Road branch-line locals. By this time the Luce Line owned three passenger gasoline-electric motor cars, one baggage and express car, fourteen passenger trailers, and a combination trailer. Traditional freight service consisted of a daily-except-Sunday train and extras during the fall grain and beet rush. Three secondhand 2-6-0 steam locomotives or a gasoline-electric motor handled these freight assignments, and occasionally a steamer pulled a regularly scheduled or special passenger train. By 1917 the company also owned 180 freight cars and an assortment of miscellaneous rolling stock. And this fleet increased; the roster in 1921 included 201 pieces of freight equipment with boxcars the dominant type. While rumors persisted that the line would come under wire, the Luces seemed satisfied with their choice of motive power. Still, early on, the senior Luce stated that he had not rejected the original plans of making the line a "trolley system," contending that traction would be cheaper, but only if the road operated its own hydroelectric plant.[11]

The presence of the first major segment of the Electric Short Line not only pleased customers with "passenger service par excellence," but also, as with every twilight railroad, an economic uplift accompanied construction and the initial period of operations. Fortunately for the Luces, their railroad building coincided with the economic boom associated with the "parity years" in American agriculture (1909–13) and the following good times that the European war fostered. "Two facts speak volumes for the high state of prosperity of this locality through progressive farming on a fertile soil. The million and half deposits in the Hutchinson banks and the large amount of building that is being done on the farms tributary to Hutchinson," remarked a Hutchinson newspaperman in 1913. "Driving through the country they may be seen in every direction." Even before rails reached Hutchinson, residents expected substantial economic gains. In 1913 and 1914 local real estate moved briskly, for "sales are undoubtedly stimulated by the assurance of the early extension to the city of the Luce Line." The March 14, 1913, issue of the *Hutchinson Leader* contained two front page maps that showed "How the Electric Short-line Affects Hutchinson," indicating that the community's trade area would increase from about 350 square miles to 480 square miles, mostly added territory to the west of town.[12]

The maps were more than tools of chamber-of-commerce boosterism; they predicted the future with a high degree of accuracy. When rails eventually reached westward to Lake Lillian and beyond, Hutchinson merchants benefited. Even before rails extended in that direction, Hutchinson and communities to the east experienced an economic shot in the arm. "Does Luce Line help the banks?" "Does it quicken commerce and increase prosperity in the territory it invades?" Early in 1916 the *Hutchinson Leader* asked these questions and the answers were a resounding yes. "Official statements dated Dec. 31 of 17 banks published recently in 7 newspapers of McLeod county indicate as much." While bank deposits declined in places that had not received the new service, "every Luce Line town shows an increase, the total for Winsted, Silver Lake and Hutchinson being $49,239.07." Hutchinson, whose citizens hoped that the Electric Short Line would propel the population past the three thousand mark, witnessed a spate of lot sales and residential and commercial construction. On November 11, 1916, for example, the Hutchinson Investment Company conducted a successful auction of sixteen half-acre tracts and thirty "choice residence lots" in a recently platted addition to the town. As often occurred with railroad-inspired real-estate sales, there were incentives for participants: "The following prizes will be given away on the grounds, absolutely free: First prize: Ladies' $25 Suit; Second Prize: $10 Gold Piece; Third Prize: $5 Gold Piece; Fourth prize: Box of good cigars." Farmers seemed pleased with the railroad's investment in a modern livestock yard in Hutchinson and arrangements with the Chicago Great Western Railroad (Great Western) for direct shipments and "prompt service" to the South St. Paul and Chicago markets. On-line residents applauded the contract the Electric Short Line signed in 1916 with the Adams Express Company, a firm different from those companies that operated on the GN and Milwaukee Road, and the U.S. Post Office decision that same year to send "pouched mail" over the road.[13]

Although Luce Lines stimulated local economic growth, the company struggled after 1916. The operating ratio, a good index of economic health, moved from a highly respectable 69 percent in 1915 to a dismal 119 percent in 1917 and remained above 100 percent for the next several years. During the war, the Luces contributed more than $100,000 ($1.7 million in 2008 dollars) of their own resources to keep the road operating, and they never drew a salary. Still, they believed that if their railroad could tap the rich grain, beet, and livestock areas beyond Hutchinson, good times would follow. They also expected that high wartime prices for labor and materials would decline after the conflict came to a victorious end and the negative ramifications of wartime federalization would likewise cease. This optimism surely explains why a McLeod county resident believed that "the promoters of the company have great future in the tremendous growth during the next ten years of the territory their lines are to traverse."[14]

The postwar decade started positively. Traffic, for one thing, improved. "The splendid service given by the line is evidenced by the fact that the business is continually growing," opined a Hutchinson journalist, "and that in the past several weeks both passenger and freight business has increased steadily and is now greater than at any other period in the history of the road." Contributing to this renewed vigor were an estimated one thousand carloads of brick and clay products annually generated by the Hutchinson Brick & Tile Company, one of the area's largest industries, that in the summer of 1920 a long-proposed spur of the Electric Short Line tapped.[15]

The Luce Lines also gained from a close relationship with the Dan Patch Lines. This company, formed in 1905 and reorganized two years later, planned to build heavy-duty traction lines from Minneapolis and St. Paul to Antlers Park near Lakeville and extend south and east to Northfield, Faribault, Mankato, Owatonna, Albert Lea, Austin, Rochester, and Dubuque, Iowa. Yet Minneapolis would be the only city ever reached. By late 1910 the road consisted of a forty-two-mile line from 54th Street and Nicollet Avenue

The Luce Line was not the only twilight-era railroad in Minnesota or the Midwest that used "motors" in freight and passenger service. For a time the Minneapolis, St. Paul, Rochester & Dubuque Electric Traction Company, "Dan Patch Lines," relied totally on this cutting-edge technology. The crew of No. 100, a General Electric product, takes the time to accommodate a photographer, circa 1915. *Courtesy of William D. Middleton Collection.*

in Minneapolis to Northfield via Antlers Park, Savage (formerly Hamilton), and Lakeville. In 1914 the Dan Patch Lines assumed for several years the operations of the Great Western's Northfield–Mankato branch (and for decades trackage rights remained). Its gasoline-electric cars provided interurban-type passenger service along its expanded 108-mile system. Initially, gasoline motors handled all traffic, but after 1915 2-6-0 steam locomotives assisted in moving carload freight.[16]

The promoter of the Dan Patch Lines, Colonel Marion Savage, was a livestock feed and mail order executive from Minneapolis. His fame, however, rested with his ownership of the beloved pacer Dan Patch. When not involved with the harness-racing circuit and other business activities, Savage thought about his railroad and concluded that better access to Minneapolis was warranted. In 1915 he extended trackage from Auto Club, via Edina and St. Louis Park, to the Electric Short Line Terminal at Luce Line Junction, and received trackage rights to the downtown Luce station. (On May 6, 1915, the Electric Short Line Railroad Company became the Electric Short Line Terminal Company.) In 1916 Savage's death and financial reversals forced the Dan Patch Lines into receivership, but two years later reorganization created the Minneapolis, Northfield & Southern Railway (MN&S) which for decades prospered as a freight hauler, deriving substantial revenues from bridge traffic that moved around the congestion of the Twin Cities. The onetime Dan Patch Lines became a remarkably successful twilight-era road.[17]

Notwithstanding the national postwar recession of 1920–21 and the beginning of hard times for some midwestern agrarians, the Luces turned once more to expansion. In May 1921 the *Minneapolis Tribune* fueled reports that Hutchinson would not long remain the western terminus. Action followed. In mid-1921 two solicitors conducted a series of meetings in the country west of Hutchinson to explain building strategies, and to ask farmers for right-of-way donations and "a small bonus of so much per acre within a few miles of the line, the terms of which those agreeing to assist are not obligated until the railroad is completed into their township." While land and an undisclosed amount of dollars came from these commitments, somewhat later the Luces won regulatory approval to issue $660,000 ($7.8 million in 2008 dollars) in fifteen-year, 5 percent bonds to help pay for the approximately fifty miles of construction. "The bonds will complete the entire financing of the project and eliminate any financial hindrance to its success." A somewhat improved bond market boded well for raising capital, but unfortunately these Luce Line bonds sold at a substantial discount.[18]

With the surveys finished, title to nearly all of the right-of-way and much of the financing arranged, construction started in May 1922 immediately west of Hutchinson. Frederickson & Company of Minneapolis won this contract, although earlier another Minneapolis firm, H. F. Balch & Company, had been the primary builder. Steady progress followed. In mid-October freight service began after rails reached Acoma, five miles from Hutchinson, when a nearby farmer shipped the first revenue cargo, a car of sugar beets consigned to the Minnesota Sugar Company in Chaska. By this time the track gang neared Cosmos, eighteen miles from Hutchinson, and grading crews worked farther

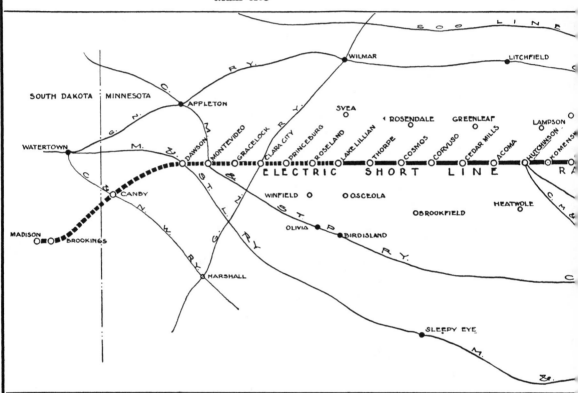

THE TIME given in this table is that at which trains are expected to arrive and depart from the several stations, BUT IT IS NOT GUARANTEED, and although every care is taken to keep the tables correct the Electric Short Line Railway Company does not hold itself responsible for possible errors or for delay or inconvenience resulting from failure to make schedule as advertised.

| E. D. LUCE | Receivers | M. MAREA | R. K. SMITH | G. W. SMILEY | Disp |
| W. J. HIELD | | Genl. Supt. | Com. Fgt. & Pass. Agt. | R. E. KENYON | |

General Offices in
Terminal Passenger Station
7th St. and 2nd Ave. North

Te

In its Fall–Winter 1923 public timetable, the Electric Short Line Railway told readers that the line was headed further into western Minnesota and ultimately to Brookings and Madison, South Dakota. The company did not miss the opportunity for self-promotion, including an advertisement for the Luces' Hampshire Arms Hotel in Minneapolis.

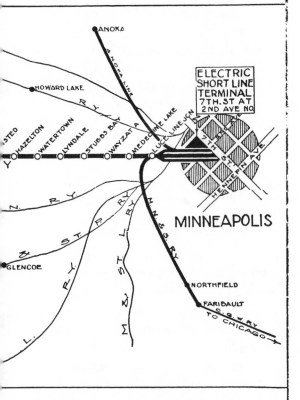

MINNEAPOLIS

For information regarding commutation fares and tickets, call Information or see Ticket Agent, Minneapolis,

Children under 5 years of age in charge of adult, free; those over 5 and under 12, half fare, and those over 12 full fare.

Freight and Express Tariffs in effect. U. S. Mail Handled.

General Office	-	-	-	-	Geneva 2753
Ticket Office	-	-	-	-	Geneva 9114
Freight Office	-	-	-	-	Geneva 3164
Genl. Supt. Office (Shops)	-	-	Cherry 2265

ELECTRIC SHORT LINE RAILWAY

E. D. LUCE
W. J. HIELD } Receivers

**PASSENGER and FREIGHT DEPOTS
7th St. at 2nd Ave. N.**

Fall & Winter TIME TABLE No. 32

Effective 12.01 A. M.

Sunday, Sept. 9, 1923

12.01 A. M.

*AVOID WASTE
Keep This Time Table*

west. But delays caused by heavy autumn rains prevented them from reaching Cosmos until the second week of November. Then shortly before Thanksgiving, residents of the Cosmos area celebrated. A young Cosmos woman received the honor of driving the ceremonial "golden spike," an object that had been displayed for several weeks at a local hardware store. Not until December 21, 1922, however, did Cosmos welcome the first Minneapolis through freight train that consisted of several cars of coal and lumber. On the return seventy-five-mile trip, five cars of livestock were loaded in Cosmos for the journey to the South St. Paul stockyards.[19]

A few days after freight service to Cosmos began, the Electric Short Line extended to Thorpe, four miles beyond the Cosmos station, and immediately established mixed-train service. This "combination freight, express and passenger train" left Hutchinson at 5:00 a.m and arrived in Thorpe two hours later, after scheduled stops at Acoma, Cedar Mills, Corvuso, and Cosmos. The eastbound train departed Thorpe at 5:30 p.m. for the two-hour return trip to Hutchinson.[20]

The completion of the western extension into a rail-starved section triggered several encouraging responses. "The long-waited for has been achieved, and farmers west of Hutchinson now have railroad connection with the outside world." These agrarians took advantage of their vastly improved transportation situation by launching several marketing groups, including the Cedar Mills Farmers Shipping Association. They either cooperatively established or backed the construction of stock pens, grain elevators, creameries, and related agribusiness facilities. Even before Luce Line motors reached Cosmos, the Cosmos Townsite Company advertized newly platted lots that adjoined the village. And a host of businesses appeared in these trackside communities. A garage, hardware store, and lumberyard, for example, emerged in Corvuso, and the old settlement of Cedar Mills relocated to the station site, resulting in the erection of a grain elevator, lumberyard, and sugar beet scale house and loading dock.[21]

Boosters seemed especially excited about the prospects for Cosmos. On June 28, 1923, the Interurban Development Company of Minneapolis sponsored a sale of lots in Cosmos: "BIG AUCTION SALE OF COSMOS TOWNSITE LOTS. THE BIG NEW TOWN ON THE ELECTRIC SHORT LINE RAILWAY EXTENSION." This Luce-controlled firm used a hard-sell approach for this particular promotion: "Many will double and treble their money by buying at this sale. There has been no such sale opening a new town for many years. Investors made thousands of dollars in the early days buying lots on the west extensions of railway lines, and you will be able to do better there where money is plentiful. Don't tell your children in years to come you could have bought lots in COSMOS, but show them your profits by buying at this AUCTION SALE." The development company reminded readers, "Nicollet avenue land could be bought at $40 an acre at one time; now it cannot be bought for $6,000 a running foot; same in proportion in many good Minnesota towns, with not the same chance that COSMOS has." Buyers were told, "All streets have been graded and arrangements for 1,000 trees have been made to beautify the City of COSMOS." And two years later another "valuable lot" sale occurred. "These lots are all located south of the railroad tracks on Main Street and by the School. ALL THE FREE WATERMELON YOU CAN EAT, COME EARLY AS AT 1 P. M. A VALUABLE PRIZE WILL BE GIVEN THE ONE WHO CAN EAT A LARGE MELON FIRST. OH! OH! DOCTOR! ON HAND." The sales went well, the village grew, and on July 31, 1925, the weekly *Cosmos News* made its debut and continued to boost the community. "Since the advent of the railroad Cosmos has made rapid growth and the necessity for a newspaper to help keep up the good work was beginning to be felt," wrote A. G. Abrahamson, the editor and publisher, in the inaugural issue.[22]

As Cosmos took on cosmopolitan airs, the extension terminus did not long remain at Thorpe. Even before snow flew in the autumn of 1922, the line had been largely completed another five miles westward, workers needing only "to lay gravel on the grade and level the track." Beginning in April 1923, with the frost out of the ground, crews labored to finish the track to Lake Lillian and shape the grade beyond to Clara City. "Two of the new steam engines constructed for the Luce Line this winter will be used on the gravel trains when they start work," reported a local journalist. "Plans of the officials look forward to finishing the line to Clara City by fall."[23]

In 1923 Lake Lillian, located on the south shore of a beautiful prairie lake, became the newest community on the Luce Line and, likely, in the state. As had happened frequently in the birthing of railroad-created towns, a "splen-did" celebration took place. On June 21 "probably there were 2,000 people in the town for the official opening of the railroad." More than four hundred of these well-wishers were those who arrived on a ten-car special from Minne-apolis. The train made a ten-minute stop in Cosmos with "the 135th Infantry band playing a few selections and the crowd getting out to look over the new addition to this thriving city." After detraining at the Lake Lillian station, the visitors, joined by others who came by auto, strolled to the lake, about a half mile from the townsite, where the military band entertained and celebrants enjoyed a barbecue luncheon supervised by the chef of the Luces' Hamp-shire Arms Hotel. Short talks were given by several dignitaries, including Colonel Luce and George Dayton, the Minneapolis department store mogul, but a downpour literally put a damper on the speech-making. When the rain

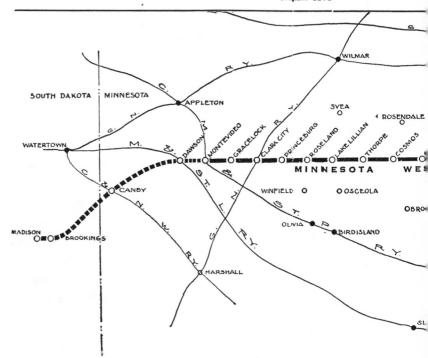

MINNESOTA WESTERN RAILROAD CO.

Passenger and Freight Depots
7th St. at 2nd Ave. N.

TIME TABLE No. 9

Effective 12:01 A. M., Sunday, Dec. 12, 1926

As late as December 12, 1926, the Minnesota Western Railroad, successor to the Electric Short Line, continued to plug its services, promoting the new communities served between Lake Lillian and Grace Lock (Gluek). The notice that rails were about to reach Montevideo proved untrue.

rthwest. There is now a demand for General Stores, Gar-
s, Produce Dealers, Hardware Merchants, etc. For in-
mation concerning these new towns address R. K. Smith,
m'l Frgt. & Pass. Agt. at Passenger Station, 2nd Avenue
rth and 7th Street, Minneapolis.

fices at ve. No.	Telephones:	Ticket Office - - - - - - - -	Geneva 9114
		Freight Office - - - - - - - -	Geneva 4654
		Gen Office and Shop - - - - - -	Cherry 2265
		Dispatcher - - - - - - - -	Geneva 4096

MINNESOTA WESTERN

stopped, "the crowd went 'down town' to see what there was to see," and later the packed train left the station and the other attendees drifted away.[24]

Lake Lillian grew rapidly, paralleling what was happening in Cosmos. While not unique in the history of town-building, this village on the shores of Lake Lillian benefited enormously from the decision of Thorpe businessmen to relocate in Lake Lillian, five miles west, leaving Thorpe but a speck on the map. "Thorpe will move bodily, taking the creamery, the bank and every other business institution with them," reported the *Hutchinson Leader* in May 1923, and this soon happened. The Thorpe State Bank, for example, became the First State Bank of Lake Lillian, and this financial institution prospered. The bank, reported the *Willmar Tribune* in January 1926, "shows a reserve greater than 400 percent of that required for a bank of its capitalization. At a recent meeting of the board of directors a seven percent dividend was declared on the capital stock." The community saw expanded public services with the building of a schoolhouse, establishment of a post office, and formation of the First [Swedish] Lutheran Church. Like Cosmos, Lake Lillian got its own newspaper, the *Lake Lillian Echo*, which began weekly publication in March 1926. The remarkable growth of the town prompted the editor to reflect, "Picture an ordinary country-side with nothing save growing grain, meadow grass, gophers and muskrats to break the monotony of nothing and you have a view of Lake Lillian's townsite a little less than three years ago. Then the railroad came, buildings were moved in, and others erected new. Boom business was conducted in a dozen and more places." The commentary ended with these thoughts: "Today we have over twenty-five different business places and enterprises in our thriving village. Last Thursday, village officers were elected, as a first step in the organization of a village council. Thus it is that Lake Lillian enters upon the roll of villages."[25]

While Lake Lillian celebrated and contemplated future growth, the Luces and their associates became involved in a corporate reorganization. On June 23, 1923, the board of directors ordered the filing of a petition for receivership on behalf of the unsecured creditors. Yet this event did not signal disaster; indeed, management supported this action. "It is understood here that the receivership was brought by a 'friendly suit' to facilitate the calling in of the common stock of the Electric Short Line Railway Company," explained the *Minneapolis Tribune*. "The common stock was given with each share of preferred stock bought and is counted as capital by the Interstate Commerce Commission. In order to build the extension west planned by the Luce Line officials it is now necessary to reduce the capital stock." Before the Interstate Commerce Commission (ICC) authorized additional bonds for construction beyond Lake Lillian, the company needed to retire at least 80 percent of its common stock. Colonel Luce, who would serve as co-receiver with W. J. Heild, a company director, told the public, "The value of the property exceeds the debts and outstanding preferred stock." Nevertheless, reorganization meant that common shareholders would lose their investments.[26]

On April 12, 1924, a new day dawned for the Luce Line. On that Saturday a crowd of about two hundred of the mostly curious gathered on the steps of the Fourth Street entrance to the Hennepin County Courthouse in Minneapolis. In a droning voice Special Master in Chancery Howard Abbott read the notice of sale, announced the terms of the bankruptcy auction, and called for bids. Abbott explained that already the court had established the condition that anyone intending to participate must deposit $50,000 in cash or $150,000 in bonds and that the required minimum bid would be $250,000 ($3.1 million in 2008 dollars). Abbott then informed the audience that only one prospective bidder had met the qualifications and that was the Luce-controlled reorganization committee. Acting for the group, Walter Thorpe made the sole offer of $275,000 ($3.4 million in 2008 dollars), and Abbott declared the property officially sold.[27]

As in most railroad bankruptcies, the stockholders suffered, and in this case, with ownership passing to the bondholders, both preferred and common shareholders were wiped out. Since the par value of the outstanding bonds was approximately $1.3 million ($16.2 million in 2008 dollars) and some $800,000 ($1 million in 2008 dollars) of those bonds were held by the Luce family, no change of ownership occurred. An effort, however, had been made on behalf of stockholders to have the court protect their investments, but this strategy failed. "A large amount of the stock of the company is held in this vicinity, some of which was purchased as an investment, and some as a bonus or gift to secure the building of the line," observed the *Hutchinson Leader*. "As an investment the stock has proven to be no exception to the rule that the original stockholders of a new railroad seldom realize anything on their purchase, but the service given a larger territory and to the people of the country traversed has justified the expenditure of those who are residents of the territory served." These insightful thoughts may have brought comfort to the disadvantaged investors.[28]

The reorganization brought about a name change. The Luces jettisoned the not-so-apt Electric Short Line Railway moniker. One newspaper writer thought that the reconstituted road should be called the Minnesota, Hutchinson & Western Railway or the Minnesota Western Railway, "bearing a name indicative of its larger scope." When company officials filed incorporation papers for their eighty-one-mile railroad with the State of Delaware (as a tax strategy), they opted for the more succinct Minnesota Western Railroad, which, incidentally, had been the name of one of the first railroads incorporated in Minnesota.[29]

Minnesota Western also became the core name of an affiliated company, the Minnesota Western Transportation Company. In the 1920s, steam railroads, large and small, at times established motor bus subsidiaries. For example, the giant Great Northern organized Northland Transportation Company, predecessor of Greyhound Lines, and the fifty-four-mile Missouri Southern Railroad launched the Missouri Southern Transportation Company. Motor-transport ventures allowed the parent railroad to extend and coordinate service, or as GN president Ralph Budd put it, "Maximum of service with the minimum of cost." Also during the 1920s, scores of electric interurbans, often desperate to maintain their very existence, created bus subsidiaries.[30]

At the time the Minnesota Western Railroad made its corporate debut, so did the Minnesota Western Transportation Company. The concept was to strengthen the passenger sector by offering connecting buses at Lake Lillian to points in western Minnesota and eastern South Dakota, including Fergus Falls, Marshall, Morris, Pipestone, and Willmar in Minnesota, and Big Stone Lake, Milbank, and Watertown in South Dakota. To handle this service, the Luce bus company purchased quality vehicles, namely six Fageol and three Reo buses. "The bus equipment is the last word in luxury and comfort in the new form of transportation." And the parent railroad made its own improvements, providing "two fast through trains each way daily between Minneapolis and Lake Lillian" and equipping the cars "with chair seats with air cushions." In an advertising blitz, the company announced:

> Effective November 30th, 1924, the Minnesota Western Transportation Company will operate new Fageol Chair Car Buses to the western part of Minnesota and to parts of South Dakota from Lake Lillian, Minn., connecting with limited all steel chair car trains from the Twin Cities. Lunches and Newspapers will be Furnished to all Passengers Gratis, on the Trains.
> Cheaper–Quicker–Safer[31]

Initial reports of the coordinated rail-bus service revealed that the Luce Line had filled a transportation need. "The first day of business found about 40 through passengers from Lake Lillian to the cities on the first of the eastbound trains and the business since then has been equally good," reported the *Hutchinson Leader* in early December. "While the bus lines are starting at the most unfavorable time of the year, this is partially compensated by the approaching holiday season and business was even exceeding their expectations."[32]

Yet operations of the Minnesota Western Transportation Company can be measured in weeks and not months or years. At the end of December the firm sold its fleet of Fageol buses to the Boulevard Transportation Company of Minneapolis. "The bus lines had enjoyed a very considerable patronage during the holiday season and at any time that weather was favorable." Perhaps, though, the company was not too sanguine about future business. Management announced, "The offer of the Boulevard Transportation Company was so attractive that it was decided to accept it at this time." With connecting bus service terminated, the railroad readjusted its passenger schedule, operating a single daily train between Minneapolis and Lake Lillian and providing an additional daily run between Minneapolis and Hutchinson.[33]

While the Luce administration quickly exited the coordinated rail-bus business, it had no intention of abandoning plans for construction west of Lake Lillian. In October 1925 the company applied to the ICC for permission to build fifty-seven miles through Clara City to Dawson that a bond issue of $850,000 ($10.3 million in 2008 dollars) would help to finance. But as the *Minneapolis Tribune* noted, "No survey for the right of way has been made, and details of the route to be followed have not been decided, except that the extension is to be built through Clara City."[34]

The further penetration by the Luce Line into western Minnesota did not please carriers that served the region. Just as neither the GN nor Milwaukee Road applauded the arrival of company rails in Hutchinson, these roads, joined by the M&StL, protested to the ICC, arguing that there was no need for more trackage. The Commission, however, accepted the Minnesota Western position that the extension would develop the territory, reduce freight rates, and protect the financial health of a not-too-robust railroad.[35]

With a green light from regulators, the Minnesota Western speedily conducted surveys, acquired rights-of-way, and awarded contracts for the construction between Lake Lillian and Clara City. By October 1926 considerable work had been accomplished. "The grade at present extends 18 miles west of Lake Lillian or within about seven miles of Clara City," noted the *Hutchinson Leader*. "The work is being done with an elevating grader, an ordinary tractor, which is used as the 'pusher,' and some 10 dump wagons in each crew. It is a very interesting sight to see the efficient way in which the dirt is moved, and to the uninitiated it seems that wonders have been accomplished." Unusually wet weather, unfortunately, delayed the advance westward.[36]

As crews labored to reach Clara City, plans for a new town took shape, creating what was one of the last railroad-inspired town sites in Minnesota and the Midwest. Reports circulated in the fall of 1926 about Kester, located in southern Kandiyohi County, where the Minnesota Western would cross State Highway 4 seven miles west of Lake Lillian and four miles east of Roseland, a village also on the emerging line. On November 7, 1926, two promoters from nearby Olivia conducted a town-lot sale at the Kesler site and offered, "Your choice of residential and business opportunities in a wonderful business territory." Unlike Cosmos and Lake Lillian, Kester never amounted to much; a subsequent name change to Blomkest made no difference. Only a depot, elevator, stockyards, gas station, and a few residences appeared. Stations at Prinsburg, Pierson, and Roseland, west of Blomkest, had not much more than a depot, grain elevator, and stock pens. Still, rumors persisted that if the railroad entered South Dakota, "it will mean the establishment of at least six new towns along the route." Yet the time for additional railroad communities had ended, although in the not-so-distant past little towns had pushed up like prairie wild flowers.[37]

The year 1927 saw the birth of Kester and the completion of the thirty-one miles of rails west of Lake Lillian at a cost of more than $600,000 ($7.3 million in 2008 dollars). During the first week of October the last steel was installed to Grace Lock, quickly renamed Gluek, seven miles west of Clara City. ("How the name of the new town is pronounced is not entirely settled. The local pronunciation is 'Gluek,' but the head of the elevator company says it 'Glook.'") More track work ensued and trains began running on October 24, following a favorable inspection by Minnesota Railroad and Warehouse Commission personnel. Then on November 8 a grand opening of sorts took place when a "big trade and friendship tour" came to Kester, Clara City, and Gluek, the "west end," in a seven-car passenger special packed with businessmen from Minneapolis and several on-line communities, and the Hutchinson Cornet Band.[38]

Even though the Luces never intended rails to end at Gluek, the place soon became a railroad terminal. Railroad employees installed a turntable, a two-stall car barn, and a fuel tank. They also erected a small depot, several outbuildings, and a bunkhouse for crews who laid over after evening trips. More construction occurred, including several stores and houses, a restaurant, a lumberyard, and a thirty-thousand-bushel elevator owned by the Victoria Elevator Company and managed by R. G. Cargill Jr., who was distantly related to the Cargill family of Minneapolis, owner of a giant grain combine.[39]

As Lake Lillian had before, Gluek became a transfer point for additional service. The Minnesota Western received state regulatory permission to provide a connecting bus and truck service under the banner of the existing subsidiary, Minnesota Western Transportation Company. Specifically, buses and trucks would take the gravel road from Gluek two miles south to State Highway 49 and then proceed west to Montevideo and Dawson, south to St. Leo "an inland town on No. 5 and No. 7 state aid roads," and finally west on

Highway 49 to Canby. Operations began on October 30, 1927, with a single daily bus run that used the Reo equipment, and truck service that was dispatched as needed. A traveler could leave Montevideo at 6:45 a.m. and arrive in Minneapolis at 11:45 a.m. and return from Minneapolis at 5:15 p.m., arriving in Montevideo at 10:45 p.m. "Those passengers traveling west will be served lunches on trains gratis." While ridership statistics are not known, residents of Montevideo already had attractive options to and from the Twin Cities, namely main line trains on the Milwaukee Road and buses operated by Northland Transportation Company.[40]

Not long after Gluek received freight and passenger service, the Luces left the Minnesota Western. Although their reasons are not really known, they likely wanted to concentrate on their real-estate ventures. Even though traffic prospects looked promising for the railroad, especially for grain and sugar beets, it seemed doubtful that capital could be easily raised for the one-hundred-mile extension to Brookings, South Dakota, via Montevideo, even though preliminary surveys had been made. Frankly, rails had just reached Gluek when the company ran out of financial steam. But fortunately, a buyer beckoned. Father and son Luce sold controlling interest of the Minnesota Western Railroad and the Electric Short Line Terminal Company to Harry E. Pence Sr. and several of his associates. A savvy businessman who headed the Minneapolis, Northfield & Southern, Pence coveted the Luces' Minneapolis facilities and recognized the potential of a belt route around the Twin Cities. This explained the recent construction of a several-mile extension of the MN&S from Glenwood Junction to the Minneapolis, St. Paul & Sault Ste. Marie Railway (Soo Line) in Crystal, and the trackage rights over the Soo Line to its Shoreham Yard which provided an easy connection with the Northtown Yard of the Northern Pacific Railway. The company soon pronounced, "Terminal Delay Eliminated: Interchange is effected within a few hours, where *days* are required for the same interchange at other and more congested terminals." Pence also believed that the Minnesota Western offered the possibility of substantial freight revenues. While a corporate merger had not taken place, he became president of the two former Luce properties and oversaw a 243-mile rail system with assets of more than $7 million ($86 million in 2008 dollars).[41]

The Luces' withdrawal revealed good timing. The coming of the Great Depression, and horrific drought conditions that coincided with hard times, dramatically reduced railroad revenues. The old adage of "when there is no rain on the plains, there's no grain in the trains" was sadly true. As with so many carriers, large and small, the devastated economy pushed the Minnesota Western Railroad into receivership in 1932, and the subsequent reorga-

In 1956 the Minneapolis & St. Louis Railway acquired the former Luce Line. On a blustery March 16, 1958, the Minnesota Railfans Association arranged a special trip over the freight-only trackage between Minneapolis and Watertown, Minnesota. The train featured F-7 diesel No. 412, with heating car, two business cars, three Soo Line coaches, and an observation car. *Photograph by William D. Middleton.*

nization by bondholders created the Minnesota Western Railway, a company that produced a modest annual operating profit during most of the 1930s. The MN&S continued to operate the property.[42]

In 1942 Cargill, Inc., the privately held grain concern, became involved in the Minnesota Western, not so much for wheat transport as for military production. Patriotic Cargill planned to open a shipbuilding facility to construct AOGs (auxiliary oil and gasoline carriers) for the U.S. Navy in Savage, situated on the Minnesota River and served by the Chicago, St. Paul, Minneapolis & Omaha Railroad (Omaha Road), part of the Chicago & North Western System (North Western), and the MN&S. But Cargill management discovered that the Omaha Road refused to place the boatyard location within the Twin Cities switching district, and the MN&S was also reluctant to make such a financial concession. Since the MN&S would grant the desired switching rights to the Minnesota Western, the solution appeared to be the acquisition of the former Luce property. "[Buying the Minnesota Western] would leave us in the position of paying only the actual transportation costs plus a nominal profit to the Minneapolis, Northfield & Southern," wrote a Cargill family member. "It would also put us in a magnificent competitive position in Central Minnesota as we could then afford to buy grain aggressively at Clara City and do an elaborate business consisting of trucking grain to Clara City and coal and gasoline out." The plan was to buy the railroad privately. With a $100,000 investment ($1.3 million in 2008 dollars), John MacMillan Jr. and Cargill MacMillan, rather than Cargill, Inc., became the owners, and this arrangement avoided censure by the ICC. After the war, the MacMillans spearheaded the creation of a holding firm, Minnesota Western Company, which controlled the railroad and another venture, the Wesota Company, which owned the on-line elevators. And it would be the more soothing Wesota moniker that Cargill would use to rename Gluek, replacing a name that no longer had a tie to the owners.[43]

While Cargill interests retained the Minnesota Western Railway, MN&S involvement continued in the role of train operations and maintenance. Moreover, in 1955 the MN&S formally acquired the Electric Short Line Terminal Company from the Minnesota Western, terminating the long-standing rental agreement. A year later MN&S involvement ended when the M&StL bought out the Cargill position for $300,000 ($2.3 million in 2008 dollars). Cargill executives believed that their "little railroad" was a bother, and the anticipated financial rewards never really developed. Yet for the five years previous to the sale, the Minnesota Western had average revenues of more than $800,000 and an average net railway operating income of $83,000. The M&StL praised the acquisition as an important step in its "industrial development program." While the old Luce property possessed "great potential" for grain gathering, the M&StL wished to increase revenues from new shippers in Hutchinson and near Minneapolis, particularly in Golden Valley and Plymouth. In fact, the M&StL expected that a warehouse then being built by the Standard Oil Company in Golden Valley would produce "carloadings in excess of 1,000 a year." That traffic mix led to another name change; the road became the Minneapolis Industrial Railway in 1959. But the following year, the North Western acquired the M&StL, and this sprawling Chicago-based carrier was not particularly excited about the M&StL's acquisition of the Minnesota Western, especially since no large rail customers used the line. Under North Western control, track maintenance deteriorated, and in 1967 service between Hutchinson and Gluek (no longer called Wesota) ended. In the early 1970s the North Western retired the track west of Plymouth at milepost 11, even though some shippers had attempted to save rail service.[44]

Presently, only a short segment of this quintessential twilight railroad of the Midwest remains in operation. The Union Pacific, which purchased the North Western in 1995, still serves customers in the Minneapolis area. While access to the rails has greatly diminished, some of the businesses that were fostered or founded because of the Electric Short Line and Minnesota Western remain, and even prosper, underscoring once again the positive economic impact of these latter-day carriers. Yet those villages launched during the euphoria of the 1920s never developed into the little cities that their backers had wished for or expected.

The Luce name, though, has gained a degree of immortality through the popular "Luce Line State Trail," part of Minnesota's extensive rails-to-trails program. This sixty-five-mile recreational path between Plymouth and Cosmos came into being in 1976 to serve bikers, hikers, horseback riders, and snowmobilers. As the state suggests: "The Luce Line is truly like a jaunt down a quiet country road." Such an experience, however, had not been the intention of father and son Luce. They sought to build a viable carrier that would enhance their economic situation and prompt growth and development along a wide corridor west of Minneapolis.[45]

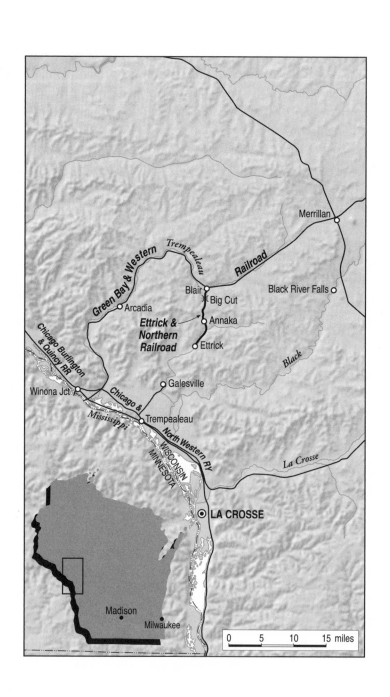

Chapter 5

Ettrick & Nothing:
Ettrick & Northern Railroad

Nestled in the picturesque "driftless" or nonglaciated region of western Wisconsin is Trempealeau County. A portion of this 745-square-mile county borders the mighty Mississippi River, which historically provided some residents access to major markets, but interior sections were mostly isolated during the settlement process. For decades, a modest network of primitive wagon ways meandered through the hilly countryside. The area's most famous pike, the strategic, albeit coarse Galesville and Eau Claire Road, crossed over a heavily wooded and substantial sandstone barrier known as "The Ridge" or "Blair Ridge" that separated the southeastern and central parts of the county, becoming at times badly rutted, muddy, or snow clogged. In order to develop economically and ultimately to prosper, the residents knew that they needed railroads.[1]

In 1870 the Railway Age came to Trempealeau County. The La Crosse, Trempealeau & Prescott Railroad, later a component of the Chicago & North Western Railway (North Western), completed a twenty-nine-mile line between Winona Junction, Wisconsin, near La Crosse, and Winona, Minnesota. After the Mississippi River was bridged, the road reached another North Western affiliate, the Winona & St. Peter Railroad. This route between Chicago and Dakota Territory sliced through the lower portions of the county. Later, in 1883, a seven-mile stub, constructed under the banner of the Galesville & Mississippi River Railroad and shortly thereafter absorbed by the North Western, began operations between the Winona line at Trempealeau and Galesville. Not long after that, the Chicago, St. Paul, Minneapolis & Omaha (part of the North Western System) finished its thirty-seven-mile Mondovi branch, which served Eleva, Strum, and Osseo in the northern part of the county. About this time, the Chicago, Burlington & Northern Railroad, a satellite of the Chicago, Burlington & Quincy Railroad (Burlington), opened a direct route between the Windy City and the Twin Cities, and in the county this trackage often hugged the bank of the Mississippi River. Citizens of Caledonia and Trempealeau cheerfully boasted direct access to two trunk carriers, the North Western and the Burlington.[2]

Although the initial entry of the North Western into Trempealeau County was lauded, the populace applauded even more loudly an expansion of rail service that took place in 1873, when the Green Bay & Minnesota Railroad—a predecessor of the Green Bay & Western Railroad (GB&W)—built through the heart of the county. The line largely followed the winding valley of the shallow Trempealeau River. This rail artery would become Wisconsin's historic east–west railroad. With the arrival of the iron horse, such communities as Arcadia, Blair, Dodge, Independence, and Whitehall reaped the economic and social advantages of modern transportation. Area residents benefited from a better way to ship their agricultural products, initially dominated by wheat and later by dairy products and livestock, and to acquire the goods of the industrial age. Everyone profited from the state's expanding railroad network, which by 1890 had increased to more than five thousand miles and by 1910 reached nearly 7,500 miles, peaking a few years later at slightly more than 7,800 miles. And in several areas, especially in greater Milwaukee, the nearly four hundred miles of electric interurbans, which had been built before World War I, enhanced transport, especially for travelers.[3]

Even with the Burlington, GB&W, and North Western main lines, and the Galesville and Mondovi branches, part of Trempealeau County remained without rail service. The most important area that lacked convenient access to the iron horse was Ettrick Township and the Beaver Creek valley situated in the rather rough terrain between Blair and Galesville. By the post–Civil War years, scores of settlers had arrived in the township, many coming directly from their native Norway. By the turn of the twentieth century, nearly two thousand residents lived in this prosperous dairy-producing and stock-raising section that a local observer described as "some of the richest farms in western Wisconsin, absolutely without railroad facilities." Not to be overlooked were small, albeit profitable, plots of black-leaf tobacco, although by World War II this production had nearly disappeared. And in the heart of the township, pioneer Iver Pederson had platted the village of Ettrick in the 1870s and "increased its material prosperity by erecting a flouring mill and woolen mill and a creamery."[4]

Citizens of Ettrick Township wanted rail service. The reason was simple: "Money and time spent in reaching these [shipping] points [at Blair and Galesville] greatly increased the cost of producing and marketing products of the farms in the Ettrick region." Residents continued to recall their earlier bad luck: the GB&W had run a survey through their neighborhood, but the company opted for the more economical Trempealeau River route.[5]

But what could be done to bring rails to Ettrick? The GB&W, which struggled financially, showed no interest in building the nearly dozen miles south from Blair. And the North Western refused requests by Ettrick representatives to extend its Galesville branch northward for about the same distance. The company could have afforded such an investment, but likely concluded that the volume of projected traffic would not justify the investment, in part because some of this business already flowed through the Galesville station.[6]

Yet those Ettrick residents who wanted a railroad were surprisingly slow to act. The possibility, or at least the hope, persisted that the GB&W or the North Western might eventually serve the township, and such a belief may have delayed action. The crushing depression that engulfed the nation for much of the 1890s greatly dampened railroad-building enthusiasm, yet the general prosperity that followed the Spanish-American War renewed interest in construction.

At any time, though, a self-help scheme might have succeeded. Even during the depths of the depression, several successful efforts developed in the Upper Midwest and Great Plains for what was commonly called the "farmers' railroad movement." In its purest form, the concept involved local residents, farmers, merchants, and others filing incorporation papers, making surveys, and embarking on construction. Since capital would be limited, farmers and townspeople—anyone who lived along the projected line—would be asked to donate land and to contribute their labor. (For those who helped, company stock would be their immediate reward.) Available animal teams, plows, and scrapers would be used to shape the roadbed, and crossties would be harvested from nearby stands of timber. With grading completed and ties furnished, management would then bond the road to raise funds to purchase inexpensive but suitable rolling stock, rails, and other track materials. The ultimate fate of the completed project would remain flexible. Perhaps the line would be sold or leased to a connecting carrier, or it would be operated as a consumer-owned enterprise.[7]

Finally, in the years immediately before America's entry into World War

I, residents of the Ettrick area took action. They believed that their isolation must end, and they had little faith that better internal combustion vehicles and the emerging crusade for improved public roads would resolve their transportation problems. "[This was] the 'B. A. era' in Wisconsin—Before automobiles," noted an officer of the Wisconsin & Northern Railroad, a company that built its 120-mile line from near Crandon to Neenah between 1907 and 1919. "[A] railroad meant much to the communities by way of convenience, business and pleasure." And these sentiments continued to be shared by other Wisconsinites. Furthermore, times were generally good. Area property owners surely appreciated the strong increase in land values. Based on real-estate sales compiled by the Wisconsin Tax Commission, the estimated price per acre for Trempealeu County stood at $26.00 in 1905, rose to $37.75 in 1910, and reached $51.75 in 1915. Even the most thrifty individual might feel inclined to invest in a railroad.[8]

Unlike some contemporary railroad proponents, including those who supported the Creston, Winterset & Des Moines and the Electric Short Line, Ettrick enthusiasts did not seriously consider an interurban option. Their desire was much more for freight than passenger service. An electric road, with its high initial costs of overhead wires and poles and power distribution equipment, hardly made financial sense, and ridership levels would never warrant frequently scheduled cars. A conventional, affordable, steam-powered operation, that could handle passengers, mail, and express, but focus on freight shipments, would be the sensible strategy.

In late 1914 and early 1915, plans for an Ettrick railroad evolved. Several local "live wires" decided to organize a company and to seek a state charter. Leaders of this classic local initiative effort included Hans Claussen, who served as treasurer of the Ettrick Creamery Company and the Ettrick Telephone Company and in 1911 had organized the Bank of Ettrick; Alexander Ekern, president of the mutual Scandinavian Insurance Company and the Ettrick Creamery Company; Mathias Pederson, an Ettrick merchant and onetime county sheriff; Andrew Hagestad, a prosperous dairy farmer and "one of the best-known agriculturists in this county"; and John Raichle, a road contractor from nearby Osseo. Also in the leadership group was John Gaveney, an attorney and former state senator from Arcadia. On June 17, 1915, the Ettrick & Northern Railroad (E&N), with Gaveney listed as president, officially filed its incorporation papers with the Wisconsin secretary of state. Company representatives then began to conduct stock solicitations.[9]

Officers of the Ettrick & Northern decided that building the ten miles north to the GB&W at Blair would be preferable to going south to link with the North Western at Galesville, even though the former route would necessitate carving a deep cut through the Blair Ridge and filling in two hollows on either side of the cut. While never stated, the E&N leadership probably considered the GB&W to be a friendlier interchange partner than the North Western, involving better switching services and more favorable rate divisions. Also, an Ettrick resident suggested that there was no love lost between the citizens of his hometown and Galesville, for there was "a long standing feud with the Galesville Baseball Team." Moreover, a railroad to Blair would create a tie-in with a main line operation rather than a lightly used appendage. And Blair seemed to be a thoroughly dynamic place, even though its population in 1910 stood at 486, or about half the population of Galesville. "That Blair is a good shipping point is evidenced by the fact that 105 cars were shipped from here during the month of October [1915]," related the *Blair Press*. "Of these 60 were cattle, 2 of horses, 26 of hay, 12 of potatoes, 3 of grain, 1 of flour and 1 of junk."[10]

Progress continued on two fronts: financial and physical. Area residents expressed enthusiasm for the project, although favorable sentiment for a railroad was not universal. "For two weeks the campaign for the new line was waged, meetings were held almost nightly," observed the *Osseo News*. "The village [of Ettrick] was almost solidly for the bonds while the farmers were divided." On September 20, 1915, the township held a special election on a $75,000 ($1.57 million in 2008 dollars), 5 percent construction bond issue, and the ballot proposal carried by a substantial margin, 298 to 148. According to one account, "The victory was celebrated at Ettrick with bonfires and a band to help make things lively." Another report noted that "the 400 people of the village and the many farmers paraded up and down the streets, speeches were made and in every way possible the community showed its exultation." Opponents graciously accepted the loss. "Those who were not in favor of the bond issue have gracefully submitted to the verdict of the majority and will be numbered among the enthusiastic boosters for the road," opined an area journalist. It did not take long for it to be reported that "over 400 farmers in the territory to be served have subscribed to the stock." The bond issue ultimately generated $144,000 ($3 million in 2008 dollars). The company also issued bonds that totaled $50,000 ($1 million in 2008 dollars). The general feeling was that the railroad could take shape rapidly. Although there was a deadline of December 31, 1917, for completion, "it is hoped that it may be finished a full year ahead of time."[11]

Following the election, surveyors entered the countryside. Much of the work took place in October and November 1915, with most of their efforts focusing on how to cross the Blair Ridge. And they also needed to decide how to manage the hills between the Ridge and Ettrick. Then in December "the final survey" was run. Even before the route had been fully determined, the company began to accept donations for the right-of-way and to buy additional parcels, a process that took more than a year to complete, in part because it became necessary to institute several condemnation proceedings.[12]

During this gestation period, rumors spread that the Ettrick & Northern might become more than a Lilliputian affair. As early as November 1915, published reports indicated that residents of "inland" North Bend "are gay to hold a special election to see whether the Ettrick & Northern can be induced to extend to their village." If this were to happen, the railroad would more than double in length, North Bend being about a dozen miles southeast of Ettrick. During the winter of 1917 a more widely discussed possibility occurred when talk centered on a thirty-five-mile line that would reach La Crosse through North Bend, Melrose, Mindoro, Holmen, and Onalaska. According to this thinking, the E&N would use a four-mile out-of-service appendage between Onalaska and North La Crosse, which was owned by the Chicago, Milwaukee & St. Paul Railway (Milwaukee Road) and which the company would officially abandon in 1918. This scheme would likely receive support from the Milwaukee Road and, according to the *La Crosse Leader Press*, "would give the Milwaukee road direct connections with a line tapping a rich agricultural section." This newspaper went so far as to announce that "the line has been surveyed and other preliminary work has been done looking to the construction of the railroad, but the project has not been financed." While the latter observation was surely correct, the former was improbable. Still, as late as the era of World War I, speculations about railroad construction continued to appear in the regional press. Such reports made for interesting reading and gossip, and underscored the ever-present spirit of civic chauvinism.[13]

As rumors circulated about the scope of the E&N, the building process between Blair and Ettrick moved forward, although slowly. Once the rights-of-way had either been acquired or condemnation suits undertaken and funding arranged, the company in July 1916 let the construction contract. John Raichle and E. J. Matchett, a road builder associate of Raichle's who also lived in Osseo, won the bid that totaled $135,000 ($2.6 million in 2008 dollars) and set a completion date of January 1, 1918. Optimism abounded. "The letting of the contract expels all doubt as to whether or not the road will be built. There has always been a question in the minds of many whether or not the road would ever be built, and the action of the promoters in letting the contract shows that they mean business."[14]

In September 1916 work began. Action took place on two fronts, grading the right-of-way and building bridges. Although the latter went smoothly, with the ten relatively short wooden spans being completed by the end of the year, the former became a challenge, with the Blair Ridge as the principal obstacle. Laborers struggled to blast and dig through the sandstone, ultimately creating an impressive cut that was ninety feet deep, three hundred feet wide, and one hundred feet long. Even with this massive passageway, which some claimed to be the largest railroad cut in Wisconsin, the approach grades were a staggering 4 percent. This construction strikingly resembled efforts of a few years earlier, when workers pushed the Creston, Winterset & Des Moines through the West Macksburg hillside. Graders on the E&N also had to fashion two deep fills that adjoined the cut, one of which was twenty-five feet deep and two hundred feet wide. Overall, the railroad project consumed 350,000 feet of lumber and required the movement of about twelve

From the time of construction to the end of operations, the Achilles' heel for the Ettrick & Northern Railroad was the deep cut through Blair Ridge, a few miles south of Blair. During the building period, workers remove rubble from the site, a process that consumed resources and time. *Courtesy of Murphy Library, University of Wisconsin–La Crosse.*

E. S. N. R. R ETTRICK, WIS,

During the summer of 1917 an elderly 4-4-0 locomotive, No. 7 (borrowed from the Green Bay & Western), four flatcars, and more than a score of laborers tend to a huge fill that had been fashioned near the Blair Ridge cut. *Courtesy of Charles H. Stats Collection.*

thousand cubic yards of earth per mile. And there was a death caused by a construction accident. A laborer on the steam shovel working on the Blair Ridge was hit by a swinging bucket.[15]

The contractor encountered additional problems. America's entry into World War I in April 1917 caused an acute labor shortage; enlistments and the draft took away a sizeable number of able-bodied workers. Also, costs escalated for materials, especially steel products; prices for secondhand lightweight rails, fastenings, rolling stock, and the like skyrocketed. And scarcities developed.[16]

Notwithstanding the physical terrain and labor and economic concerns, the railroad emerged. While costs could not be easily controlled, residents of the Ettrick area volunteered to assist physically with the construction. A cross section of citizens braved the winter weather to help the contractor meet the December 31, 1917, deadline for their hometown railroad. During the two days before Christmas, "fifty-five men from Ettrick and surrounding country worked with the railroad men," reported the *Blair Press*, "and on [Christmas

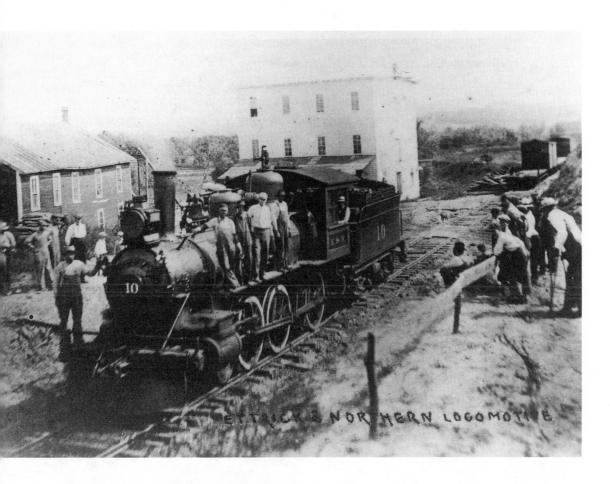

Eve] another crowd of like size—business and professional men, farmers, nobody barred, all working side by side at anything that was to be done." And females joined the workforce. "Women and girls donned overalls to go out and work on the road bed, with pick and shovel." Their collective labors paid off; the work train, with Frank Wall at the throttle, proudly steamed into the village on December 27, 1917. "The whistle of the Ettrick & Northern railroad can now be heard by the Ettrick people, and it is a welcome sound to all." At last Ettrick lost its status as an inland community.[17]

Since the final phase of construction was a rushed affair, much remained to be done before revenue service could begin. Throughout most of the construction season of 1918, workers labored on the track structure, put in sidings, built a frame depot and engine house in Ettrick, installed cattle guards, and made other improvements. The E&N, though, never had a turntable or a wye track in Ettrick, and that forced the locomotive to run in reverse from Blair. Likewise, the road lacked a water tank of its own, using the GB&W standpipe in Blair. It was August before the short line began revenue opera-

The workhorse for the Ettrick & Northern was a big ten-wheeler, No. 10, built in 1895 by Brooks, and formerly owned by the Lake Shore & Michigan Southern. For some reason the 10 spot has attracted a crowd along the railroad corridor in Ettrick. *Courtesy of Murphy Library, University of Wisconsin-La Crosse.*

tions, although the Railroad Commission of Wisconsin waited until November to conduct an official inspection.[18]

Differing from typical contemporary roads, the E&N avoided acquiring a broken-down piece of used motive power. Rather than an old 4-4-0 American Standard, a wheel arrangement already obsolete, a 2-6-0 Mogul, or a four- or six-wheel switcher, management selected a muscular secondhand 4-6-0 ten-wheeler, the No. 10. Although this Brooks-built product dated from the 1890s, according to railroad historian Stan Mailer, No. 10 rivaled the largest locomotives of the GB&W. The ten-wheeler was a good choice. The E&N encountered those steep approach grades to the cut, and even with a small train, high horsepower became essential for moving tonnage. The company made arrangements with the North Western and GB&W to provide major

E, &N, FREIGHT ETTRICK WIS,

Possibly the first freight train to leave Ettrick is captured in this photograph from 1918. The large oil lamp on the locomotive tender allowed for the train to move safely in reverse from Blair. The company never owned a turntable or wye, so the engine couldn't be turned around at the Ettrick terminal. *Courtesy of Charles H. Stats Collection.*

repairs and prepare for the annual boiler inspection required by the Inter-state Commerce Commission. When No. 10 temporarily left the property for maintenance, the E&N borrowed power from the road where the work was being done.[19]

But the E&N made the barest additions to its rolling stock. Unlike most short lines there never were any company-owned freight cars or other pieces of equipment, such as a caboose or ditcher. The E&N embraced a frugal strat-egy and believed that paying per diem charges for freight equipment was the prudent course. The only major expenditure was for an attractive secondhand combination coach, No. 100, which arrived in January 1919. This classic wood and steel "combine" could easily accommodate passengers, mail, and small shipments of freight. In 1921 the company also acquired a Model T Ford that rode on flanged wheels and pulled a two-ton trailer. At times management substituted this homemade unit for the locomotive and combine, producing considerable savings, since such a consist was exempt from the state's full-crew law. Except for perhaps the ten-wheeler and the Model T and its trailer, there was nothing exceptional about the E&N.[20]

The actual train operations lacked complexities. Scheduling reflected the connecting service on the GB&W at Blair, where the E&N shared depot space. For the initial years of the Ettrick road's existence the daily-except-Sunday mixed train made two round-trips. The first train departed Ettrick at 8:00 a.m. and reached Blair at 8:50 a.m., with an 8:15 a.m. intermediate stop at the tiny, rural Annaka station, three miles from Ettrick. This train then left Blair at 9:10 a.m., stopped at Annaka at 9:45 a.m., and arrived in Ettrick at 10:00 a.m. The afternoon accommodation whistled out of the Ettrick station at 12:40 p.m., reached Annaka at 12:55 p.m., and chugged into the Blair terminal fifty minutes later. The final train of the day departed Blair at 6:00 p.m., paused at Annaka at 6:35 p.m., and tied up at 6:50 p.m. in Ettrick. On Tuesdays the 12:40 p.m. from Ettrick left at 3:30 p.m., probably to accommodate freight shipments for some unstated reason. Like typical interurbans and other steam short lines, "the train was accustomed to stop anywhere along the track and pick up passengers." Only during the national coal shortages of the immedi-ate post–World War I period did the E&N modify its scheduled operations, reducing service to a single daily-except-Sunday round-trip.[21]

Resembling the general nature of transportation, business on the E&N fluctuated. Just as there would be occasional extra freight movements, usu-ally stock trains, additional passenger runs also occurred. On November 7, 1919, for example, the railroad posted this notice: "The Ettrick & Northern will run an extra train Tuesday, Nov. 11th, leaving Ettrick 12:40 p.m. to make connection with train for Whitehall at Blair. For benefit of those wishing to take in the celebration [first anniversary of Armistice Day] at Whitehall." And on New Year's Eve 1920, "a number of the Ettrick people chartered a train and went to Blair to take in the New Year's ball of that place." The local paper revealed that everyone had a "joyous experience" and continued, "we expect that when we have a blow out that we too can have the opportunity of entertaining the Blair people in a like manner." Then there was the masquerade dance in Blair with music provided by Mack's Orchestra that a special train, which left the Ettrick depot on February 11, 1921, at 7:00 p.m., helped to make a resounding success.[22]

As with other twilight railroads, the coming of the E&N had a positive economic impact on its service area, with Ettrick as the epicenter. Yet before the shrill whistle of the No. 10 could be heard, local businessmen in February 1917 organized the Ettrick Lumber Company "to do a general lumber business." The organizational gathering took place in the offices of the E&N. The location of this meeting was hardly accidental; all of the officers of the lumber

In the fall of 1918 the first stock train is about to whistle out of the Ettrick station. The new depot stands to the right of the six-car movement. The string of flatcars is likely part of a work train. Courtesy of Murphy Library, University of Wisconsin–La Crosse.

company had a direct connection to the railroad and wished to prepare for the new road. As long as the E&N operated, the Ettrick Lumber Company would be a major customer. Not long thereafter the Ettrick Elevator Company erected a 20,000-bushel-capacity elevator. This facility claimed "all modern conveniences for weighing, elevating, storing, cleaning, loading and unloading grain." Some of the individuals associated with these endeavors started the Ettrick Shipping Association, "a combination of farmers who have organized for the purpose of doing their own shipping," and in 1918, the association's first year, the group shipped seventy-five carloads of livestock from its facility near the depot. The association worked with a recently formed "auto truck line" that transported livestock from the Galesville area to Ettrick. Later, local investors opened the Beaver Valley State Bank: "The New Bank—The Bank of Personal Service, ACTIVE, ALERT, ALIVE." Now residents had a choice between two hometown financial institutions.[23]

In order to take advantage of and publicize these new or expanded businesses, the community's first newspaper, the weekly *Ettrick Advance*, made its debut on October 3, 1919. Elmer Gilbertson moved to town from neighboring Melrose to become editor and publisher. "Ettrick has been without a paper," observed the rival *Blair Press*, "and the business men there realize the advantages of having a paper to advertise their business and their town. It is such enterprise and aggressiveness that makes the difference between the dead towns and the growing ones." Ettrick appeared to be on an upward trajectory.[24]

Civic pride and optimism fostered by the coming of the rails led to the incorporation of Ettrick. Since the early 1860s, when Ettrick Township was formed, the village had lacked the trappings of municipal government, being controlled by township and county agencies. The change in the legal structure came in 1920 when a grassroots organization, the Ettrick Advancement Association, pushed successfully for incorporation.[25]

As seems to have been nearly universal, even at a late date in the construction period, the advent of rail service triggered an urban land boom. The first burst of activity took place in Blair in October 1918 when the Louisville Real Estate and Development Company of Louisville, Kentucky, announced a public auction of thirty residential lots in the eastern part of town. The advertising copy announced, "Blair On the Map to Stay," and called the place "a progressive village of 700 inhabitants, beautifully situated along the Trempealeau River near the eastern boundary of Trempealeau County, in the midst of one of the finest farming communities in Wisconsin." Local transportation services were not overlooked: "Blair is located on the Ettrick & Northern and the Green Bay & Western railroads, 38 miles northeast of Winona and 43 miles north of La Crosse on the State Trunk Highway System." But the big sale did not go off as planned. An outbreak of the deadly Spanish influenza, the pandemic that ravished Europe and America, prompted a postponement. Finally, on April 28, 1919, the auctioneer cried the sale and these out-of-state promoters expressed pleasure at the results. The following year a somewhat smaller auction took place in Ettrick. On May 22, 1920, the U.S. Real Estate & Development Company of Spring Valley, Minnesota, another outside firm that sensed the positive impact of the Ettrick road, offered fifteen lots in an eastside addition opposite the school. Just as the Louisville company lauded Blair, the Spring Valley firm glorified Ettrick as being "in the heart of the best diversified farming section in Wisconsin, and is a thoroughly modern city of about 700 population, located on the Ettrick & Northern Railway." The sale went well, and in October the *Ettrick Advance* reported, "There are six new residence buildings under construction in the village at the present time."[26]

Once the railroad opened, and before the postwar recession of 1921–22 struck, optimism throughout the Ettrick community was widespread. "It requires a little time to change customs that have been in vogue for the past half century," wrote Elmer Gilbertson in the *Advance* on October 10, 1919, "but when railroad facilities and a closer market is [*sic*] offered the numerous productive farming and dairy sections of this locality, it is natural that the near market will get the business. Such is the case and condition in Ettrick. Every month shows a greater increase in shipping and freight receipts over the Ettrick & Northern." Gilbertson believed that "this increase will continue from month to month until the natural trade territory is covered," and concluded that these events "will pull for larger population, giving the village further opportunity for growth."[27]

Although signs pointed to a successful railroad, the E&N never became a moneymaker. In part because of the higher than normal costs of improving and maintaining the track, especially in the area of the big cut, the financials for the first several years surely disappointed everyone who wanted the little pike to prosper. Gross earnings for 1919 totaled $13,426, but operating expenses reached $25,224. A year later the situation worsened; gross earnings increased to $14,724, but operating expenses climbed to $29,314. However, 1921 saw somewhat better gross earnings ($17,257) and a substantial drop in operating expenses ($15,349), producing for the first time a modest surplus of nearly $2,000. But 1922 proved disastrous. Gross earnings plummeted to a dismal $7,298, while operating expenses remained approximately static, $16,088. When other expenses were added, the annual deficit reached $16,575 ($211,000 in 2008 dollars).[28]

Several forces buffeted the E&N. Troubles stemmed from postwar-era inflation; a soft regional economy, especially for livestock; steadily improving public roads; and greater numbers of motorized vehicles. Increased automobile usage led to a free fall in passenger revenues. In 1920 earnings stood at $2,240, but two years later plunged to $852.[29]

Backers of the Ettrick & Northern realized that a crisis loomed. A series of meetings in 1921, designed to place the company on a solid financial footing, led to a plan of action. Voters of Ettrick would be asked to authorize another bond issue, with the proceeds going to the railroad. A committee would then attempt to sell additional stock that an infusion of public funds would make more attractive to investors. "Let's keep the whistle 'tootin' and the bell a ringing" became the battle cry. "The life of the road depends on the people of Ettrick and those tributary to Ettrick," argued the *Advance*. "It can be saved and it must be saved and it will take the cooperation of everyone."[30]

In July voters expressed considerably less support for their hometown carrier than they had in 1915. Although the tally gave the bond proposal a slim six-vote margin of victory, R. J. Herreid, "an Ettrick taxpayer," took legal action against the funding scheme. In November a state court ruled in favor of his suit, arguing that it was illegal to "give the town's money away to keep the road in operation."[31]

Problems mounted. Not only did the railroad fail to raise adequate funding, but more bad luck plagued the company. In late spring 1922, "locomotive troubles" (undisclosed headaches with No. 10 that stemmed from a serious derailment in March 1921), and a deteriorating roadbed, especially in the big cut area, forced a suspension in service. The inability to meet interest payments and other obligations caused grave concern for future operations.[32]

These troubling events prompted a new course of action. The board of directors decided that it had no alternative but to seek court protection. On June 22, 1922, the E&N declared bankruptcy. Circuit court judge R. S. Cowie in La Crosse appointed area businessman H. R. Madsen to serve as receiver and manager, and supporters hoped that the railroad could be saved. The expectation was that the property could be revitalized with creditors held at bay, and through the sale of $8,000 of receiver's certificates.[33]

During much of the summer of 1922, efforts were under way to bring "Our Railway" back to life. Madsen supervised the renaissance on several fronts. Work on the track became a priority and the company repeatedly advertized for section men: "WORK WILL LAST UNTIL LATE IN THE FALL. WAGES 35 CENTS PER HOUR." The company also sought straight, eight-foot hardwood ties, preferring white oak to red oak. "The prices they are offering are good and should be an inducement to bring in a nice bunch of ties." Madsen also made arrangements for a machinist from the Milwaukee Road in La Crosse to supervise the overhaul of No. 10. Even the dowdy combine was not being overlooked. "The coach is also undergoing a thorough remodeling," reported the *Blair Press*. "John Fillner of Ettrick is at work painting the coach now." Court protection and the sale of $7,650 of receiver's certificates made these betterments possible. And on September 15, 1922, both freight and passenger service resumed.[34]

Advocates of the Ettrick railroad were not complacent. They stressed repeatedly that the company must have the "COOPERATION of the COMMUNITY." Since freight traffic was essential for success, potential customers were urged to route shipments "via E&N," even though rates might not be the lowest. For example, it cost 31.5 cents per hundredweight to transport cattle from Ettrick to Chicago, but twenty-eight cents from several neighboring stations. The differential for hogs to the Windy City was a comparable 4.5 cents per hundredweight. In an effort to bolster livestock traffic, the owner of the Ettrick stockyards announced that "in view of a small difference in freight rates and as a protection to the railroad I have decided that parties cannot use the stock scales or yards unless they signify their willingness to patronize this line." This was the action of a truly public-spirited citizen.[35]

A functioning and somewhat stronger E&N returned to life. Freight traffic increased and revenues reached nearly $15,000 for the income year of 1923. This encouraging trend led to an annual surplus of slightly more than $2,000. Even though the mixed train made two daily-except-Sunday round-trips, passenger revenues remained dismal, amounting to just $834 for the year. Admittedly, service had been suspended for several months and automobile travel continued to grow, but in June a bus company, Mohawk Stage Line, began operations between La Crosse and Eau Claire, offering twice-daily service through Ettrick. And this competing form of public transport definitely had a negative impact. For one thing, Santa Claus, who annually visited Ettrick stores and handed out apples, candy, and nuts to the children, had come to town since 1918 on the train from Blair, and youngsters were told, "His team of reindeers were left in the woods some place west of here." Instead, for a few years after 1924 the jolly old man arrived on a Mohawk bus.[36]

While the mid- and late 1920s were a time of general prosperity for residents of Trempealeau County, the E&N grew financially and physically weaker. The company continued to handle freight, mostly outbound livestock and inbound building materials and fuel, and remained a source of community pride. Then in the fall of 1927 management suspended service due to motive power and track problems and steadily mounting deficits. This second shutdown would last until the following April when somehow the railroad managed to deliver a car to the Ettrick Lumber Company.[37]

Abandonment seemed imminent. When, in late 1927, the bankruptcy judge ordered liquidation and the posting of an official sale notice, the fate of the E&N appeared to be sealed. The front page of the *Blair Press* on March 15, 1928, proclaimed, "E.& N. RAILROAD IS SOLD FOR JUNK." For advocates of continued rail service, the sad news revealed that the New Brunswick Iron & Wrecking Company, based in Albany, New York, had purchased the rails, the disabled locomotive, and the coach for a paltry $8,000 ($99,000 in 2008 dollars). The report indicated, however, that "the depot, roundhouse and office equipment are still for sale, and the bill of sale to the Albany company probably gives it the right to resell the road." Added the *Press*, "Should the wrecking company take up the tracks the right of way will revert back to the original owners." Soon the court accepted a bid of $800 for the bridge timbers, ties, and depot. Surely, the death warrant had been signed.[38]

Even though liquidation of the Ettrick & Northern Railroad Company generated a distribution of only $3,944.91 to investors, some Ettrick residents badly wanted to retain their railroad, and this desire turned to action. Spearheading this desperate effort were two local businessmen: Maurice Casey, agent for Ford automobiles and McCormick-Deering farm implements; and Obel Pederson, meat butcher and storekeeper. Casey and Pederson swiftly struck a deal with the scrap dealer whereby they agreed to lease the railroad for thirty days with the expectation that a sale could then be arranged. The men deposited $1,000 and pledged another $8,000, if funds could be raised. "In case of failure," commented the *Advance*, "M. Casey and Obel Pederson at least took a sporting chance."[39]

Casey and Pederson did not blindly respond to an emerging community crisis. These two sparkplugs, or as the *La Crosse Tribune* called them, "a mixture of Irish and Norwegian perseverance," developed a sensible business plan. The company would be reorganized and stock sold, track structures would be modestly improved, and motive power replaced. The railroad, however, would not be a conventional steam operation, but rather it would acquire an internal combustion locomotive that would be cheaper to operate and less likely to experience mechanical problems. Also, the road would become freight only, with no pretense of being a passenger carrier.[40]

The saviors of the E&N labored effectively. Casey and Pederson raised the necessary cash to satisfy the junk dealer, and they arranged for the purchase of the other assets with the sellers realizing a modest profit. In late April the new corporation, recast as the Ettrick Railroad, secured clear title to all of the property, although the official articles of incorporation were not signed until early October 1928.[41]

Still another hurdle needed to be overcome. The railroad had to raise about $7,000 to buy the internal combustion locomotive, and so more funds were solicited. Said Pederson, "After a fair trial is given the part of soliciting, and is found that the money cannot be raised, the road will then eventually be junked. It is now only a matter of power equipment." But the money came, and a thirty-ton, four-speed gasoline engine arrived in time for the fall shipping season from the Whitcomb Locomotive Works of Rochelle, Illinois, a unit of Baldwin Locomotive.[42]

The little locomotive, Ettrick Railroad No. 1, was a wise purchase, performing well and saving money. Charles Sherwood, the general manager, praised the No. 1 in a letter to the manufacturer. "On this line we have a 4½ percent grade, with sharp curves on each side. We have pulled 226 tons over this grade in second gear. While the condition of the track will not permit much speed, the short distance makes a gasoline locomotive an ideal power for us." Fuel consumption for the twenty-mile round-trip totaled only about twenty-five to thirty gallons and, of course, there were no boiler flues to renew or other costly maintenance procedures. "We will be able to make some money," concluded Sherwood, "which would be out of the question with steam power." The Ettrick road had a piece of motive power to be prized.[43]

The reconstituted company worked hard to maintain freight service, and from every indication, the Whitcomb and the two-man train crew and tiny office and maintenance force served customers well. The traffic mix of this Spartan operation continued to be lumber, petroleum products, household furnishings, and coal and livestock in season. Low operating costs and a dedicated labor force, however, could not guarantee traffic. A combination of competition from trucks, which traveled an improved State Highway 53, and, after 1929, the crippling national depression doomed the struggling railroad.[44]

Still, the Ettrick carrier survived for nearly a decade. But by the mid-1930s revenues had declined precipitously, and in April 1937 stockholders, without dissension, voted to liquidate. It did not take long before the company received regulatory permission to abandon and to find buyers for its principal assets. Harry P. Bourke, a scrap dealer from Escanaba, Michigan, paid $15,100 ($224,000 in 2008 dollars) for the steel rails and related materials, and the Iron and Steel Products Company of Chicago acquired the locomotive for an undisclosed price. Subsequently, the pint-size Whitcomb made its way through the used locomotive market, eventually rusting away on a siding in Louisiana.[45]

The passing of the plucky little railroad was duly noted. On August 20, 1937, the final words in the *Advance* appeared with the headline, "Last locomotive." Said the newspaper, "A full train crew with locomotive, flat cars and caboose were in here Tuesday to pull the last curtain on the Ettrick railroad.

The 'toot' of the whistle, which will be the last heard here, brought out many of the citizenry." Added the newspaper, "It is a regrettable fact to see the rails pulled up, but it is a condition that is happening to many of the smaller lines. Trucks have changed the mode of transportation throughout the entire nation." Yet no obituary writer remembered that the Ettrick & Northern had had meaningful economic impact on Blair and, most of all, on Ettrick. It was hardly fair to call the road the "Ettrick & Nothing" as some residents jokingly did when the company experienced that financial crisis in the mid-1920s.[46]

Repeating a familiar theme of twilight railroads, the timing of the Ettrick road was unfortunate. Admittedly, construction and operation bolstered the service territory, but arguably, rails appeared two or three decades too late. As Stan Mailer correctly observed, "The town waited too long and by World War I, when many short lines were withering due to highway competition, Ettrick bravely decided to foster the Ettrick & Northern." Backers of rail service struggled gallantly to achieve and maintain their transportation outlet, and during the Ettrick Railroad phase they imaginatively embraced dependable, internal combustion motive power. If the community had had a volume shipper, for example a furniture factory or a brick works, the ending might have been different. And making the company part of System No. 14, "Burlington," which the *Complete Plan of Consolidation of the Interstate Commerce Commission* of December 9, 1929, had called for under terms of the Transportation Act of 1920, might have led to corporate salvation and a somewhat extended life. Alas, these two possibilities were not to be.[47]

Yet Ettrick did not wither away when the railroad closed. In time, the town grew to a population of more than 1,200 residents and the community mostly prospered. Residents could rightly take pride in accomplishing the difficult construction and satisfaction that their little road had spawned such businesses as a bank, lumberyard, and newspaper, providing that economic base for further growth.

Ettrick area residents can still be reminded of their remarkable railroad heritage by some physical remnants. A snowmobile trail uses the somewhat-filled-in Blair Ridge cut and approaches. The depot serves as a storage facility, and the engine house has been converted into apartments. And several lengths of the roadbed remain visible between Ettrick and Blair.[48]

The Ettrick & Northern Railroad stands as a testimonial to local initiative and drive. If there was ever a "farmers' railroad," this little hometown pike wonderfully represents a mostly forgotten genre.

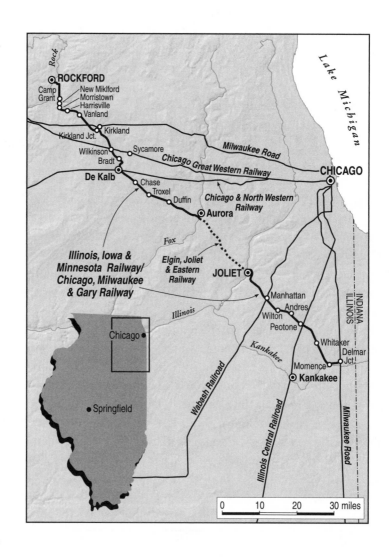

Rock

ROCKFORD
Camp
Grant
New Miklford
Morristown
Harrisville
Vanland
Kirkland
Kirkland Jct.
Wilkinson
Bradt
Sycamore
De Kalb
Chase
Troxel
Duffin
Aurora

Milwaukee Road

Chicago Great Western Railway

*Chicago & North Western
Railway*

CHICAGO

Lake Michigan

***Illinois, Iowa &
Minnesota Railway/
Chicago, Milwaukee
& Gary Railway***

Fox

*Elgin, Joliet
& Eastern
Railway*

JOLIET

Manhattan
Andres
Wilton
Peotone

Whitaker
Delmar
Jct.

Momence
Kankakee

Illinois

Kankakee

INDIANA
ILLINOIS

Wabash Railroad

Illinois Central Railroad

Milwaukee Road

Chicago

Springfield

0   10   20   30 miles

The Rockford Route: Illinois, Iowa & Minnesota Railway and Chicago, Milwaukee & Gary Railway

As the twentieth century dawned, Illinois resembled other midwestern states by possessing a well-developed network of railroad lines. In fact, by 1900 the Illini State claimed the greatest amount of trackage, at 11,002 miles, with Iowa a distant second at 9,185 miles. Unique among these eight states, mileage in Illinois increased after 1910, reaching an impressive 12,188 in 1920 and peaking at 12,506 a decade later. No one should have been surprised by this extensive grid of steel rails. By the post–Civil War years, Chicago had developed into the meeting place between East and West, becoming the undisputed railroad mecca of America. Not only did trunk roads radiate from the Windy City, St. Louis also had evolved into a major railroad hub, with strategic routes crossing Illinois to reach the Missouri metropolis. Illinois grew rapidly, gaining nearly 1.8 million residents between 1880 and 1900, adding another 800,000 by 1910, and 850,000 more by 1920. Chicago was the nation's second-largest city, having more than 2.1 million residents in 1910, and the state counted an impressive number of thriving industrial centers. In addition to Chicago, places like Aurora, Decatur, Joliet, Moline, Peoria, Rockford, and Rock Island produced an astonishing array of products, ranging from farm machinery and furniture to candy and books.[1]

Following the short, disruptive Panic of 1903, most talk about additional railroad building in Illinois centered on electric interurbans. Both America and the Midwest were about to experience an extensive wave of traction promotion and construction. Eventually, interurban mileage in Illinois reached 1,422 miles, ranking the state fourth nationally. Some of these interurbans transported conventional freight equipment that carried coal, grain, lumber, and other goods rather than rolling stock that accommodated short-haul passengers and package express. It was no surprise that the four-hundred-mile Illinois Traction System (McKinley Lines) served scores of elevators, and the 160-mile Chicago, North Shore & Milwaukee Railway switched a number of industries.[2]

Although electric traction dominated discussions about twilight railroad proposals in Illinois, steam road construction continued. Projects frequently involved adding additional tracks to existing routes, reducing grades and curvatures, and building cut-offs, often designed to reduce freight congestion. Still, new lines appeared after 1905, including major expansions undertaken by the Chicago, Burlington & Quincy (Burlington) and Chicago & North Western (North Western) railroads. In 1905 the Burlington, through a subsidiary, began construction of a fifty-five-mile extension from Centralia to Herrin, in the southern portion of the state. Opening a year later, this route gave the Burlington access to major coal mines. This desire to tap additional coal tonnage prompted the company, in 1909, to build from Herrin to Neilson, where the road obtained trackage rights over the Chicago & Eastern Illinois Railroad (C&EI) to West Vienna, and in 1910 to continue expansion south to the Ohio River community of Metropolis. Shortly after the nation entered World War I, the Burlington bridged the Ohio River and reached Paducah, Kentucky, 112 miles from Centralia, for even more freight traffic, including coal from the vast Kentucky fields. While the North Western did not seek Paducah or another Ohio River city, the railroad wished to exploit the St. Louis Gateway. In 1901 the North Western satellite, Peoria & North Western Railway, built the eighty-five miles south from the "Overland Route" main line at Nelson to Peoria. Then in 1913–14 another subsidiary, St. Louis, Peoria & North Western Railway, constructed a ninety-mile line southward from Peoria to Girard, where the rails met the coal-carrying Macoupin County Railway, also in the orbit of the North Western. The latter firm gave the North Western a connection with the Litchfield & Madison Railway and direct access to St. Louis.[3]

While most of the trackage constructed by steam roads in the early part of the twentieth century offered passenger service, the thrust of these latter-day projects, including the Burlington and North Western extensions, was for freight, which, after all, paid the bills. And business in the state was brisk. "The number of tons of freight carried earning revenue during the year ending June 30, 1906, was 146,127,773," reported the Illinois Railroad and Warehouse Commission in 1907, "an increase over the previous year of 23,543,686 tons." It was this desire to capture carloadings that explains the building of the Illinois, Iowa & Minnesota Railway (II&M) and its successor, the Chicago, Milwaukee & Gary Railway (Gary), collectively known as the "Rockford Route."[4]

As Chicago grew and railroad density increased, a belt road became essential to move freight around the urban congestion, especially to avoid older, inner-city yards. As the nineteenth century closed, the Elgin, Joliet & Eastern Railway (EJ&E) dominated belt operations. Organized in 1887 the company acquired the recently completed Joliet, Aurora & Northern Railway, which spanned the twenty-five miles between Joliet and Aurora. The EJ&E rapidly completed its core 129-mile route that linked Waukegan, Illinois, on the north, with Porter, Indiana, on the south. The EJ&E served such interchange points as Chicago Heights, Joliet, and West Chicago, Illinois, and Griffith, Indiana, thus running in a radius of approximately thirty miles from the center of Chicago. By World War I additional appendages and leases gave the EJ&E an operating network of more than eight hundred miles. "This line performs a general interchange of carload traffic between all Eastern, Western, Northern and Southern roads and Fast Freight lines operating via Chicago," announced the company in 1917. "Traffic routed via the E. J. & E. Ry. will avoid the congested terminals in the City of Chicago." This "Chicago Outer Belt Line" provided a valuable service to a vast number of customers, large and small, and made United States Steel Corporation (USS), then the owner, handsome profits.[5]

As greater Chicago burgeoned, a group of promoters envisioned another belt route, but mostly to the south and west of the EJ&E. Their plan initially involved building in a northwesterly direction from Momence, a town of approximately five thousand residents near Kankakee in Kankakee County and served by the C&EI (Frisco System) and Indiana, Illinois & Iowa (New York Central System) railroads, through Aurora, De Kalb, Rockford, and Freeport, to East Dubuque, in Jo Daviess County, opposite Dubuque, Iowa. There, it could make connections with the Chicago Great Western (Great Western) and Illinois Central (IC) railroads. In November 1903 this "Chicago Inner-Line Belt" scheme became public when a party of individuals, including several businessmen linked to the St. Louis Union Trust Company, received an Illinois charter for their Illinois, Iowa & Minnesota Railway Company. Area newspapers and the trade and financial press announced the undertaking, noting that the railroad was capitalized at $100,000 (soon increased to $5 million) and would be headquartered in the prestigious Rookery Building in the heart of Chicago. Halleck Wager (H. W.) Seaman, it was reported, had taken the throttle as president and general manager.[6]

Described as "painstaking, vigilant, untiring" and known for his "indefatigable energy and perseverance," H. W. Seaman, head of the evolving II&M, was an Iowa native, having been born on September 26, 1860, in the Mississippi River town of Clinton. After attending local schools, Seaman entered the University of Iowa "where he made an excellent record," and in 1881 received a degree in civil engineering. But this academic achievement did not end his educational training. Seaman returned to his hometown to read law and a few years later won admission to the Iowa bar, becoming subsequently a partner in "one of the strongest firms in the state."[7]

With training in engineering and the law, Seaman possessed the qualifications to undertake a wide range of pursuits, and this he did until his death in 1941. He became involved in Black Hills gold mining and the affairs of inland waterways. An avid participant in professional organizations, Seaman served two terms as president of the Western Mining Congress, and was a longtime member of the executive committees of the Mississippi Valley Association and the Upper Mississippi Waterways Association. While not linked to any commercial firm, he lobbied politicians and bureaucrats for river enhancements, and did so with considerable effectiveness, especially for locks and dams.[8]

While best remembered as a "pioneer river advocate," Seaman became heavily involved as a twilight era railroad promoter, builder, and executive. Both steam and electric projects attracted his attention. Although the sequence is unclear, he had a hand in numerous small steam roads, including the Davenport, Rock Island & Northwestern (DRI&NW); Groveton, Lupkin & Northern; Lorain & West Virginia (L&WV); Manistee & Grand Rapids; Minneapolis & Rainy River; Muskogee Southern; Ozark & Cherokee Central (O&CC); and Tremont & Gulf. In each case, Seaman served as a ranking officer, often president. These carriers varied in success, with the DRI&NW, L&WV, and O&CC having the best records, either in terms of revenues or profits generated by their sale. Noted one observer, "It is hard to see why he would spend so much effort promoting a system of disconnected short lines which never really earned very much money."[9]

Although engaged in these widespread steam railroad schemes, Seaman devoted time to at least one interurban project, the Gary & Southern Traction Company. Initially designed to coordinate with the developing II&M at Momence, "the proposed interurban was an electric feeder line, not like most interurbans." Conceived in 1908 the fifteen-mile electric railway opened four years later going northward from Crown Point, seat of Lake County, Indiana, to the new, mushrooming steel town of Gary. Yet the Gary & Southern planned to extend beyond Crown Point, specifically southwestward through Cedar Lake and Momence to Kankakee. While never a freight hauler as contemplated, or completed as projected, the little juice road eventually became part of the Gary Railways, and the Seaman segment operated until the early 1930s.[10]

Seaman and his associates envisioned a strategic steam railroad in the Chicago region. By early 1904, reports indicated that the line would "make a half circle" from Michigan City and Valparaiso, Indiana, to Dubuque, Iowa, and St. Paul, Minnesota, "tapping all the important trunk lines entering Chicago." A year later, though, the public learned that the road would not seek out Dubuque, but would expand directly to the Twin Cites from Rockford. The Illinois, Iowa & Minnesota moniker left open routing options.[11]

Rather than building from an announced end point, work began in 1903 and focused on the twenty-eight mile section from Aurora to DeKalb. It's likely the sponsors believed that good, local traffic could be generated immediately. The building of the first and subsequent components was under the supervision of the Kenefick Construction Company of Kansas City. The owner, William Kenefick, had been involved with Seaman in the O&CC and had also built railroads elsewhere. In typical fashion, backers of the II&M expected to reap the benefits from the money the II&M paid the construction firm. The railroad took shape as bridge builders and tracklayers did their jobs and laborers erected depots, coal chutes, and water tanks at strategic locations. "The track is in excellent condition throughout," reported the *Aurora News* later in 1904, "being laid with 70-pound steel rails and ballasted with gravel." But the *News* failed to note the absence of true "air line" qualities because "the company always went around any rise in the ground." This decision helps to explain why its heaviest grades were only one-half of 1 percent.[12]

It would be on October 24, 1904, that the first section of the II&M opened. "Thirty-eight cars of revenue freight were delivered into the DeKalb terminals of the Great Western (which the company had arranged to use) as the initial send off for the new road." Two days later an excursion of 150 members of the Elks, riding in borrowed coaches, journeyed from Aurora to DeKalb, "the occasion being the initiation of a large class of candidates into the DeKalb lodge." Progress had been delayed for a couple of reasons. Some property owners went to court to object to the proposed right-of-way "badly cutting their farms," a complaint that property owners repeatedly made even back to the canal-building era, and a viaduct needed to be completed over the North Western main line outside DeKalb. But this construction could not start until a condemnation suit with a large landowner had been settled.[13]

Major events soon took place. Beginning on November 2, 1904, the II&M advertized a single daily-except-Sunday mixed train between the two temporary terminals, but quickly the service doubled. And the road announced that the American Express Company received the right to conduct package operations along the line. Four secondhand 2-6-0 Mogul locomotives and a "handsome" passenger coach made these operations possible. As these trains moved over the new track, construction crews, with "over 300 teams at work," concentrated on the sixteen miles from DeKalb, officially DeKalb Junction, northward to Kirkland. The cry became "On to Rockford."[14]

Preliminary work was also taking place between Joliet and Momence, a distance of thirty-six miles. The II&M expected that the intermediate connection would be achieved through trackage rights over the EJ&E between Aurora and Joliet, and on February 21, 1905, this rental agreement took effect. The charges, however, were steep, seventy-five cents per car mile. But the II&M intended to close the missing link, wanting to develop on-line business opportunities and not wishing to be delayed by EJ&E trains. But most importantly, this parallel line would end cash payments to host EJ&E.[15]

With only the Aurora-to-DeKalb portion in operation, the II&M had not become much of a belt or bridge-line operation, although there were interchanges with the Burlington, EJ&E, and North Western in Aurora, and the Great Western and North Western in DeKalb. The company needed to rely on customers at either end and from on-line shipping points. The II&M, though, did not serve the industrial heart of Aurora, but rather terminated at the West Aurora yards of the EJ&E.[16]

Not surprisingly for the IM&M, DeKalb, rather than Aurora, became the leading source for early revenues and was where the railroad had a greater impact. This seat of DeKalb County boomed, being the birthplace of the barbed wire industry and home to a state normal college, and having a population of about 6,000. "DeKalb has been growing so fast of late years," editorialized the *DeKalb Evening Chronicle* in July 1904, "that people have grown to expect a whirl here all the time." With arrival of the II&M, the newspaper observed, "Scores of new houses are under way and many have been started during the past few weeks." And advertisements appeared frequently, offering residential building lots in developments and additions. Although the North Western, the dominant road, monopolized the passenger business in the "Barb City," several manufacturing firms shared their in- and outbound freight with the three local carriers, including the II&M. The town's newest road reached these sites over the Great Western, which a ninety-nine-year lease allowed. The American Steel & Wire Company emerged as the best revenue producer, and within several years the II&M handled nearly all of the raw materials and coal to this teeming plant, and more than half of the finished products. The arrival of the II&M prompted the Melville-Clark Piano Company to locate on its rails, becoming another important customer after the music firm achieved full production.[17]

Even in this well-populated region, the coming of Rockford Route still resulted in town creation. While the farming village of Chase, located twenty-one miles from Aurora, already existed, the presence of the II&M led to a cluster of new structures, including a large grain elevator. And soon the Chicago, DeKalb & Rockford Electric Traction Company (later the Chicago, Aurora & DeKalb Railroad), a twenty-eight-mile steam road between Aurora and DeKalb that had been projected as an interurban and in time came under wire, gave this Kane County community another line. Yet Troxel, named for the II&M's chief engineer I. W. Troxel, sixteen miles from Aurora, became a village that owed its existence solely to the new road and would not receive additional rail service. Early in 1905 surveyors staked out the townsite and within a short time this hamlet, located in the southwestern corner of Kaneville Township, became "the most important shipping point between Aurora and DeKalb." It did not take long before Troxel sported a grain elevator, gristmill, coal yard, lumberyard, two general stores, and a collection of houses. Another place, Duffin, ten miles from Aurora and honoring II&M general

The Illinois, Iowa & Minnesota did much to enhance manufacturing activities in DeKalb, Illinois. The Melville-Clark Piano Company became one shipper of importance. This photograph of the impressive brick factory dates from 1906, not long after the plant and railroad opened. Courtesy of Embree Collection, Regional History Center, Northern Illinois University.

superintendent J. C. Duffin, also sprung up from the prairie, but little building activity occurred in this crossroad settlement. Yet great expectations existed for rural stations, both on the first segment and then on the trackage between DeKalb and Rockford and Joliet and Momence. "The railroad passes through one of the richest farming sections in Illinois, and will have a magnificent local traffic," proclaimed the DeKalb newspaper.[18]

Although for years Seaman and his colleagues held fast to their intention for major expansion at both ends, not until 1905 did the II&M complete nearly all of its trackage. Rails reached the north end, Rockford, first and somewhat later the south end, Momence.

But irrespective of future plans for this belt railroad, serving Rockford was critical. Although widely called the "Forest City," by the early twentieth century Rockford boosters promoted their hometown as the "New Industrial City of Illinois," and for good reason. In 1903 this Winnebago County seat counted nearly 35,000 residents, many of whom were foreign-born artisans, and produced a diverse and increasing number of products, dominated by furniture (second only to Grand Rapids, Michigan), agricultural implements, hardware, and hosiery.[19]

Rockford, though, hardly lacked adequate transportation. Rails radiated outward in every direction; the Burlington; Chicago, Milwaukee & St. Paul (Milwaukee Road); IC; and North Western all offered service. Also, the Rockford & Interurban Railway operated three electric intercity lines, but its non-passenger business consisted almost entirely of package and milk shipments. There was arguably room for another railroad, especially for a road that could carry freight around, rather than through, Chicago.[20]

With Rockford and points beyond in mind, II&M management directed construction parties to head north from DeKalb Junction. In early 1905 these crews reached the main line of the Great Western at Wilkinson, five miles distant, and by July 1905 arrived at Kirkland Junction, eight miles beyond the Great Western crossover and interchange. At this point workers installed a mile of track into Kirkland, a town of six hundred residents, to reach the east–west stem of the Milwaukee Road, further enhancing business. Also, several commercial houses selected the new railroad, including grain and lumber concerns, and the company acquired for its depot a large two-story house on South Main Street and built a forty-eight-by-twenty-four-foot addition. The II&M expected its station agent at Kirkland to be busy, satisfying local customers and also managing the connecting traffic with the Milwaukee Road.[21]

The last twenty-one miles of construction turned out to be more challenging than the previous work. Laborers faced some heavy grading assignments, and in May 1905 torrential rains seriously interfered with their progress. "In

A remodeled private residence with a large, added-on freight house functioned as the depot in Kirkland, Illinois, until the Milwaukee Road, which already served the community, took control. *Courtesy of Embree Collection, Regional History Center, Northern Illinois University.*

many places the embankments have been washed away and will have to be entirely replaced." And considerable time was consumed spanning the occasionally tyrannical Kiswaukee River six miles from Rockford. Not until November 12, 1905, did trains ply the rails between Kirkland and Rockford.[22]

Just as town development occurred at Kirkland, four stations appeared on the latest section, Vanland, Harris, Morristown, and New Milford. The first three places, which were new sites, never developed much beyond being shipping points for grain and livestock. New Milford attracted similar customers, but this village of 250 residents already had Burlington rails, being on the twenty-seven-mile Rochelle–Rockford branch.[23]

After the Rockford extension started to take shape, construction commenced on the thirty-five-mile Joliet-to-Momence leg. By late June 1905 the relatively easy grading and bridge building were largely finished, and tracklaying and ballasting followed. Work had begun at the EJ&E connection and had progressed southeastward. By early September track gangs reached Peotone and then continued toward Momence. The routing between the two end points included two established towns, Peotone and Manhattan. The

former community of 1,500 residents offered access to several local industries, including the Continental Bridge Works, but no immediate interchange with the IC. The latter, a town of one thousand, with a handful of customers, including two coal yards and a lumberyard, offered a tie-in with the Wabash. As crews built track during the summer of 1905, the II&M established several new stations: Wilton, three miles southeast of Joliet; Andres, three miles beyond Wilton; Whitaker, five miles from Peotone; and Yeager, four miles

Occasionally the
Rockford Route,
both as the
Illinois, Iowa &
Minnesota and
the Chicago,
Milwaukee &
Gary, provided
special excursions.
No. 4, a shiny
2-6-0, is the
power for this
two-car train at
Kirkland, Illinois,
about 1910.
*Courtesy of
Embree Colleck-
tion, Regional
History Center,
Northern Illinois
University.*

farther down the line toward Momence. As with the stations between DeKalb
and Rockford, these places along the Momence extension were mostly agricultural shipping points for the convenience of nearby farmers. In order
to economize, the company rented space in the EJ&E depot in Joliet, but
planned to have its own structure later.[24]

The "big day" for the Rockford Route occurred on November 20, 1905,
when the entire route between Momence and Rockford opened for through

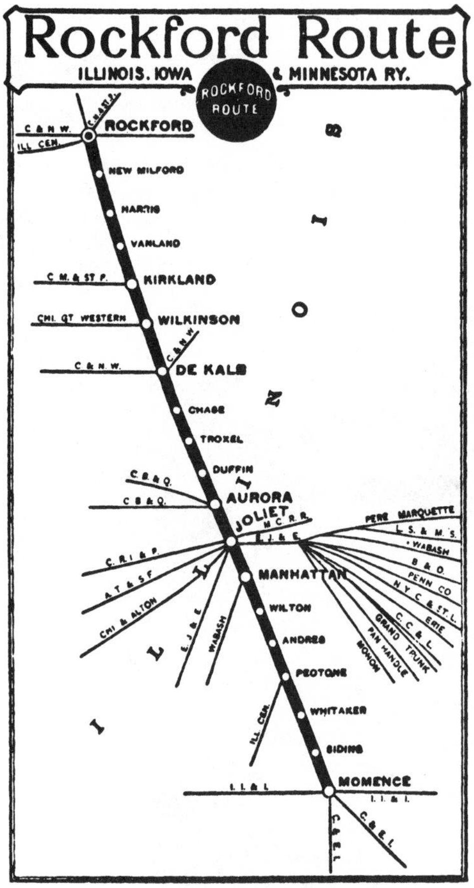
Rockford Route
ILLINOIS. IOWA & MINNESOTA RY.
ROCKFORD ROUTE
ROCKFORD
NEW MILFORD
HARRIS
VANLAND
KIRKLAND
WILKINSON
DE KALB
CHASE
TROXEL
DUFFIN
AURORA
JOLIET
MANHATTAN
WILTON
ANDRES
PEOTONE
WHITAKER
SIDING
MOMENCE
C & N W.
ILL CEN.
C. M. & ST. P.
CHI. GT WESTERN
C. & N. W.
C B & Q.
PERE MARQUETTE
L. S. & M. S.
WABASH
B & O.
PENN CO
ERIE
GRAND TRUNK
PAN HANDLE
MONON
C. R I & P.
A T & S F
CHI & ALTON
E. J. & E.
ILL CEN.
I. I. & I.
C & E I.
I L L I N O I S

ROCKFORD ROUTE

SCHEDULE OF TRAINS

BETWEEN

ROCKFORD
KIRKLAND
DeKALB
AURORA
JOLIET
MOMENCE

EFFECTIVE FEBRUARY 15, 1906

B. H. HARRIS
Traffic Manager
CHICAGO

STROMBERG, ALLEN & CO., CHICAGO.

Illinois, Iowa & Minnesota Railway Co.

SOUTH BOUND TRAINS		Miles	STATIONS	Miles	NORTH BOUND TRAINS	
Mixed Daily ex Sunday	Mixed Daily ex Sunday				Mixed Daily ex Sunday	Mixed Daily ex Sunday
No. 18	No. 16		Effective Feb. 15, 1906. Supersedes all Previous Schedules.		No. 15	No. 17
PM	AM				**PM**	AM
6.00	7.00	0	Lv.. ..Rockford ....Ar.	125.00	**5.40**	6.00
		2.60	..... Rockford Jct......	122.40		
6.45	7.45	6.00	...New Milford.....	119.00	**5.00**	5.10
7.00	8.05	8.70	.....Harrisville	116.30	**4.40**	4.50
7.15	8.20	14.20	........Vanland.....	110.80	**4.20**	4.30
7 55	9.00	21.10	.....Kirkland.....	102.90	**3.40**	3.45
		22.10	....Kirkland Jct......	101.90		
8.30	9.45	30.10	.....Wilkinson.....	94.90	**3.00**	3.10
		35.95	.....DeKalb Jct.....	87.69		
9.15	10.20	37.31	.....DeKalb......	86.33	**1.50**	2.15
10.10	11.25	44.45	.....Chase......	80.55	**1.05**	1.25
10.35	11.45	49.31	...Troxel.....	75.69	**12.40**	1.00
11.05	12.10	55.37	...Duffin.....	69.63	**12.10**	12 30
		64.37	...Aurora Jct......	58.83		
12.10	1 00	65.27	.....Aurora.....	59.73	11.00	11.00
1.40	2.35	89.27	....Joliet....	35.72	9.30	9 30
2.10	3.10	98.19	...Manhattan...	26.80	9.00	8.50
2.28	3.30	101.88	...Wilton....	23.11	8.40	8.27
2.43	3.50	104.76	.....Andres	20.23	8.25	8 12
3.10	4.20	110.75	....Peotone.....	14.24	8.00	7.50
3.35	4.55	116.84	...Whitaker.....	8.15	7.30	7.25
		120.00	...Yeager........	5.00		
4.10	5.35	125.00	Ar.....Momence.. .Lv.	0.00	7.00	7.00
AM	PM				AM	PM

A. M. time in light type.   P. M. time in **black** type.

CONNECTIONS.

At Rockford—With I. C. R. R., C. & N.-W. R'y, C., M. & St. P. R'y.
At Kirkland—With C., M. & St. P. R'y.
At Wilkinson—With C. G. W. R'y.
At DeKalb—With C. & N.-W. R'y, C. G. W. Ry.
At Aurora—With E. J. & E., C. B. & Q. R'y, C. & N.-W. R'y.

At Joliet—With E. J. & E. R'y, C. R. I. & P. R'y, A. T. & S. F. R'y, C. & A. R'y M. C. R. R.
At Manhattan—With Wabash Railroad.
At Peotone—With Illinois Central Railroad.
At Momence—With C. & E. I. R. R., I. I. & I. R. R.

H. W. SEAMAN,
PRESIDENT,
CHICAGO.

J. C. DUFFIN,
GEN'L SUP'T,
ROCKFORD, ILL.

B. H. HARRIS,
TRAFFIC MANAGER,
CHICAGO.

The Rockford Route never offered the traveling public much in the way of regularly scheduled passenger service. The public timetable for February 15, 1906, suggested a road oriented toward carload freight. *Courtesy of Arthur D. Dubin Collection.*

traffic. In addition to interchanges with trunk roads in Momence, Manhattan, Joliet, Aurora, DeKalb, Wilkinson, Kirkland, and Rockford, the company offered more: "In connection with the E.J. & E. Ry. we have a through route to all points in the east via the various eastern trunk lines." Potential customers were urged to route their "through-consigned freight" around Chicago on the II&M. Although officials bragged of being a 125-mile railroad "with a rosy future," the EJ&E remained the expensive connector between the two newly built sections. A wag later described the road as "two tails without a middle." To enhance freight revenues in Rockford, in February 1905 the promoters organized and then quickly built the five-mile Rockford Belt Railway that ran "through the factory districts" in the southeastern part of the city. Rockford, too, became the center of the road's train operations and repair facilities.[25]

The II&M continued to offer passenger service, albeit with a mixed-train consist. Yet the *Rockford Republic* believed that the company would acquire gasoline motor cars for passengers, mail, and express, and that "as it is the only direct route Aurora-DeKalb-Rockford, a good passenger business can be worked up." After rails reached Kirkland, the company dispatched two daily mixed trains and one daily-except-Sunday mixed run between Aurora and DeKalb, and a daily and daily-except-Sunday mixed consist between DeKalb and Kirkland. Throughout 1905 the railroad made adjustments, with essentially the same frequency of operation. Then in February 1906 the road implemented through mixed-train service between Rockford and Momence. Train No. 16 left the Forest City at 7:00 a.m. and was scheduled to arrive in Momence at 5:35 p.m. No. 18 departed at 6:00 p.m. and steamed into Momence at 4:10 a.m. The northbound timetable showed No. 15 leaving Momence at 7:00 a.m. and reaching Rockford at 5:40 p.m. and No. 17 departing at 7:00 p.m. and making its final stop at 6:00 a.m. Somewhat later the road dropped one of the two mixed trains between Aurora and Rockford, likely due to competing electric car service between Aurora and DeKalb.[26]

But as had happened when train service began between Aurora and DeKalb, a variety of passenger specials, with mostly borrowed equipment, took place as needed. In August 1905, a "cheap excursion" took about 250 residents from DeKalb and the surrounding area to visit the Orphan's Home and the Illinois State Penitentiary in Joliet, and the following July a packed train left Aurora to bring merrymakers to Rockford so that they might enjoy "boat and automobile riding."[27]

Rumors spread that other passenger arrangements would become part of daily operations. The Great Western, it was reported, would run through trains between Chicago and Rockford via the II&M interchange at Wilkinson

Crossing, but such service never materialized. The belief that the road would have dedicated passenger trains likewise proved false.[28]

The passenger service that existed on the II&M, and later the Gary, generated little revenue. For the fiscal year that ended June 30, 1906, the company received slightly more than $8,500, but the following year income dropped to $6,812. For the most popular destinations, travelers had options. When the Chicago, Aurora & DeKalb Railroad (CA&D) opened between Aurora and DeKalb in 1906, trains were convenient and tickets inexpensive. Although the II&M had the most direct route between DeKalb and Rockford, a combination of interurban and steam roads allowed for relatively handy trips. Yet in 1909 the CA&D, at last electrified, indicated that it might build between DeKalb and Rockford because "directors figure that there is a fruitful field for an interurban road in the territory through which that road passes. The villages [en route] are thriving little towns which now have no interurban connection with DeKalb." In fact, the initial plans of what became the CA&D had been to link Aurora and Rockford. Between Aurora and Joliet, where II&M trains held trackage rights, the public had access to parallel service provided by the frequently dispatched cars of the Joliet, Plainfield & Aurora Railway (JP&A), a road that opened in 1904. Significantly, the JP&A was part of a semicircle of traction lines around Chicago, extending from Carpentersville to the north to Chicago Heights to the south. Probably few individuals wanted to travel between Joliet and Momence, but in those communities served by other steam railroads, trains to Chicago were easy to catch.[29]

Since the II&M used mixed trains, arrival and departure times varied. Crews had to pick up and set out cars, snake their way through freight yards, and navigate junctions. In the latter part of 1907, a resident of Aurora, who owned a farm near Troxel, complained to the Illinois Railroad and Warehouse Commission about the dreadful state of affairs, wanting passenger service that was faster and on time. The company willingly admitted that its mixed trains operated on schedules that were slow and "nearly always from one to three or four hours late." Such operations gave real credence to the popular expression "to lie like a timetable." In fact, the commissioners concluded that the "carriage of passengers between Aurora and Rockford [is] so inadequate, and the running of the trains so uncertain, that it may be fairly presumed that no person would patronize the road except in case of absolute necessity." But since the II&M consistently operated in the red, the regulators sided with the railroad. "In as much as the respondent's whole line is being operated at a loss, and these additional trains would entail a further loss upon the company, and because such facts would probably be considered by the courts a

The Chicago, Milwaukee & Gary's No. 1, a 2-6-0 Mogul, was ideally suited for switching and light road assignments. In August 1909 the No. 1 pauses in the yards in Rockford, Illinois. *Photograph by F. R. Ritzman. Courtesy of Embree Collection, Regional History Center, Northern Illinois University.*

sufficient reason for refusing a *writ of mandamus*, the prayer of the petitioner is denied." Passenger operations remained unchanged.[30]

Company officers invested little in passenger rolling stock, although two more coaches were later acquired, probably for excursions. If a mixed train lacked a passenger car, the conductor and rear brakeman shared space with ticketed riders in one of the road's nine cabooses. But major expenditures on equipment involved freight cars. By 1913 the road owned two hundred furniture cars, designed to serve the several manufacturers in Rockford, about fifty flat and gondola cars, and two refrigerator cars. Fifteen mostly small and older 2-6-0 and 2-8-0 locomotives provided the power.[31]

The II&M was no moneymaker. The overall deficit for 1906 was a modest $2,948, but the following year the amount soared to $59,012. And for the entire history of the corporation, earnings totaled $657,381 ($15.5 million in 2008 dollars) with operating expenses of $624,289 ($14.7 million in 2008 dollars), but after additional obligations net income stood at a negative $11,401. The II&M never paid bond interest or dividends. In 1908 management nevertheless gave the financial situation a positive spin. "The present line has been in full operation but a short time and has shown very satisfactory earnings, when it is considered that it is only the middle section of an incomplete property and not yet in possession of its principal terminal points." If the railroad could reach Milwaukee and some point in Indiana, now ideally Gary, the economic health of the company would undoubtedly improve. This reasoning led to reorganization in March 1908, whereby the property took a name that indicated its plans for future success: Chicago, Milwaukee & Gary Railway.[32]

Yet before reorganization, rumors circulated that the developing II&M might enter the orbit of a major carrier. In September 1905 some observers believed that the St. Louis–San Francisco Railway (Frisco), then in an expansive mode, would take control. "Should the new road pass into the hands of the Frisco, it is probable that the line will not stop at Rockford," speculated the *Rockford Gazette*, "but push on further north, giving the road a line which might be extended to Minneapolis." Others thought that the Great Western or Michigan Central would gain ownership. Reports also suggested that the II&M might join the Wisconsin Central Railway, Southern Indiana Railway, or the recently constructed but faltering Chicago, Cincinnati & Louisville Railway. But more commentators expected that the EJ&E, the USS affiliate, would use the II&M to reach new markets and to protect its position as the principal belt road in the region. Although the owners of the II&M might have gladly sold out, nothing happened, prompting a concerted effort to become a major player in the railroad operations of Chicago.[33]

In spring 1908 the principal backers, led by men linked to the St. Louis Union Trust Company, believed that they had waved a magic wand over the sputtering II&M. An Illinois charter for their Gary road granted authority "to acquire, by purchase and construction, a line of standard gauge steam railroad from Milwaukee, Wis., to Gary, Indiana." Financing would come through the sale of $20 million worth ($465 million in 2008 dollars) of 5 percent, forty-year gold bonds. A portion of these securities, $5.5 million, would be used to buy the assets of the II&M and the Rockford Belt Railway, and much of the remaining $14.5 million would be used for construction. The company expected to allocate $2.225 million ($52.6 million in 2008 dollars) for the forty-mile extension from Momence to Gary; $6.595 million ($156 million in 2008 dollars) for the 100-mile Rockford-to-Milwaukee line, including terminal costs, and $1.180 million ($28 million in 2008 dollars) to close the gap between Aurora and Joliet. Stated officials, "This leaves a margin of $4,500,000 ($10.6 million in 2008 dollars) of bonds for future requirements."[34]

Optimism reigned again. "The line encircles Chicago. . . . It forms a complete Outer Belt from lake to lake and crosses and connects with the 32 main truck lines radiating from Chicago, and 12 important branch lines of big systems, making a total of 44 foreign line connections and points of interchange." Then there were these thoughts: "The extension to Milwaukee will place the CM&G in touch with the largest city in the State of Wisconsin, while Gary, on the south extension, will soon enjoy the distinction of being the largest city in the State of Indiana." In a later report, the company expected to deliver to the Gary furnaces twenty thousand tons of soft coal daily. "This is approximately 500 cars daily of 80,000 pounds capacity each, or an annual consumption of more than 7,000,000 tons of soft coal, equal to 175,000 cars."[35]

Although Milwaukee, with a 1900 population of 400,000, continued its dominance as the premier city of Wisconsin, Gary, about thirty miles east of Chicago, had had only a brief existence. Indeed, this northeastern Indiana community was truly a "magic city," much more impressive than the rapid growth of several other self-described "instant" cities in the Midwest, including Barberton, Ohio, the Diamond Match Company town founded by O. C. Barber in the 1890s, and Pullman, Illinois, home of the Pullman Palace Car Company that George Pullman established somewhat earlier. In 1906 the United States Steel Corporation created Gary and nurtured its development. This "city of the century" became the site of a massive complex of mills and finishing plants owned by the Indiana Steel Company, a USS subsidiary, and where the Gary Land Company, another USS entity, oversaw the planned community. By 1908 the population surpassed ten thousand and two years later reached sixteen thousand. By the era of World War I, Gary had more than fifty thousand residents. Yet the population of this "future great city" failed to reach 300,000 the number that prognosticators had expected.[36]

With the dynamic growth of Gary, it is hardly shocking that railroaders set their eyes on this burgeoning metropolis. There was now less reason for the Rockford Route to build to Michigan City or another point on Lake Michigan. Yet access to the steel works might be difficult; after all, USS owned the EJ&E and had interests in other terminal properties. And it would be the EJ&E that benefited from the steel business. Journalists made much of a remarkable day in February 1912 when the total number of trains handled in and out of Gary by the EJ&E was one hundred, consisting of 3,573 loaded and 1,991 empty cars.[37]

Not long after the formation of the Gary, Albert T. Perkins, "the railroad expert of the [St. Louis] trust company," replaced Seaman as president, and appeared to possess the necessary executive talent. This native of Maine had graduated in 1883 from the prestigious Boston Latin School and four years later from Harvard College. In 1888 Perkins joined the freight department of the Burlington, and in time became an operating superintendent in Missouri and also a consultant on several non-company railroad projects. Why Seaman stepped down is not clear; he may have wanted to focus on the Gary & Southern interurban and waterway interests. Still, Seaman remained associated with the Gary until 1916.[38]

Notwithstanding the leadership provided by Perkins, the Gary went nowhere, except for completing in 1910 the three miles eastward from Momence to Delmar and a connection with the Chicago, Terre Haute & Southeastern Railway (or the Terre Haute), formerly the Southern Indiana. For years, reports circulated that various outside parties contemplated taking over the Gary and extending the road to Milwaukee and Gary and closing the break between Aurora and Joliet. Even during these mostly good economic times, company bond sales apparently faltered. Surely, too, USS interests were not thrilled with the prospect of a competing belt road.[39]

The reality of the unfinished Rockford Route was that revenues remained relatively flat with no net profits. Yet this red ink did not reach the point where a receivership became necessary. Operations continued much the same as during the Seaman years, although there was a huge spike in passenger income during World War I ($77,658 in 1918 and $41,484 in 1919 but a paltry $98 in 1920) when the company handled troop movements generated by Camp Grant, the new army post located between Rockford and New Milford. In 1921 the Valuation Bureau of the Interstate Commerce Commission (ICC) gave the final value of the road as of June 30, 1915, at $2,990,974 ($62.9 million in 2008 dollars), and tabulated the cost of construction at $3.3 million ($69.4 million in 2008 dollars). "No dividends have ever been paid on the stock and no interest has ever been paid or even accrued in the accounts on the first mortgage bonds." In the early 1920s the Gary board of directors admitted to the ICC that "the road as now constructed has proven a failure,"[40] and members probably took little or no offense to the company's popular nickname: "Cold, Miserable & Grouchy."

During this decade or so of stagnation, the principal owners, known as the "St. Louis Syndicate," repeatedly sought a buyer. The major stumbling blocks involved the high rental agreement with the EJ&E and the cost of building a parallel line between Aurora and Joliet. "The management [of the Gary] has struggled for the past ten years with an incomplete and ill-equipped property, the business of which has been so restricted by the ill-advised trackage contract [with the EJ&E] as to make its profitable operation as an independent carrier impossible," concluded the St. Louis Trust Company. "The deficit has been assuming large proportions. Every possible effort has been made to lease or sell the property."[41]

Although the assessment made by the St. Louis bank augured poorly for the future of the Gary, a remarkable event happened. On January 1, 1922, the Milwaukee Road took control. The deal involved the Milwaukee Road guaranteeing the principal of $3 million worth of the first mortgage bonds of the Gary and all interest that would accrue after January 1, 1924, as well as acquiring all $1 million of capital stock. President Harry E. Byram of the Milwaukee Road told shareholders and the financial community that "control of the Chicago, Milwaukee & Gary enables [the Milwaukee Road] to transport Company and commercial coal originating on the Terre Haute Division [formerly the Terre Haute], as well as on the lines of the Chicago & Eastern Illinois Railway, direct to points on its lines west and north, without hauling the same through the expensive terminals of Chicago, and the shorter haulage. This not only expedites movement, but greatly reduces the cost of transportation." At this time the Milwaukee Road also received regulatory permission to construct trackage parallel to the EJ&E, thus filling the troublesome gap.[42]

But the explanation for the attractive arrangement was more complex, smacking of nefarious backroom deals. Although the public knew that the Gary had finally found a corporate home and that the property gave the Milwaukee Road ready access to another recent acquisition, the Terre Haute, the real story did not come to light for several years. Business observers, though, realized that the Milwaukee Road had faltered dangerously after the end of federal control in March 1920, in part because of the enormous expense of constructing and operating the Pacific Coast Extension. And their concerns were correct; the company five years later entered a receivership.[43]

In 1926 the ICC conducted hearings to probe into the Milwaukee Road bankruptcy. These widely publicized inquiries revealed much that was either sinister or stupid. At the least, bad executive decisions explained the financial disaster that had befallen this once "blue chip" property. President Byram may have been an able operating man, but he seemed to lack good business sense. The examination indicated that neither the Terre Haute nor the Gary should have been acquired, having increased "interest burdens at a time when it [Milwaukee Road] already had more than it could bear."[44]

The ICC examiners explored the Gary lease, and they made several discoveries. About 1915, at a dinner in St. Louis, a representative from the Syndicate discussed a possible sale with Percy Avery Rockefeller, Milwaukee Road board member and son of the powerful businessman and Milwaukee Road investor William Rockefeller. The younger Rockefeller then conveyed the proposition to Albert J. Earling, the road's president. Earling wanted nothing to do with the Gary, realizing that the unfinished belt road with its pricey trackage rights agreement offered little. Much later Albert Perkins, the emissary for the St. Louis interests, contacted Harry Byram, who had replaced Earling in 1917, about a possible acquisition. Initially Byram was not anxious either for his railroad to become involved with the Gary.[45]

Yet what appeared to be the same old story of the "orphan" Gary not being able to find a corporate home changed dramatically. The investigation revealed that Samuel Pryor, a business associate of Percy Rockefeller in the Owenoke Corporation, a private investment firm, played a pivotal role in sealing the deal. And Benjamin Winchell, vice president of the Piece Oil Corporation, with ties to the St. Louis Syndicate, served as an intermediary between the Gary and Pryor. Apparently Pryor convinced Rockefeller to pressure Byram and the board of directors to take the road. For his good work, Pryor received a hefty commission, amounting to $150,000 ($1.8 million in 2008 dollars) in Gary bonds. Then for some reason he turned over his windfall to the Owenoke Corporation. In the testimony, Rockefeller denied any knowledge of Pryor's compensation. "I told him [Pryor] President Byram was the man to see. I never told Mr. Byram to look into it. I never told him to buy it." And Pryor denied that Rockefeller had much involvement. The resourceful investigators of the ICC, however, found a communication from Pryor to Byram in the files of the executive department of the Milwaukee Road that had not gone directly to him but passed initially to Rockefeller to be forwarded to Byram, a circuitous and incriminating path.[46]

Notwithstanding the ICC investigation, the Gary became a satellite of the Milwaukee Road, and major changes followed. Since the Milwaukee Road already served Rockford via Davis Junction, there was no need for the Kirkland Junction-to-Rockford trackage. Therefore, on December 15, 1923, the company petitioned the ICC to abandon the line; in fact, service had ceased when the lease began. A group of farmers protested, and regulators

Railroads (both old and new) had countless loading pens for livestock. The Rockford Route created such a place at Bradt, three miles north of DeKalb Junction, benefiting neighboring farmers. This photograph of the rather seedy cattle yard, siding, and main track dates from the early 1940s when the Milwaukee Road owned the line. *Courtesy of Charles H. Stats Collection.*

postponed abandonment. But several years later the Milwaukee Road reinstated the application, arguing that only a few customers would be adversely affected and that the track structure had badly deteriorated. The company, though, promised not to lift the rails between Rockford and Camp Grant. The ICC agreed, and the fifteen miles were soon dismantled. Beginning with the takeover of the Gary, the Milwaukee Road discontinued mixed train service, dispatching three scheduled daily freights over the line, but this service gradually declined. In the mid-1920s, DeKalb boosters applauded the Milwaukee Road for painting and repairing the former Gary facilities. Also, track conditions generally improved, allowing heavy coal drags to use the old Rockford Route.[47]

The legal ties between the Gary and the Milwaukee Road (after 1927 the reorganized Chicago, Milwaukee, St. Paul & Pacific Railroad Company) also changed. On December 13, 1929, the Milwaukee Road asked the ICC for a Certificate of Authority to acquire the Gary. It did not take long to win approval, the decision coming on February 8, 1930. The impact of a well-researched muckraking book on the Milwaukee Road bankruptcy, *The Investor Pays*, by Max Lowenthal, which appeared in 1933, came too late to have any impact. And the new owner shelved plans to build between Aurora and Joliet.[48]

Resembling many other lines, as the nation's railroad network contracted, dismemberment of the former Gary took place piecemeal. Even with formal ownership, the Milwaukee Road had lost interest in the line. On the eve of America's entry into World War II, the company indicated that it would abandon most of the remaining trackage. This did not occur as federal officials insisted that the Momence–Kirkland line be kept open as part of an emergency bypass around Chicago in case of some wartime disaster, perhaps destruction of railroad facilities by the Germans or Japanese. But matters changed after the war. In 1947 the ICC allowed removal of the Aurora-to-DeKalb section and termination of operations over the EJ&E. At the time, the Milwaukee operated a local freight only three times a week between Aurora and DeKalb. The DeKalb-to-Kirkland Junction and Joliet-to-Momence lasted much longer, being retired in the 1970s.[49]

The saga of the Rockford Route turned out to be more success than failure. The company was not a financial disaster; neither the II&M nor the Gary sought protection from a bankruptcy court. Moreover, the concept of an outer-outer belt around the central section of Chicago held real merit. If built as announced, the Rockford Route might have thrived as a bona fide belt operation. Even though the Milwaukee Road got involved for not altogether rational reasons, the Gary provided an efficient avenue for connecting traffic to and from its Terre Haute Division. Yet the EJ&E lease haunted the arrangement and diminished the attractiveness of the Gary. And, there was that seemingly unbridgeable gap.[50]

Even though the Rockford Route never became a strategic beltway, the road fostered discernable economic growth. Several new villages appeared and other communities grew, providing benefits to farmers, businessmen, and other residents. More than any place, DeKalb received a boost to its economy with the coming of II&M rails. Industrial development accelerated, causing a strong demand for housing, consumer services, and the like. Similarly, Rockford remained an industrial powerhouse, aided by the II&M main line and the satellite Rockford Belt Railway.

Yet public perception of the Rockford Route had probably little to do with economic expansion or the movement of freight, but rather with passenger operations. With its miserable service, the company could not use quality passenger trains to enhance its reputation as a freight carrier. But it seems that with Milwaukee Road control and then ownership, customers felt better about the line. After all, the Gary joined one of the largest carriers in America and a major player in the Midwest. This relationship surely prevented an early abandonment of this twilight road and briefly offered hope that a true and lasting outer-belt line could be achieved.

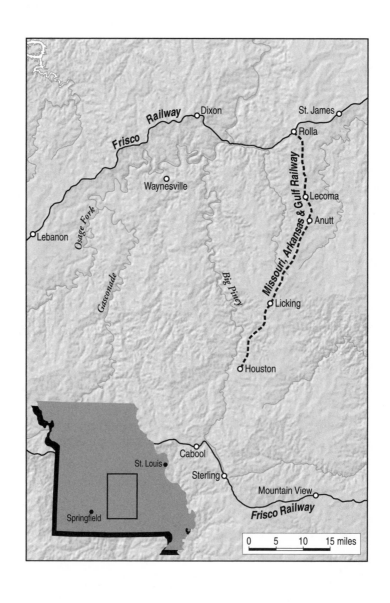

Chapter 7

Ozark Short Line: Missouri, Arkansas & Gulf Railroad

Before the modern era of vehicular travel, Missourians understood the importance of the railroad. As in other midwestern states, this desire produced considerable railway construction. On the eve of the Civil War, the state's network stood at 817 miles, but by the close of World War I, mileage had reached 8,529, although sections of the sprawling Ozarks region lacked extensive and, in the minds of many, adequate rail coverage.[1]

It is unsurprising that one of the last frontiers in America, the Ozarks of south-central and southern Missouri, with its abundant stands of pines and hardwoods, ample water, valuable minerals, and moderate climate, became the center for an array of proposals and some construction during the twilight railroad-building era. A few trunk roads, most notably the St. Louis–San Francisco (Frisco) and Missouri Pacific, already operated main stems and a modest network of feeder lines in the region. And several, mostly lumber-carrying, "tramways" offered additional, albeit limited service, although in some cases these little pikes lacked common-carrier status. Notwithstanding the presence of both large and small roads, many places had yet to see the iron horse.

The most painful effort to expand the rail grid involved efforts between 1908 and 1914 to construct the Ozark Short Line, initially under the corporate banner of the Missouri, Inland & Southern Railway (MI&S), and later the Missouri, Arkansas & Gulf Railway (MA&G), and finally the Rolla, Ozark & Southern Railway (RO&S). Although collectively these attempts failed, workers cleared and graded portions of the route between Rolla and Houston, assembled ties and bridge timbers, built concrete culverts, erected two depots, and laid some rail. And in the process, the repeated theme of economic development became a legacy of even this ill-fated railroad venture.[2]

For good reason, residents of Dent, Phelps, and Texas counties had long griped about inadequate railroad service. By the early years of the twentieth century, they had to make do with the main line of the Frisco, which linked Cuba, St. James, Rolla, and Dillon between St. Louis and Springfield, a branch that extended southward from Cuba to Salem, and another Frisco route, the former Kansas City, Fort Scott & Memphis Railroad between Springfield and Memphis, Tennessee, which served the Ozark communities of Mansfield, Cabool, and Willow Springs. In 1904 citizens who lived on the northern edges of the Ozarks rejoiced when the Chicago, Rock Island & Pacific Railroad (Rock Island) forged a through line between St. Louis and Kansas City, providing rail service to Belle, Eldon, and Meta. Yet there remained a massive hole in the railroad map south of Rolla and Salem and north of Cabool and Willow Springs. Complaints about the lack of rails were widespread and seemed most intense in Texas County. "Houston [seat of Texas County], being off the railroad, is subject to many inconveniences, and not the least of these is the exorbitant charges at the station at Cabool both [for] express packages and boxes shipped from here to other points," grumbled a Houston journalist. "In many instances the shipping charges on small packages are far greater than the value of the packages, and in many instances are beyond all reason." Another newspaperman observed, "Best of all would be the development of the resources of the country. Many desirable citizens would locate among us, giving us the advantage of their capital, and of enterprises, not now practicable, if there was convenient means of transportation."[3]

Although proposals to pierce the greater Houston area had been floated as early as the 1880s, the dream of the Ozark Short Line had its start about 1908. That summer the *Texas County Star* reported that a "conference on the railroad question" took place in Rolla, the Phelps County seat. Seemingly, the possibilities of connecting Rolla with Houston by rail appeared encouraging. By November the newspaper happily told readers of prospects for an "Electric Road from Mountain Grove to Rolla or St. James via Houston and Licking." Already, representatives of the Houston Commercial Club had canvassed the locality and indicated that a "bonus of $20,000 ($473,000 in 2008 dollars) or more can be raised" for what was then known as the Inter-Ozark Electric Railroad. By January 1909 area residents continued to beat their drums for the project: "There is no doubt but it would be a paying proposition from the start, as a short line from Mountain Grove or Cabool to Rolla would put passengers from the south into St. Louis about five or six hours earlier, to say nothing of the reduced cost of travel and shipping." More benefits were expected: "All land and property within a reasonable distance of the road would be advanced in many cases to two or three times their present value, [and] new businesses would take hold."[4]

Talk of an electric rather than a steam railroad was hardly surprising. It would not be until about 1910 that the interurban map in the Midwest had nearly jelled, and in Missouri the largest electric road, the seventy-nine-

NO. 4808

Boosters of the Ozark Short Line produced this picture postcard of the "Prop. Electric Line between Rolla & Licking, Mo." by taking a photograph of an existing trolley car and track and suggesting that such a scene would soon appear. Mailed from Rolla on December 23, 1909, the sender of this example of postcard fakery wrote in part, "Now do you like this? It will be very nice to not need your automobile." *Courtesy of John F. Bradbury Collection.*

mile Kansas City, Clay County & St. Joseph Railway, did not open until 1913. During the time citizens of Rolla, Licking, and Houston were contemplating an interurban, several other projects were rumored to be under consideration in the greater Ozarks, including lines between Jefferson City, Carthage, and Joplin; Columbia, Jefferson City, and Rolla; and Mansfield, Ava, and Gainesville. The continuing profitability of the pioneer Southwest Missouri Electric Railway, which between 1893 and 1906 built a network of lines radiating out of Joplin, may have stimulated such talk, and other interurban success stories bombarded the public.[5]

Enthusiasts for an electric road between Rolla and Houston conceived of more than a rural trolley. Resembling what contemporary traction promoters in the Midwest often envisioned, they wanted their route to be "well graded and well constructed in every department [so that] full cars of freight and stock can be hauled." It was expected that the interurban would dispatch convenient passenger runs and that ultimately the road would be more economical to operate than a steam railroad. Also excess electricity, generated by company-owned hydroelectric plants, could be sold to commercial and residential customers. Some backers believed that "steam roads control money in the East and can shut off small [steam] roads in bond sales." This did happen, having been an unpleasant experience for the Creston, Winterset & Des Moines Railroad.[6]

Every successful railroad project, whether electric or steam, needed effective leadership. The Ozark Short Line found a promoter who was supremely motivated and seemingly capable of turning dream into reality. This individual was Elbert E. Young, better known as E. E. Young. Information on Young's background is sketchy. He was born in 1884 on a farm near Licking and spent his childhood in that Texas County community. As a young adult Young moved to the Pacific Northwest, then briefly lived in Alaska, and later he called San Francisco, California, home. By 1909 the handsome Young, who stood slightly more than five feet, ten inches, weighed about 145 pounds, and had dark black hair and light blue eyes, married and fathered a child. The *Texas County Star* described Young as being "a railroad promoter and is said to be a builder of railroads." Another account mentioned that he hailed from Spokane, Washington, and had been "identified with great development corporations of the Northwest, but his heart and his hope has [*sic*] never slackened for opening up and development of his old home of Texas County." Still another newspaper believed that "he has amassed a fortune of $200,000." These published reports likely contained elements of truth, but there is no evidence that Young had become wealthy while in the American West.[7]

In early 1909 Young became identified with the interurban proposal.

"[Young] has taken hold of the enterprise and promises to push it to completion," reported the *Houston Herald*. "Knowing the need of a railroad through this part of the state and knowing the large territory to be developed, he has interested the western capitalists in building this road." Young quickly held meetings with prominent individuals and civic groups along the proposed route, focusing his energies in Houston, Licking, and Rolla. He sensed that public interest in the flanged wheel was keen, especially in Texas County. "Houston wants a railroad; wants it badly; will pay any reasonable sum to get one." This part of Missouri was potentially a paradise for railroad promoters.[8]

Young told railroad-hungry residents that his project lacked great complexities. He underscored the advantages of a "high speed electric interurban" and indicated that financing was feasible. Although the estimated cost was initially reported to be an astounding $2.5 million ($59.1 million in 2008 dollars), the public would need only to invest $250,000 ($5.9 million in 2008 dollars). Young urged civic groups to create canvassing committees so that stock subscriptions might be raised. "This is no hot-air talk," he asserted, "but a red-hot proposition."[9]

The next step for Young involved incorporation. In May 1909 he filed the necessary documents with the secretary of state for the Missouri, Inland & Southern Railway Company, modestly capitalized at $400,000 ($9.4 million in 2008 dollars), and paid $225 ($5,300 in 2008 dollars) for the privilege, apparently money from his own pocketbook. For reasons that are not clear, the MI&S would not stretch between Rolla and Cabool or even Houston. "That the railroad shall be constructed from Rolla in the county of Phelps . . . to Licking, in the county of Texas . . . that the length of the road, as near as may be, is forty miles." The incorporators, in addition to Young, who listed his residence as Licking, were three other local men, another backer from nearby Lecoma, and two who hailed from Spokane, Washington, giving credence to Young's ties to "western capitalists."[10]

It is doubtful that Young had ruled out service to Houston. The strategy of the MI&S seemed to be to open the northern segment and to later push southward. Furthermore, money-raising in the Houston area had fallen short of expectations. "Citizens of Houston have subscribed liberally but farmers are holding back," observed the annoyed editor of the *Houston Herald*. Moreover, Young faced a competing project. In July 1909 a group of Houston citizens, led by "Doc" Perry Andre Herrington, a young, dynamic, and entrepreneurial druggist, had launched the St. Louis & Houston Mineral Belt Railway Company (StL&HMB). According to papers filed with the secretary of state, this electric railroad, also capitalized at $400,000, "shall be constructed from, at or near Cabool, in the County of Texas to Houston, county of Texas, that the length of the road as near as may be sixteen (16) miles." By September the StL&HMB fielded a small force conducting a preliminary survey, likely made possible when nine backers, including Herrington, took $3,500 ($83,000 in 2008 dollars) of the road's stock.[11]

Journalists believed that the StL&HMB would become part of a much greater project. Several accounts indicated that the "Herrington Road" would join a steam railroad that "midwestern capitalists" proposed building between St. Louis and Harrison, Arkansas, by way of Salem. Ultimately this trunk road would connect with the Atchison, Topeka & Santa Fe Railway at Paris, Texas, or extend beyond to a port on the Gulf of Mexico. The absurdness of this scheme failed to dampen optimism for some type of railroad, steam or electric, to serve Houston and Texas County.[12]

Undismayed by happenings in the Houston area, Young, officially president of the MI&S, forged ahead. Supporters took heart when the company hired Hugh Palmer, chief engineer of the Chicago, Kankakee & Champaign Electric Railway and the Yorkville & Morris Railroad, two speculative interurban projects in Illinois, "to make all surveys, draw all specifications and superintend the entire construction." Palmer strongly endorsed the MI&S. "I can very safely say that the road is bound to meet all its obligations in the way of bond interest and operating expenses, and besides to be in a position to pay a dividend on its capital stock soon after the cars start running." No one, however, questioned publicly the veracity of a somewhat suspect expert. Reports circulated that surveyors had entered the field and that "work of construction will begin by September 15 [1909]."[13]

Yet all was not well with the MI&S project. In late May, Young told individuals who had gathered at a promotional meeting in Licking, that it would be essential to raise "$15,000 more in order to guarantee the road." The reason was clear: "This was made necessary to Licking on account of dropping out all the territory south of this place and building the road just to Licking, at least for the present." But need for more financial support from Licking was only one concern. Shockingly, in early June the Dent County sheriff arrested Young. Reported the *Salem Monitor*, "He had committed fraud in some land deals in this country." Young posted bond and resumed his railroad work. This highly publicized event may have damaged the credibility of the gestating road, although the burning desire of residents for rail service played to his advantage.[14]

Young soon had more on his mind. Several weeks after his dustup with the law, the press indicated that Young had become gravely ill: "The malarial fever has developed into typhoid of the worst form." Yet the exact status of his health was not really known. Considering his recent legal concerns, the "malarial fever" may have been more mental than physical. By mid-August, Young had recovered and told the *Licking News*, "During the past month this railroad question has not been from my mind one hour at a time, while awake, regardless of my illness."[15]

The MI&S was hardly stillborn. By July, the surveyors had completed their preliminary assignments and seemed satisfied with their work. "The engineers declare that the grade is all that could be desired," announced the *Rolla Herald-Democrat*. The only negatives were Coon Hill, south of Rolla, where the anticipated grade would be 1.5 percent, steep but not disastrous, and another 1.5 percent grade at Salem Lane, near Licking. The railroad would start at a connection with the Frisco on the east side of Rolla, extend in a generally southerly direction to reach what is known as the Ozark divide, a relatively level ridge (present-day U.S. Highway 63) near Elk Prairie in Phelps County, and then pass through the Dent County villages of Lecoma, Victor, and Lenox and the Texas County hamlet of Maples, to Licking. The *Rolla Times* described the profile as looking "like a prairie road's" and this assessment had merit. But as late as the end of 1909, Young announced that he still wanted "some additional survey work."[16]

The reported progress caused a stir. The promotional efforts of Young and his associates had a positive impact on real-estate activities. In July 1909 the W. S. Nichol Realty Company of Licking advertised, "20 farms on and near line of proposed new railroad from Cabool to Rolla to sell at bargain prices," and newspapers indicated a number of sales along the projected route. Others expected values for agricultural land and town lots to increase, and even soar, if a railroad shattered the area's isolation.[17]

Yet the MI&S failed to attract the financial support that backers wanted. In July 1909 an unsigned letter in the *Licking News* indicated that "only one third of the stock subscribers had paid their five per cent. To each one the amount is small, but all of it to Mr. Young is of great importance, besides this dallying and indifference threatens the very existence of the road." Added the writer, "Mr. Young has spent much time, done lots of hard work, used up a tremendous amount of nerve force, contracted obligations, purely as much for the benefit of the community as for himself, and to be treated this way is the unkindest cut of all." Still, most farmers along the route planned to donate land for rights-of-way, a common way that many electric interurbans and steam short lines managed this expense.[18]

Throughout the summer and early fall of 1909, fund-raising languished. In October, a disgusted Young told stockholders, "Now, if you want this road all you will have to do is to come up and subscribe or donate your part, and if you do not do this, why, the road will not be built and you will still be left in the 'sticks.'" He issued this ultimatum, "I will abandon the enterprise and you will see that you will never get another proposition as liberal as the one I have secured for you."[19]

About the time Young was haranguing actual and potential investors, he scored a modest triumph. Somehow the MI&S president brought in A. C. Harrington of Indianapolis, Indiana, a bona fide consulting engineer "who represents an eastern trust company who is interested in the purchase of our bonds." Initially, Harrington was not too enthusiastic about the Ozark Short Line, but after an on-site examination, he changed his mind. He told Young and MI&S backers that their road should be steam and not electric. Harrington concluded that a steam road "would be cheaper to construct and would have the advantage of conveying transferred cars with less trouble." Talk of an interurban subsided, and Houston area residents became interested in rejoining the MI&S scheme. In fact, Young indicated that the MI&S would terminate in Houston and not Licking.[20]

Press coverage of the Harrington connection may not have revealed the entire story. Harrington and associates at Carnegie Trust Company in New York City, together with Young and his investor friends, may have expected Rock Island support. Maybe this sprawling carrier would push a branch southward from its newly opened St. Louis route at or near Belle to Rolla, forging a direct connection with the MI&S or, even better, the Rock Island might buy or lease the MI&S whether projected, partially built, or fully operational. The *Houston Herald* categorically stated, "The Rock Island was behind the [MI&S] enterprise." The system map of the Rock Island revealed numerous appendages to main and secondary lines, including some recent additions in Arkansas and Texas. The trans-Missouri route, however, lacked any direct, independent feeders, except for the five-mile Versailles & Sedalia Railroad that would suspend operations about 1915.[21]

The reaction to the altered plans of the MI&S lifted hopes. Since only $150,000 ($3.5 million in 2008 dollars) was needed to be raised and all stock subscriptions were to be null and void unless construction commenced by a prescribed time, likely June 1, 1910, "the proposition looks good, so let our citizens get together and get to work."[22]

As 1910 unfolded, residents of Phelps, Dent, and Texas counties had reason to believe that the Ozark Short Line would materialize. "Conditions are becoming brighter and better each day and there is a greater feeling of confidence and certainty among our citizens," reflected *Licking News* editor J. A. Prigmore. "Don't become discouraged, friends, this road is certain to be built."[23]

Young himself reaffirmed his intentions to bring the MI&S into operation: "WE ARE IN SHAPE AND WILL BEGIN GRADING WITHIN SIXTY DAYS FROM THE TIME THE SUBSCRIPTIONS ARE ALL IN. THIS WILL BE A WINNER. IT MUST BE, I'LL WORK HERE AS LONG AS I HAVE LIFE IF THE PEOPLE HERE WILL STICK TO ME." This pronouncement closed oddly, "Yours until death, E. E. Young."[24]

Early in 1910 plans were announced for the formation of the Inland Construction and Realty Company (IC&RCo), a firm in the classic mold that would manage building and equipping the MI&S, and also develop real estate, particularly town lots. For decades such an ancillary organization offered promoters an opportunity to reap profits from the construction phase. Significantly, IC&RCo brought together the area's two leading railroad promoters: Young served as corporate secretary and Doc Herrington, "the man who does things," assumed the presidency. The Houston druggist would contribute more of his energies to the MI&S, in addition to the on-again, off-again StL&HMB project. And it was Herrington who showed a strong taste for modern technology, having been the "originator, promoter, financier, and builder" of a hydroelectric plant outside Houston which enabled the town to have its first electric lights in 1908.[25]

The IC&RCo pushed ahead vigorously. The firm arranged a two-day town-lot sale in Licking for July 4–5, 1910, telling potential buyers about the attractive terms. "Not a Red Cent to be paid until the M. I. & S. is built." Explained the company, "If the road is built, the lots will be worth more than you pay for them, thereby making a profit off of the building of the road, besides encouraging one of the greatest enterprises ever launched in this country. If the road should not build, you will not take the lots but it is foolish to consider this under the circumstances." As an added incentive, the company would "give away one dozen of the best residence lots in Licking to the holders of the lucky numbers." The results of this real-estate promotion were impressive, generating between $30,000 ($668,000 in 2008 dollars) and $40,000 ($913,000 in 2008 dollars) in paper sales. "This is a big boost to the railroad," concluded the *Licking News*, "and seems to make the railroad a certainty."[26]

The IC&RCo continued to peddle property. On July 23, 1910, the company conducted a lot sale at Lenox and on July 29–30 held one at Anutt, a village in Dent County. Arrangements for similar events at Lecoma and Elk Prairie and then in Houston were also publicized. The IC&RCo did well in Lenox and Anutt, although organized sales in the other communities never transpired. The Anutt event attracted a large crowd, estimated at more than one thousand. "There were several stands on the grounds, where you could get any kind of refreshment you desired, also a swing for the young people and

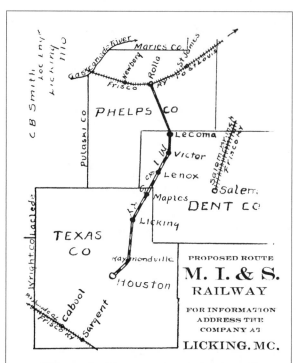

PROPOSED ROUTE

M. I. & S.
RAILWAY

FOR INFORMATION
ADDRESS THE
COMPANY AT

LICKING. MC.

This road will serve one of the best dairy countries in the U. S. Also adapted to all other branches of farming, including fruit growing and the raising of live stock. Our country offers hundreds of opportunities to investors, both large and small, in fruit, farm, mineral and timber lands, which sell cheap, will more than double cost upon completion of this road.   Correspondence solicited.

Instead of employing a fake image of an intended electric car or train, the Ozark Short Line, then using the name Missouri, Inland & Southern Railway, issued this advertising postcard in 1910 to show the location of its intended route and publicize the service territory.

several other kinds of entertainment." The popular Victor Cornet Band provided the music. Young spoke to the assembled crowd, reassuring listeners that trains would soon arrive. The IC&RCo generated $6,300 ($143,000 in 2008 dollars) with the sale of forty-five parcels and in an advertised drawing gave away a choice residential lot.[27]

Coinciding with the labors of the IC&RCo, the MI&S pushed forward with construction. Because of their low level of stock subscriptions, Young threatened (or bluffed) Rolla residents with a northern terminus near Dillon, "where town site and terminal grounds will be donated." Yet he relented. In July 1910 the intermittent building process on the previously announced survey began north of Licking, a sensible choice since it was the easiest part of the route and the best section to demonstrate progress. A crew working with a dozen teams cleared the right-of-way and started to shape the roadbed. The following month, additional workers appeared in the vicinity of Elk Prairie. "At first they [construction men] did not do very good grading," reported the *Rolla Times* in November, "but they made every fill and every cut necessary until they passed through Lecoma." Added the *Times*, "They quit work one half mile south of town and have now gone back over the work they had done and made fills higher where it was necessary and cuts deeper until they are getting it in good shape." Laborers also installed several concrete culverts and cleared a route several additional miles south of Lecoma. About the same time, the *Rolla New Era* believed that "about twelve miles of roadbed is [sic] now ready for the ties." A later edition of the *Times* expected that "a large part of the road bed" would be ready for rails by January 1911.[28]

While construction reports encouraged backers of the MI&S, the actions of prominent promoters, however, generated negative publicity. In December 1910, a Dent County jury found Young guilty of the earlier charge of fraud. Remaining out of jail on bond, he successfully appealed the verdict. A few months later a U.S. Secret Service agent arrested Young; his brother-in-law, Bode Payne; and Carl Evers, an MI&S compatriot, on charges of counterfeiting. The government contended that Evers had made several hundred dollars of fake currency and that Young and Payne had committed criminal possession of counterfeit money. Once more, Young remained free on bond, but the affair surely stained his reputation. Herrington also faced legal problems, having recently been convicted for illicit alcohol sales. All of these happenings prompted the *Houston Republican* to editorialize in a humorous vein: "With several convictions against Dr. Herrington for selling whiskey and the promoter of the railroad to Licking under arrest for counterfeiting, we wonder that the Appeal to Reason [a leading Socialist Party newspaper] doesn't charge that the Plutocratic Legal Department is conspiring to keep Texas County from getting a railroad."[29]

The growing scandals that plagued the MI&S leadership surely explain why Young resigned in April 1911 as president, and the company went through a reorganization. Gilbert Lay, a bank cashier from St. Clair, Missouri, succeeded Young, and on April 12, 1911, the Missouri, Arkansas & Gulf Railway (MA&G), the second Ozark Short Line, paid its incorporation fee to the state treasurer. "Many of the names appearing on the list of officials of the new company are well known here," observed the *Texas County Star*. "They are not only financially responsible but they have a reputation for integrity which will greatly strengthen the project." Immediately, the MA&G absorbed the assets of Young's firm, buying "the right of way, the donations, real estate and all assets of the Missouri, Inland and Southern Railway Company." Moreover, the MA&G, capitalized at $2 million ($45.6 million in 2008 dollars), had big plans. Rather than linking Rolla with Houston, the successor company announced a 125-mile line southward from Rolla through Willow Springs to the railroad-starved community of Bakersfield in Ozark County. In an early map, the MA&G route surprisingly bypassed Houston, running to the east through the Texas County villages of Raymondville and Yukon.[30]

The relationship between Herrington and the MA&G is mystifying. The new corporation may have decided to miss Houston because Herrington wanted to push ahead with the StL&HMB, now to use steam rather than electricity, between the Texas County seat and Cabool. As the year 1911 progressed, Houston journalists showed a newfound optimism. Said the *Herald*, "You can wager your old hat that Doc Herrington will build this railroad." Using his own resources, Herrington purchased eleven "heavy" mule teams, constructed a large barn, and contracted with local sawyers for crossties made from nearby stands of oaks. In February the Herrington forces, in a cleverly arranged publicity stunt, staged a railroad parade though Houston, led by a steam traction engine, "showing people that the preparations for building the railroad was [*sic*] not all a bluff." In May, Herrington acquired a husky Peerless traction engine that would "be used in moving the dirt for the new railroad."[31]

Then a monumental shift occurred. Herrington took renewed interested in the Ozark Short Line. In July 1911, the *Houston Republican* reported that he had signed a contract for grading part of the MA&G between Rolla and Licking. And the *Houston Herald* indicated that Herrington "at least for the present [has] given up the proposition of a railroad from Houston to Cabool, the latter place not taking a very active interest in the matter." Since he needed additional railroad-building equipment and tools, Herrington sold $1,000 worth of ties that he had stockpiled for the StL&HMB.[32]

The change in railroad-building strategy neither alarmed nor angered Houstonians. Although stock subscription agreements would need to be altered, backers concurred that a rail outlet through Rolla was preferable to one via Cabool. "We believe this will be highly satisfactory to everyone," concluded a Houston editor, "for we realize that a connection with the St. Louis market is what we want and need so badly."[33]

With Herrington and his supporters behind the MA&G, the general feeling along the proposed route, which would again terminate in Houston, was one of optimism. "The road has now passed the experimental stage," surmised the *Rolla Times* in July 1911, "and the officers are setting down to business." In early August, the *Houston Herald* happily reported that Herrington "received here a shipment of 19 dump cars, tent, [cooking] range, blacksmith outfit, etc., and his great 30 horse power traction engine left to begin the construction work on the railroad between Rolla and Licking."[34]

Work advanced during the remainder of 1911. In Rolla, the Frisco installed a switch near the future yards and depot, located on a ten-acre parcel owned by the MA&G. Soon thereafter the company completed 2.5 miles of grade southward from the Frisco interchange. Even though officials had not finalized a route survey beyond Licking, construction began in Houston, but not until a gala celebration transpired, displaying again the power of publicity, and the desperate longing for a railroad. The afternoon of the "big September day" became a time to remember:

> The band played, the stores closed, and everybody went to the north-east corner of Mart Coyle's pasture to see work started on the new

railroad which is to be built from Houston to Licking to join the one from there to Rolla. The school was dismissed and most of the children attended. The exercises consisted of an address by Mayor Carmical, followed by prayer by Rev. J. J. Carty. Mrs. Coyle then threw the first shovel of dirt, after which the plow teams started. Mayor Carmical turning the first furrow, followed by Garwitz's [traction] engine and the graders.[35]

Once dirt had been turned in Houston, the Herrington Construction Company divided efforts between the immediate Houston area, where some grading took place and preparations began to bridge the Big Piney River, and the Rolla-to-Licking segment. This strange strategy likely stemmed from the desire of Herrington and MA&G backers to convince residents of the Houston community that a railroad would come, thereby attracting badly-needed financial support.[36]

Although the increased railroad activities may have surprised doubters, the return of E. E. Young to the railroad scene surely astonished everyone. In November, a judge sentenced Carl Evers and Bode Payne, the two men charged with counterfeiting along with Young, to jail terms, but Young had

The maker of this card (featuring a real photograph) caught the teams and wagons that "Doc" Harrington had assembled. The exact date is unknown, but the location is Licking, Missouri, hometown of promoter E. E. Young and the on-again, off-again southern terminus of the Ozark Short Line. *Courtesy of John F. Bradbury Collection.*

his indictment dropped for lack of evidence. A few months later he became general manager of the MA&G.[37]

The events of 1912 would soon make or break the Ozark Short Line. Because of winter conditions construction had slackened. "Owing to the severe weather only a small force of men could be kept employed." Then in March, press reports indicated renewed activities. "A car load of grading

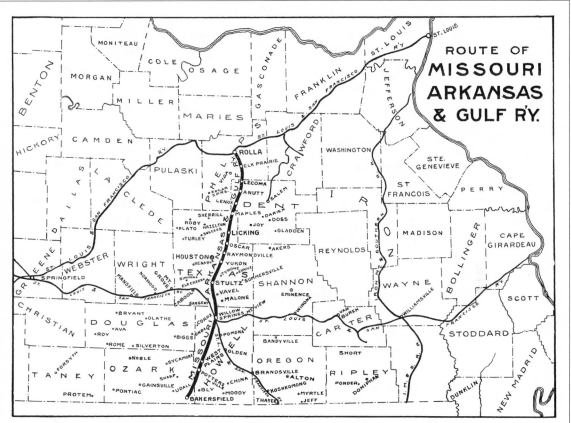

Map showing the route of the Missouri, Arkansas & Gulf Railway and relative positions of St. Louis, Springfield and other places. This road runs one hundred and twenty-five miles through a well-populated country, which is rich in timber and minerals, is adapted to farming in all its branches and as a dairy country it has no equal.

We wish to call your attention particularly to the counties of Shannon, Oregon, Wright, Douglas and Ozark; while our road does not operate through these counties, when completed to Willow Springs, where it connects with two other roads, it will serve practically all of south Missouri, because it will shorten the distance to St. Louis one hundred and fifty miles for this entire territory, which can be seen by reference to the above map; hence, it will save them $7.50 railroad fare on each round trip to St. Louis and twenty-four hours of time. All of the St. Louis business of this district now goes by the way of Springfield, therefore, when you consider that this railroad will put the entire population of south Missouri twenty-four hours nearer the great markets of the east and that it will serve a territory one hundred and twenty-five miles long and fifty miles wide, WITHOUT ANY COMPETITION WHATEVER, you will readily see that this road is destined to become one of the best dividend payers the country has ever known.

—2—

About 1911 the Ozark Short Line, flying the corporate banner of the Missouri, Arkansas & Gulf Railway, produced a lavish promotional folder that included a map and commentary about this twilight-era project.

machinery of the latest and most approved kind was unloaded at Rolla this week with which to do the grading on the Missouri, Arkansas & Gulf Railroad," announced the *Rolla Herald*. "The work of grading is being pushed with all possible speed." In June, the Frisco delivered two carloads of rails to the MA&G switch. Also two depots took shape, first in Rolla and then in Houston, and the company, in a burst of optimism, hired an experienced immigration agent for development work.[38]

But as 1912 progressed, the MA&G faced mounting problems. The raising of funds became paramount. Apparently local residents had contributed all that they could (or would) and the sale of bonds to outside parties never produced the hoped-for results. Efforts to attract foreign investors came to naught, and toward the end of the year, the company coffers were nearly empty. Part of the woes involved some bad luck that had befallen Herrington. Spring floods had temporarily knocked out his hydroelectric plant on the Big Piney River outside Houston. By summer, however, the generating facility was "operating better than ever before," and Herrington resumed railroad construction. Then in September another flood struck. Instead of damaging the impoundment dam, the raging waters scoured out a new course, necessitating the expense of putting the stream back into the old channel. A few weeks later a fire erupted at the plant. These events left Houston in the dark and Herrington in a financial bind. Eventually power was restored, but high water in January 1913 again damaged the facility. "This is another hard blow for Dr. Herrington," commented the *Houston Herald*, "coming as it does on the top of his other misfortunes and losses." Later, in 1914, the *Houston Republican* recalled that this last flood was too much. "The doctor's means are so exhausted that he is forced to sell his railroad equipment and abandon the [MA&G] proposition."[39]

And once again Young confronted legal problems. In the wake of serious money woes, as MA&G general manager he sought to cash $28,000 ($617,000 in 2008 dollars) of promissory notes that were not to be redeemed until the railroad opened. In December 1912, directors of the MA&G won a court injunction that prevented Young from taking this questionable action. About the same time, Young illegally cashed a note for $100 that had been made out to Carl Kimmel, a company director from Lecoma, and Young soon found himself in the Phelps County jail. A trial swiftly followed. After a guilty verdict, the judge sentenced Young to a two-year term in the state penitentiary. He did not appeal, and in May 1913 the twenty-nine-year-old "promoter" became inmate No. 14681 in the Jefferson City facility.[40]

As 1913 dawned, the MA&G project was in shambles. Construction and fund-raising had ceased, yet the railroad was more than just hot air. About fifteen miles had been graded, and one account indicated that two miles of track had been laid. There were also those finished depots in Rolla and Houston. Hope had not totally evaporated. After the annual meeting of shareholders held in March, the *Rolla New Era* stated: "It was the consensus of opinion among stockholders and directors now that the affairs had been straightened out to resume work toward the completion of the road at an early date." That was wishful thinking.[41]

But the Ozark Short Line saga was not yet over. Even though Young had been incarcerated and Herrington had moved to Lewiston, Idaho, after another run-in with the law over the illegal sale of whiskey and losing his light plant through foreclosure, the MA&G was sold on December 29, 1913, for a mere $100 ($2,100 in 2008 dollars) on the steps of the Phelps County courthouse. "It is generally supposed that Mr. [W. T.] Denison bought the road for a syndicate of Rolla financiers and that the road will be built next summer," optimistically observed the *Rolla Times*. The sale, though, did not include the Rolla depot and about three-quarters of a mile of track, suggesting that the earlier report of two miles of rails was unlikely. The exemption of the depot and track may have been due to bondholder liens.[42]

In early 1914, the Ozark Short Line gasped its last breath. On April 15, 1914, a group of Rolla area investors filed incorporation papers for the Rolla, Ozark & Southern Railway Company. But these men had in mind a truncated line: "That the railway shall be constructed from Rolla, in the County of Phelps, to Anutt, Dent County; that the length of the road, as near as may be, is eighteen (18) miles." Capitalization was modest, only $200,000 ($4.2 million in 2008 dollars). Press reports again contained optimistic expectations. "It seems that something is about to be done at last on our long wanted railroad," commented J. A. Prigmore of the *Licking News*. "While the company is chartered under a different name, it is virtually the same company and men who are the most interested in the building of this road." Concluded Prigmore, "While the charter was only taken to Anutt, which is about half way between this place and Rolla, there is no doubt that the road will continue right on down the ridge through Licking and on to the South."[43]

There was never to be a railroad that would link Rolla with Anutt, Licking, Houston, Cabool, Bakersfield, or anywhere else. Still, Houston could claim to be the only town in Missouri, perhaps in the nation, to have a depot without ever having an operating railway, and Rolla had an unused depot not far from the Frisco main line that became a private residence. There were to be other physical remains, including sections of the graded rights-of-way, crumbling culverts, and three parallel streets on the east side of Rolla named Missouri, Arkansas, and Gulf.[44]

Even though the concept of the Ozark Short Line hardly smacked of crazy thinking, much went wrong. Financial shortcomings became the major stumbling block. If adequate outside funding had materialized, perhaps underwritten by the Rock Island, chances for a successful outcome would have dramatically improved. Although local enthusiasm existed, the number of individuals who were able to contribute was limited. The area contained only a small population: Rolla, the largest community, claimed about three thousand residents, Houston one thousand, and Licking five hundred. Surely, too, the legal problems that Young faced damaged the project, prompting some to view him as nothing more than a flimflam man. Although Herrington repeatedly experienced setbacks with his power plant, and had other personal problems, this energy-packed and resourceful entrepreneur failed to focus on either the Houston and Cabool or the Houston and Rolla projects. If Herrington had pushed the former, which was a smaller and, hence, a less expensive proposition, rail service for his hometown would likely have been achieved. Yet a Cabool line would probably have had a fate similar to the nearby Kansas City, Ozarks & Southern Railway, a steam road, originally projected as an interurban, that after 1909 linked Mansfield with Ava, fifteen miles to the south. This little pike slipped into bankruptcy, and a subsequent reorganization kept the operation alive only until the Great Depression. These years of struggle killed off many short lines and some of the nation's last remaining interurbans.[45]

Time had run out for the unfinished Ozark Short Line. By 1914 lumbermen had harvested much of the area's commercially valuable trees, and wood products would have constituted a sizable portion of the railroad's freight traffic. Significantly, too, the motor age was evolving steadily. By then Houstonians could use the commercial services of a firm that regularly operated three two-ton Kissel trucks between Houston and the Frisco station at Cabool. Even though a network of good roads had not yet appeared in Phelps, Dent, and Texas counties, longer car trips became practical. In July 1914 a Houston resident drove his Maxwell to Rolla, taking three hours and thirty-five minutes to travel the fifty-five miles. "Formerly with a good team," observed the *Rolla Herald*, "it was an all day trip and some times parties would use part of two days in making the trip." No wonder so many enthusiastically embraced the "good roads" movement and agitated for an all-weather highway through the region known as the "Ozark Trails Route."[46]

The advancement of internal combustion road transport doomed most small steam short lines in Missouri and the Midwest, with some becoming junk as early as the era of World War I. Promoters and backers of the Ozark Short Line can hardly be damned for lacking clairvoyant powers. Probably some were gullible in their enthusiasm for the Young scheme, but they can be admired for struggling to improve Ozark transportation during the final period of extensive railroad building. Remarkably, even as they stumbled, these advocates of improved transport saw economic benefits resulting from what was not much more than a "paper" project. These Missourians, who sought to shrink distances, turned to improving roads. In time, residents experienced easier and cheaper transportation, the advantages that they had long sought.

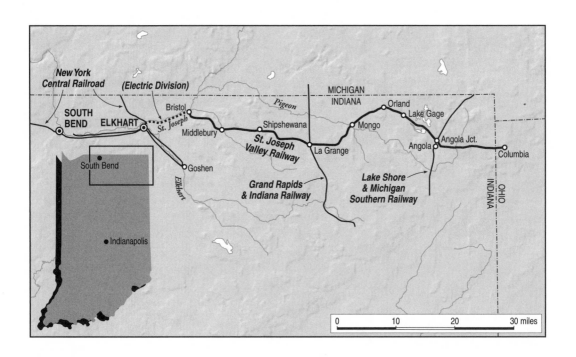

New York
Central Railroad

SOUTH
BEND

ELKHART

(Electric Division)

Bristol

St. Joseph

Middlebury

Shipshewana

MICHIGAN
INDIANA

Pigeon

Orland

Lake Gage

Mongo

*St. Joseph
Valley Railway*

La Grange

Angola

Angola Jct.

Columbia

*Grand Rapids
& Indiana Railway*

*Lake Shore
& Michigan
Southern Railway*

OHIO
INDIANA

Goshen

Elkhart

South Bend

Indianapolis

0   10   20   30 miles

Chapter 8

The Arnica Salve Line:
St. Joseph Valley Railway

"A n institution," insisted American philosopher Ralph Waldo Emerson, "is the lengthened shadow of one man." Had Emerson lived in Indiana early in the twentieth century, he could have had the St. Joseph Valley Railway Company (Valley Line) in mind as the institution, and Herbert "Herb" E. Bucklen (1848–1917) as the man. It was Bucklen who created and sustained the Valley Line and, in the process, contributed to the economic development of its northern Indiana service territory. In the public's mind he personified this Indiana carrier much as James J. Hill represented the Great Northern, A. B. Stickney the Chicago Great Western, and the Luces the Electric Short Line. No twilight railroad in the Midwest was more associated with a single individual than the St. Joseph Valley.[1]

Bucklen was a Horatio Alger–like figure. Born on July 19, 1848, in the central New York village of Winfield, he received a common school education, typical for lads of his generation, although later he briefly attended a business college. When Bucklen was seven years old, the family relocated to Elkhart, Indiana, a developing trading and manufacturing center. Barely a teenager, the energetic Bucklen began his work career in his new hometown, clerking in his father's drugstore. It was here that he demonstrated his business acumen when he persuaded the senior Bucklen to add a soda fountain. "Some of the village skeptics looked aghast but the shrewd young business man knew far better than they of the importance and necessity of keeping abreast of the times." It would be during his clerkship (his father later made him a partner) that Bucklen acquired a knowledge of drugs, utilizing "rooms over the store to carry on his experiments with the result that he soon had a number of propri-etary medicines on the market." In 1875 the Bucklens sold their drugstore and

two years later the younger Bucklen married well, soon started a family of two sons and a daughter, and expanded his patent medicine business. Bucklen had wisely purchased a line of medications from a Dr. Z. L. King of Elkhart, and he continued to develop other profitable pharmaceuticals. In 1883 the family moved to Chicago, about 125 miles away, "believing that Chicago would be a

In Bristol in 1912 the diminutive figure of "Dr." Herbert Bucklen is found by the front entrance of gasoline motor car No. 173, a thirty-five-seat passenger unit built in 1910 by the Kuhlman Company of Cleveland. *Courtesy of Elkhart County Historical Society.*

great city." The H. E. Bucklen & Company found immense success with Dr. King's New Discovery for Consumption, an alleged cure for tuberculosis, "the white plague," which ravaged the nation during the post–Civil War decades. The firm's advertising message was strong and direct: "The *only* cure for consumption," and, "It strikes terror to the doctors." Bucklen & Company marketed another popular product, Electric Bitters, a laxative, and also the "wondrous" Arnica Salve, an all-purpose ointment. As for the latter, Bucklen inadvertently admitted the salve's lack of "scientific" properties. When asked if he had any of his acclaimed palliative, Bucklen responded, "Take some axle grease off your wagon wheel; it's the same thing." While Arnica Salve was probably safe, the consumption cure was not, being a mixture of chloroform and morphine. Notwithstanding the possible dangers and limitations of the Bucklen products, the nostrum-taking public kept the factory on South Michigan Avenue in Chicago busy. Even the crushing depression of the 1890s did not dramatically reduce sales. Bucklen likely enhanced his credibility when he adopted the title "Dr.," and by the turn of the twentieth century had become a bona fide "toadstool millionaire."[2]

Bucklen pursued other business interests. A man who strongly believed in self-promotion and hard work, he created advertisements for his proprietary medicines and launched a trade journal, *The Druggist*. He also became heavily involved in real-estate ventures, early on in the Elkhart area and then in Chicago. "At the time of his death Mr. Bucklen had the reputation of being the largest citizen holder of real estate in Chicago." Bucklen, too, invested in the natural gas boom that swept parts of northeastern Indiana and northwestern Ohio in the 1880s, and later he acquired thousands of acres of virgin timberlands in Tennessee. One project in Elkhart was the development in the 1880s of a large tract of land known as the Riverside Addition, located near the St. Joseph River about a mile from the town center. This north side industrial district became home to several plants that produced various products, including buggies and, later, Elcar and Pratt automobiles. But surely most Elkhartans associated the self-made patent medicine king with two other ventures, the Hotel Bucklen, which opened on March 20, 1889, at the cost of nearly $100,000 ($2.3 million in 2008 dollars), and the Bucklen Opera House, later renamed the Bucklen Theatre. The feeling existed among area residents that Bucklen "is patriotic in working for the improvement of [Elkhart] and the betterment of the St. Joseph valley." At the time of Bucklen's death. the editor of the *Elkhart Truth* called him "the father of Elkhart."[3]

In his desire to maximize the attractiveness of the Riverside Addition and to respond to community concerns, Bucklen entered the railroad business. Although Elkhart was already a stop on the busy Buffalo-to-Chicago main line of the Lake Shore & Michigan Southern Railway (LS&MS) and claimed a station on the less strategic Cincinnati, Wabash & Michigan Railway (CW&M), which extended between Anderson, Indiana, and Benton Harbor, Michigan, there was widespread unhappiness about the high rates, especially for freight and express shipments, charged by the LS&MS, the western anchor of the mighty Vanderbilt system. In 1892 the situation worsened when the Vanderbilts acquired the CW&M, making this property part of their Cleveland, Cincinnati, Chicago & St. Louis Railway (Big Four Railroad). In order to break the stranglehold, Bucklen proposed a new outlet for Elkhart commerce. This could be achieved by constructing about a dozen miles of track westward from Elkhart to the Chicago main line of the Chicago & Grand Trunk Railway (Grand Trunk) at Mishawaka, a few miles east of South Bend. South Bend itself could be easily reached, allowing for an interchange with the independent Terre Haute & Indianapolis Railroad or "Vandalia Line," a later unit of the Pennsylvania System.[4]

Spearheaded by Bucklen, with support from several Elkhart businessmen, backers of the Elkhart & Western Railroad (E&W) filed with the Indiana secretary of state articles of incorporation on June 1, 1888. The stated purpose was to have "said road to be constructed in Elkhart, Elkhart County, Indiana, and shall extend to or near the western limits of South Bend, St. Joseph County, Indiana." Although the construction process began in the autumn of 1890, progress was slow, largely because of problems securing real estate, crossing spongy terrain, and installing a bridge over the St. Joseph River. It would not be until August 1893 that the first freight train steamed into Elkhart from Mishawaka. Then a month later passenger service began, with the inaugural run being a ten-coach round-trip excursion from Elkhart to Chicago.[5]

But the wait was worthwhile. Despite making its debut during the worst months of the nation's most severe depression, the E&W soon became an impressive moneymaker. With direct access to most Elkhart businesses, including those located in the Riverside Addition, and with solid support from the public, the "Bucklen Line" thrived. The E&W also benefited from a cooperative Grand Trunk. "Overnight fast service from Chicago in connection with the Grand Trunk had picked up considerable former Lake Shore customers," remarked a chronicler of the E&W. "Meat from the packing houses and banana cars began to come via the new road."[6]

The E&W was a somewhat typical midwestern short line, although construction standards were high, featuring good hardwood ties and heavy steel rails atop a well-engineered and ballasted grade. "The very best material procurable has been the rule with President Bucklen, and the grading, etc., has been made to correspond," opined a veteran railroad official. "The line is much smoother to ride over, in its present new condition, than many so-called first class roads." Two used 4-4-0 American Standard locomotives provided the motive power, and a combination coach and baggage car, built new by the Pullman Company, accommodated passengers, express, and mail. The company's operating practices resembled those of scores of comparable pikes with daily-except-Sunday mixed-train service.[7]

Yet Bucklen, who served as chief executive and was the largest investor, revealed his desire to experiment, a trait he later demonstrated on the Valley Line. At the time the E&W opened, Bucklen acquired a steam handcar, designed to increase the efficiency of track workers. But the contraption did not function properly and was soon discarded. Even though the interurban era was in its birthing stage, Bucklen toyed with the possibility of electrification. Reportedly he ordered the wiring of fish plates when the rails were laid. "This preliminary spade work being done, it would be a simple matter of sixty days to string the overhead wires." Possibly cost considerations explain why the E&W never became a pioneer interurban.[8]

There may have been further ambitions for the E&W, most likely building the few miles into South Bend. But before any additional construction could occur, Bucklen and his colleagues sold the property. Several suitors had their eyes on the short line. There was speculation that the Grand Trunk would acquire this important feeder. There also existed the possibility that the Indiana, Illinois & Iowa Railroad (Three I), an independent carrier that stretched between South Bend and Streator, Illinois, might make an offer. This road apparently not only sought an Iowa destination, but also wanted to reach Toledo, Ohio, and the E&W would be an excellent fit. Then there was the LS&MS, which realized the prosperity of the Bucklen Line and wanted to protect its Elkhart and South Bend markets. Being a good negotiator, Bucklen entered into talks with Vanderbilt representatives, and on May 22, 1898, he announced the impending sale. The deal would be profitable for E&W investors, although the LS&MS would regain its monopoly on Elkhart commerce. "The road which came into being as one man's dream of breaking the Lake Shore's iron grip on Elkhart traffic, had a short life but a busy one," opined the *Goshen Democrat*. "It had been a great freight rate demoralizer as far as the Lake Shore was concerned. It had opened optional routes to shippers of Elkhart to the east, west and north with the Chicago and Grand Trunk connection. It greatly aided in the industrial development of Elkhart and Mishawaka. It was one of the few railroad promotions of the [18]90's to become an actuality and a financial success."[9]

Bucklen was surely buoyed by the outcome of the E&W venture and perhaps thought that he could repeat his triumph. If he fretted about the

Vanderbilt dominance of rail traffic in the Elkhart area, he apparently did not say so publicly, and probably for good reason. About the time of the sale, residents applauded the arrival of the cars of the Indiana Electric Railway that connected their little city with Goshen, eleven miles to the south. A year later, in 1899, the fifteen-mile Indiana Railway opened between Elkhart and South Bend. Although these two future components of the Northern Indiana Railway (later the Chicago, South Bend & Northern Indiana Railway) did not immediately handle carload freight, they provided convenient and reasonably priced passenger and express service.[10]

The appearance of juice lines between Elkhart and Goshen and South Bend was a harbinger of many more interurbans in Indiana. By the end of the building period, the state claimed the second-largest concentration of electric intercity lines in the nation, 1,825 miles, eclipsed only by neighboring Ohio. Much of the Indiana environment, both natural and man-made, proved nicely suited for interurbans. With the exception of the Ohio River counties, most of the topography was flat or gently rolling, and interior streams were relatively small and shallow, greatly reducing construction and maintenance costs. Moreover, the state, heavily settled in most areas, enjoyed a stable economy based on agriculture and light industries. Interurban promoters were further aided by closely spaced cities, towns, and villages, ideal for the typical traction road which tended to be relatively short.[11]

Bucklen became caught up in the interurban fever that swept much of the Midwest early in the twentieth century. An admirer of technology who possessed business skills, drive, and wealth, he conceived a plan to expand the interurban network in what was a prime area, northern Indiana. But

When the Valley Line issued its public timetable for August 3, 1912, it featured a map that showed what would be the completed railroad. Yet the company intended to advance toward Toledo, far beyond the Ellis station.

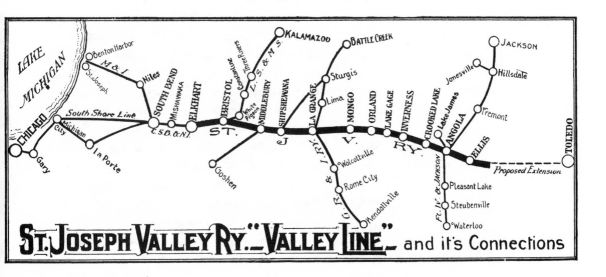

Bucklen did not envision a simple electric road that would connect a few county-seat towns and intermediate farms and villages. Service to such places would be desirable, but he had greater ambitions. As interurban construction blossomed between 1900 and 1905, it became apparent to him (and others, too) that a gap had developed between the expanding interurban systems of Ohio and Indiana. By this time, passengers could take the Lake Shore Electric Railway between Cleveland and Toledo and make connections for destinations farther west. By 1905 the Toledo & Indiana Railway operated a fifty-six-mile road between Toledo and Bryan, Ohio, and the Toledo & Western Railway had a division between Allen Junction (Toledo) and Pioneer, Ohio, a distance of about forty-five miles. Travelers could gain access to greater Chicago from Elkhart via the Northern Indiana and, after 1908, through a connection with the Chicago, South Bend & Northern Indiana Railway. But it was *not* possible to ride electric cars directly and continually between Toledo and Chicago. Although in 1907 the misnamed Toledo & Chicago Interurban Railway opened a forty-two-mile Y-shaped line between Fort Wayne and neighboring towns of Garrett, Kendallville, and Waterloo, the road was more north–south than east–west in orientation. Still, this Fort Wayne company wished to become more than a somewhat localized trolley operation.[12]

It is not known exactly when Bucklen decided to build the missing eighty-four-mile link in the Indiana–Ohio interurban network. But on March 28, 1903, he took action when he received a charter for what he called the St. Joseph Valley Traction Company (SJVT). The projected line would connect South Bend with Pioneer, where it would meet the Toledo & Western for the Glass City. The road was expected to pass through Elkhart; La Grange, seat of La Grange County; and Angola, seat of Steuben County, but the exact path remained undetermined. The SJVT would likely follow somewhat the route of the Goshen & Indiana Traction Company that in 1899 had announced its intention to connect Goshen and Angola via La Grange and Orland. Apparently, backers of the Goshen project "were in no position to compete with Mr. Bucklen," and by 1907 this potential competition vanished.[13]

Although the Goshen & Indiana never became more than a paper proposition, the SJVT would not be serving a traffic vacuum; steam roads were abundant. The LS&MS operated a raceway between Toledo and South Bend, although running about twenty miles south of the projected Bucklen road. In the 1890s the Wabash Railway had built through the same vicinity, and in places its Chicago-to-Toledo (Montpelier) line was only about a dozen miles to the south. And the SJVT would cross several steam roads on a north-south axis. Yet Bucklen's carrier would provide several places with their first rails and others with a second railroad. Bucklen believed that this section of

Indiana was ideally suited for more economic development, especially manufacturing. "It offers fine climate, plentiful water power, cheap fuel, raw materials at your door," and a location where "you can compete for the Central, Northern and Western markets."[14]

Areas along the anticipated road welcomed the prospect of a well-placed interurban. The *La Grange Standard*, which kept close tabs on business matters, applauded what seemed to be happening, warmly praising "Mr. Bucklen's ideas of building a first class road, with the latest improvements, facilities and luxuries, which will be a credit to the generous capitalist who has conceived the plan, and [will be] the pride of the people of this region." The newspaper believed that the county "will be traversed by one of the great trunk electric lines of the country," adding, "It will be the beginning of a new era of development."[15]

With charter in hand and strong public support, Bucklen moved ahead with the St. Joseph Valley Traction project. Although the financial dimensions were never clearly revealed, the company over time issued only a small amount of stock, most of which Bucklen or family members owned, and Bucklen possessed all of the bonds. As construction progressed, the SJVT received some public subscriptions and real-estate donations for the right-of-way and facilities, as was customary for steam and electric projects. The road also won, usually without much fuss, favorable franchises to operate within corporate limits.[16]

It might be expected that the SJVT would start construction at either end of the proposed route, and likely from Elkhart where Bucklen had personal and business ties. The decision, though, was to begin at La Grange and push westward toward Shipshewana and Middlebury. The precise route to Bristol, Elkhart, and South Bend remained to be determined. This uncertainty prompted Goshen boosters to pressure Bucklen to consider a line from Middlebury to Goshen, where the track could connect with the Northern Indiana Railway. But he rejected this routing strategy. Later, according the published accounts, the SJVT planned to advance eastward from La Grange toward the Toledo & Western, which in 1903 and 1904 graded a right-of-way toward the Ohio–Indiana border from its end-of-track at Pioneer.[17]

Bucklen, who possessed sound judgment with matters of personnel, intelligently selected Martin Swinehart, a civil engineer, to take charge of the building and related matters. The son of an Elkhart County farm couple, Swinehart had had experience building a trolley line in Goshen, and then took charge of a major extension of the Chicago & North Western Railway in northern Wisconsin. Later he served as chief engineer and general manager of a large irrigation project in southern California. Swinehart became an effective field general and the eyes and ears of Bucklen, and would remain involved with the company through most of the critical construction phase.[18]

Notwithstanding the skills of Swinehart, the construction process went slower than expected. Finally in August 1904 graders had completed most of the slightly more than sixteen miles of right-of-way between La Grange, Shipshewana, and Middlebury. By September, several carloads of rails, ties, and tracklaying tools had arrived in La Grange at the planned interchange with the Grand Rapids & Indiana Railway (GR&I), part of the Pennsylvania System. Soon trackmen began their labors and were assisted by a work train pulled by an elderly 0-4-4T Forney tank engine. In mid-November 1904, the editor of the *Standard* joined Swinehart for an inspection tour of the first two miles of completed track, and he liked what he saw. "Being constructed of 70-pound rails and standard gauge it looks like any new, well constructed steam railway." Workers also began to erect the "car house," a 120-by-39-foot structure, near the center of La Grange.[19]

By the second week of December, tracklayers had reached the vicinity of Shipshewana, but bad weather caused postponement of further work. Frigid temperatures and deep snows repeatedly gripped the area. Unfortunately, the proposed road lay in the heart of the Lake Michigan snow belt. But once weather conditions improved, workers returned to their assignments. As had earlier happened to LS&MS and Wabash track builders, SJVT laborers encountered occasional, nasty beds of quicksand and peat and troublesome sinkholes. Two miles west of Shipshewana, the unstable soil caused delay and expense. "The ground is innocent looking and has been farmed for years, but the railway bed has sunk in all about ten feet."[20]

While the construction crew pushed west of Shipshewana, the village happily welcomed the first train. The event took place on March 10, 1905, when the tiny tank engine steamed into town with a caboose crammed with farmers and trackmen. "The electric railway is laid to Shipshewana," reported the *Standard*. "The people attracted by the whistle as the engine approached, gathered on Main street and welcomed it with smiles, cheers and the band. The engine stopped in front of the hotel, the band played on, Superintendent Swinehart received congratulations."[21]

Once regular passenger service began between La Grange and Shipshewana in late March, travelers would not have to ride in an uncomfortable caboose. Patrons could board a piece of cutting-edge railroad technology, a thirty-five-foot, olive green gas-electric car, No. 101, built by the Hicks Locomotive and Car Works of Chicago Heights, Illinois. Long before the Luces of Minnesota gained fame for their fleet of internal combustion "motors," the SJVT road had an earlier, experimental version. "The power is electric.

Four axle motors of 40-horse power each, with a maximum power of 200, are driven by a storage battery charged by a Sprague electric generator. The generator is driven by a 90-horse power four-cylinder marine engine by the Marinette Gas Engine Company of Chicago Heights," explained the reporter. "This is the first motor car of its kind made. At a test at the factory it ran at the speed of forty miles an hour." The SJVT had also acquired a handsome trailer coach from the St. Louis Car Company, the No. 102, a piece of rolling stock that could be converted into an interurban car. Bucklen was delighted with his purchases, believing that they would be "the model of the motive power of interurban lines everywhere." The future would be with "wireless inter-urbans." Still he hedged his bet with the adaptable St. Louis–built trailer.[22]

The first public timetable, which took effect on March 31, 1905, revealed an operation that possessed both steam and interurban characteristics. Resembling a steam road, the SJVT dispatched only two trains daily over the ten-mile stretch of track, leaving La Grange at 8:20 a.m. and 2:00 p.m. and returning from Shipshewana at 10:30 a.m. and 4:15 p.m. Yet like other contemporary electric roads, SJVT motor trains made frequent, scheduled intermediate stops, four in ten miles, and the road notified patrons that "cars will stop at any point to take on or let off passengers. To stop the car, signal to the motorman by raising your hand."[23]

As the line took shape west from Shipshewana, Bucklen, the accomplished real-estate promoter, purchased land beside beautiful Shipshewana Lake and platted cottage sites. "There are forty-two lots on the bluff and thirty-one lots down by the lake." By the time of the Fourth of July celebrations in 1905, this budding resort included a boathouse, pavilion, and baseball field. Bucklen knew that money could be made through lot sales and increased summer business from cottagers and excursionists, a pattern that he would shortly repeat elsewhere. The traffic situation to the lake improved when on September 20, 1905, the seven miles opened to Middlebury, with three daily trains scheduled each way between terminals.[24]

While Bucklen expressed uncertainty about the precise route beyond Middlebury, he expected that his road would push east of La Grange into the lake country of Steuben County, and reach Angola and then western Ohio. In June and July 1905, Superintendent Swinehart considered where this construction should occur and talked about routing and financial support with residents from several communities, including Orland, approximately midway between La Grange and Angola. "He met the [Orland] citizens in the evening at the hotel and from the crowd that gathered every businessman of the village and most of the farmers in the vicinity must have been present." And Swinehart encountered a warm response. "Although Orland has seen several railway mirages to their great disappointment, they are as willing and anxious as ever to do all they are able to get a railway through their town." The company would surely receive financial support, including tax subsidies from towns and townships. Swinehart concluded that rails "would connect a number of beautiful lakes, already well known as summer resorts, and two as good, wide awake inland towns as can be found in the country." He also believed that the road would not encounter troublesome physical limitations. Although later the railroad in its official maps indicated a straight line between La Grange, Mongo, Orland, and Angola, the route was hardly as the crow flies, going out of the way to reach Orland and the lakes.[25]

On July 23, 1905, Bucklen received a state charter for the St. Joseph Valley Railway Company to build between La Grange and Pioneer, Ohio, with authorization to issue $400,000 ($9.4 million in 2008 dollars) of capital stock, but no bonds. Likely this corporate strategy came about because of the strong possibility of local stock subscriptions. Indeed, in September voters in one La Grange County township and two in Steuben County overwhelmingly approved modest subsidies, and in Mongo the vote was unanimously in favor. "Probably five hundred people gathered at Mongo the night of the election, and when the result was known there was great rejoicing. Old band instruments were resurrected, a bonfire was lit and everyone was happy." Once trackage had been completed, the SJVT and Valley Line could be united; in fact, on March 1, 1909, the Valley Line leased the SJVT "for an indefinite period."[26]

By August permanent survey work had begun. Yet Bucklen and Swinehart remained undecided on how best to enter Angola, in part because it might be possible to use existing trackage. In 1903 the Angola Railway & Power Company, one of America's smallest interurbans, opened a 3.7-mile line between Angola and Paltytown, a resort community located on Lake James. The Lake James Railway, its common name, was built to serve vacationers on this popular lake; in fact, this trolley operated only during the summer season. The Valley Line could connect with the little juice road at Paltytown and use its line into Angola. But negotiations with the road failed, prompting the company to build on its own into the Stueben County seat. To reach the commercial heart of Angola, Bucklen opted for a one-mile stub that left the main line northeast of town at Angola Junction.[27]

By the end of 1905, construction crews had entered the countryside east of La Grange and worked toward Mongo and Orland, and also at points west from Angola toward Orland. The feeling that there would be no problems building the twenty-eight miles was wrong. Workers encountered several exceptionally large sinkholes near Lake Gage, located between Angola and Orland, and they struggled to create a stable roadbed. "While it was frozen, the right of way over these places was covered with a network of tamarack poles to the width of fifty feet. Brush was thrown on the poles and covered with ten feet of dirt." Still, with the spring thaw, the roadbed sank considerably, requiring more fill. "The company has no intention of abandoning the work already done and building around the sink holes." Then workers discovered quicksand at the abutment sites for the bridge over the GR&I near La Grange, and this bad luck necessitated extra pilings to create a stable base. By late spring 1906, Swinehart reported, "Practically seventeen of the twenty-eight miles were graded and ready for the steel." These encouraging words prompted the *La Grange Standard* to believe that "without serious interruption the rails will begin to glisten in the sunlight along the roadbed to Mongo and Orland."[28]

The slowness of erecting the overhead bridge delayed tracklayers until early fall, and it would not be until spring 1907 that rails reached Mongo, nine miles east of La Grange, and soon Orland, fifteen miles from La Grange. Appropriately, on May 4 Orland had a big blowout to officially welcome the Valley Line, complete with orations, bands, and fireworks. Four special trains brought hundreds of celebrants, some of whom perched on the cab roof of one of the road's several stately 4-4-0 locomotives. Immediately, the company started three daily passenger runs that made the trip in forty-five minutes. Within in a month, this service was extended to Lake Gage, about four miles east of Orland. Finally, in early August, the *Angola Herald* announced that the last rails had arrived in Angola and that workers had installed the

Gasoline motor car No. 173 pauses at the passenger shelter at Lake Gage, Indiana, circa 1910. *Courtesy of Krambles-Peterson Archive.*

interchange connection with the Jackson, Michigan, line of the LS&MS. This phase of fashioning the Eastern Division ended on August 20, 1907, when No. 121, pulling combine No. 115 with Bucklen as a passenger, steamed into Angola to be met by town dignitaries and residents who "indulged in some oratory and cheers that seemed necessary to the occasion." The latest time-card listed three daily trains between Middlebury, La Grange, and Angola, and more movements on Sundays from Angola to serve nearby resort destinations, especially the Lake Gage Assembly where Chautauqua-like summer programs attracted large audiences.[29]

Gasoline motor car No. 172 has recently arrived from the manufacturer. Brill built this twelve-ton, thirty-five-seat vehicle in 1909. *Courtesy of Krambles-Peterson Archive.*

In anticipation of service through the Indiana lake country, Bucklen had indulged in more real-estate investments. In early 1906, he had purchased for $10,000 ($237,000 in 2008 dollars) the Shady Nook resort on Lake Gage and planned to "make of it the most popular outing place between Toledo and Chicago." More cottages appeared and all indications pointed to a smart decision by Bucklen and those who joined his efforts to make Shady Nook "acquire a fame second to none in this section of the country."[30]

Before Bucklen turned to expanding the "Western Division" and also forging an interurban connection in Ohio, he continued to experiment with motive power. As a carload freight business developed, energized by active connections with the GR&I and LS&MS that followed favorable regulatory decisions on rate divisions, the road purchased an assortment of more than thirty freight cars and additional steam locomotives. Eventually the company owned six secondhand 4-4-0 American Standards and a 4-6-0 acquired from the GR&I. This ten-wheeler handled the heaviest freight trains and occasionally passenger extras, with their head-end cars and two or three wooden coaches. Similar motive power and consists could be found throughout the country on scores of short lines, old and new. But what was different would be a parade of self-propelled units, or what one commentator called "a fantastic collection of motive power that included tiny gasoline-powered chain-drive vehicles, a battery car and conventional size gasoline-powered equipment." Although the Hicks car developed at least one major mechanical problem and then burned in early 1907, Bucklen was not disenchanted with emerging technologies. Later that year, he acquired a twenty-seat gasoline car from the Stover Motor Car Company of Freeport, Illinois, described as "hardly more than an automobile mounted on railroad wheels." Patrons soon dubbed this little vehicle "Bucklen's Arnica Salve Wagon." In 1908 the road bought a slightly larger Stover gasoline car. Bucklen met the demands of the newly opened Eastern Division by buying from the Sheffield Car Company of Three Rivers, Michigan, two similar gasoline units that a thirty-horsepower four-cylinder water-cooled Fairbanks-Morse engine propelled. This manufacturing firm had already found a few customers for its smaller inspection vehicles that could seat a dozen passengers. The Valley Line named these larger, twenty-seat cars the *Orland* and the *Angola*, and used them mostly to shuttle passengers between Angola and the lakes on Sundays and holidays. Then in 1909 the road received two thirty-five-passenger J. G. Brill cars from the famed Philadelphia manufacturer, each containing a Fairbanks-Morse kerosene-burning engine. The Nos. 171 and 173 were the first of what became a popular model type. And between 1910 and 1914, the company purchased four, thirty-five-horsepower gasoline motor cars from the G. C. Kuhlman Company, an interurban builder in Cleveland that Brill controlled. Part of this order was necessary because a fire in November 1911 consumed the shops and storage facilities in La Grange, destroying a steam locomotive and tender and five motor cars.[31]

As the Valley Line assembled a fleet of motor cars, the national press took notice. In a wire story, which appeared in the latter part of 1909, the road's passenger service received positive coverage. "The Valley Line was the first road in Indiana—and possibly the only one now—to use gasoline motorcars. The advantage of gasoline motorcars is in the cheap cost of operation. West-

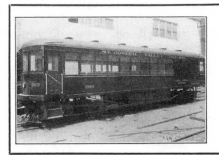

Edison-Beach Battery Cars

Cost 2 to 4 Mills per Car Mile

for all battery maintenance
(materials and labor).

Federal Storage Battery Car Co.

30 Broad Street, New York City

Fred A. Curtiss,   Pacific Coast Representative
Rialto Bldg., San Francisco, Cal.

The Federal Storage Battery Car Company proudly advertised the forty-five-passenger-capacity unit that it built in 1913 for the Valley Line. Unfortunately, the car could not hold a battery charge long enough for a round-trip on Bucklen's nonelectrified road. *Courtesy of Krambles-Peterson Archive.*

ern steam road officers figure the cost of running a passenger car at 50 cents a mile, where the cost of operating one of the Valley Line's gasoline motors is about 10 cents a mile. This means such transportation, therefore, is beginning to be regarded as the most feasible and desirable for sparsely settled communities." The piece concluded by observing, "Five fares at 2 cents a mile will pay the cost of operating the car. Neither trolley nor steam road could make ends meet at that rate." This was certainly a public-relations triumph for the Bucklen road.[32]

The quest continued for better non-steam-powered rolling stock. In 1913 Bucklen invested in a forty-five-seat Edison-Beach storage battery car built by the Federal Storage Battery Car Company of Silver Lake, New Jersey. The following year he bought a forty-passenger 150-horsepower Hall-Scott all-steel gasoline car from the Berkeley, California, manufacturer. While the latter acquisition performed well and served as a prototype for gas-electrics of the 1920s, the former was a bitter disappointment. This unit, No. 203, failed to maintain a charge for most of its runs. Bucklen protested to Federal Storage Battery officials, arguing that they had guaranteed that their battery car would run 150 miles on a charge, but that had not happened. A court case ensued, but Bucklen lost his bid for compensation. The car remained on the property until the road shut down.[33]

The all-time Bucklen passenger car roster also included two bona fide electric interurban cars, a sixty-seat Stephenson and a fifty-seat McGuire-Cummings. The former came from the John Stephenson Car Company in New York City and the latter from the McGuire-Cummings Manufacturing Company in Chicago. These acquisitions took place two years after the SJVT had reached Elkhart from Middlebury. When the lease with the electric Chicago, South Bend & Northern Indiana Railway (CSB&NI) expired on July 1, 1912, Bucklen was forced to acquire rolling stock to maintain service between Elkhart and Bristol, the only segment to sport overhead wire.[34]

The snail-like progress of creating the Chicago-to-Toledo "missing link"

The most dependable motor car owned by the Valley Line was No. 204, built by Hall-Scott in 1914. A year later the unit is about to leave the La Grange station. Observed a railfan, "She ran well enough to be specially offered with obvious confidence at the receiver's sale." *Courtesy of California State Railroad Museum.*

interurban must have frustrated Bucklen, yet the Valley Line progressed. Once he decided that Elkhart rather than Goshen would be reached, he had to battle for a street franchise from the Elkhart Common Council and hammer out a contract for an exchange of track privileges with the CSB&NI in Elkhart. Once these matters were favorably settled, he could forge ahead.[35]

Still, the process of connecting the end-of-line at Middlebury with Elkhart, via Bristol, a distance of sixteen miles, was not easy. Although some adjoining landowners deeded parcels of land, Bucklen experienced difficulty in obtaining other pieces of the right-of-way. Onlookers seemed disappointed at what appeared to be the lack of tangible progress. "We have long hoped for that extension, and we know that Mr. Bucklen realizes its importance to his railway," editorialized the *Standard* in May 1908. "Here is hoping that the skies will clear and that the sunshine will continue so far as the Valley Line is concerned, thus permitting the building of that extension."[36]

Supporters of the Bucklen road must have been cheered when in November 1908 they learned that construction at last had begun in Elkhart. Yet it would not be until the following July that most of the grading, including two large fills, were completed, and bridges over the Elkhart River and Middleton Run nearly finished. Bucklen, though, faced a hostile LS&MS that objected to a crossing at grade of its main line near Bristol, an issue that would not be resolved in favor of the Valley Line for months. The project still looked promising. "Many Elkhart citizens who have been out past where the line is being laid during the past week have been heard to remark enthusiastically about the beauty of the right of way," reported the *Middlebury Independent*. "The line for a stretch of about a mile runs beneath the shade of a long row of maple trees on the right side of the road and is exceptionally pretty."[37]

Development of the Valley Line became more complicated when Bucklen decided to electrify the nine miles between Elkhart and Bristol. As he had repeatedly stated, the entire road would be placed under wire, but he thought that the western end would be a proper beginning, and would allow city service in Elkhart. Yet it would not be until late spring 1910 that the Bristol-Elkhart segment became a true interurban. In the interim, Bucklen worked out a deal with Samuel Murdock, who controlled the connecting CSB&NI, to operate the Bristol line. Not that Bucklen wished to dispose of the property, but the Murdock road could supply rolling stock and immediately incorporate the Bristol segment into the extensive network of interconnected midwestern electric lines. On July 6, 1910, the first car made a trial run, taking thirty-five minutes between terminals. "The power was weak and only one car could be on the line at a time." Ten days later regular scheduling began with the CSB&NI operating nine daily trips. Bristol residents not only gained

VALLEY LINE BRIDGE OVER PINE CREEK.

an interurban outlet to the north, south, and west, but also a $6,000 depot, "a beauty with stucco walls and red tiled roof," and conveniently located in the center of town.[38]

With traction service established between Bristol and Elkhart, Bucklen pushed to connect Bristol and Middlebury. Again construction was slow, partly because of the failure to receive a speedy and satisfactory franchise agreement with the town of Middlebury. At last, on July 13, 1911, the ceremonial last spike was driven at the Bonneyville Road crossing, three miles east of Bristol. Then on August 1, 1911, the first motor car operated between La Grange and Bristol with a platform connection for Elkhart. Completion of this trackage "put to rest the complaints of the carping critics who have vented their spleen upon the line ever since it was proposed in the early years of the last decade."[39]

Coinciding with the closing of the gap on the Western Division, work on the Eastern Division progressed beyond Angola Junction. In the latter part of 1911, service began to Berlein station, eight miles to the east. But not until July 1915 did the Valley Line reach the hamlet of Columbia, Ohio, in part because sinkholes, including a massive one near Berlein, delayed construction and escalated costs. The road stalled at Columbia, and passenger service

For several years, electric cars of the Chicago, South Bend & Northern Indiana Railway operated Valley Line trains between Elkhart and Bristol. Car No. 215 stands atop the deck bridge over Pine Creek. *Courtesy of Elkhart County Historical Society.*

Not long after electrification, a traction freight motor, which handled express and less-than-car-load shipments, waits in front of the Bristol Opera House. *Courtesy of Elkhart County Historical Society.*

east of Angola never exceeded two daily-except-Sunday trains with a single run on Sunday.[40]

Another factor in explaining the slowness of building eastward involved connecting service and expansion strategies. Even though the Toledo & Western had graded several miles west of Pioneer, subsequent ownership changes reduced the company's commitment for an extension. By the time the Valley Line inched toward Pioneer, the T&W had fallen into the hands of Henry L. Doherty. This rising utility–holding company magnate showed much more interest in electric power than in electric railways. It would be up to Bucklen to create the link. Rumors, too, surfaced about the Valley Line continuing to Montpelier, Ohio, and establishing a connection with the Wabash or an expanding Toledo & Indiana. The latter seemed more plausible; the interurban announced several plans to reach the Hoosier State, including building northwest from Bryan to meet the Valley Line. Still, as the *South Bend Tribune* observed, "The dream of Herbert E. Bucklen is to control an electric railway connecting Chicago and Toledo, Ohio."[41]

The desire to directly unite the Ohio and Indiana traction networks attracted the attention of the promoters of the Chicago-New York Electric Air Line Railroad. Although the company pushed for a high-speed electric

railway between America's two largest cities, by 1911 the firm showed interest in a more sane construction policy. The Air Line endorsed building the
sixty-two miles between Goshen and Bryan, which would complete a tie-in
with existing traction roads and would connect in the Indiana towns of Kendallville and Waterloo with the Toledo & Chicago Interurban. Nothing happened, largely because the limited resources of Air Line went to reaching
Gary, that grand new "magic city." It is unlikely that the Air Line's wish to
close the interurban gap bothered Bucklen; the "ten-hour, ten-dollar" project
appeared to be mostly bluster.[42]

Bucklen may have contemplated other routes. Since he never developed
a cordial relationship with the CSB&NI, reports persisted that he wanted his
own line between Elkhart and South Bend. Much more speculation developed concerning an extension northward from Bristol and later from Elkhart
to Three Rivers and Kalamazoo, Michigan, a distance of about sixty miles.
"Well informed men assert that simultaneously with the development of the
Elkhart-Kalamazoo project, there is likely definite steps taken for the construction of an interurban road south out of Elkhart, tapping the Nappanee
territory and possibly connecting with Logansport." Had the Valley Line or
"Bucklen System" reached Kalamazoo, it probably would have established
a close relationship with another twilight-era carrier, the Kalamazoo, Lake
Shore & Chicago Railway, better known as the Fruit Belt Line. This hard-
pressed steam road, projected as an interurban, extended fifty-five miles
between Kalamazoo and the Lake Michigan port of South Haven. In 1911
the Michigan United Railway, a major traction road, leased the Fruit Belt
Line for a five-year period and proposed electrification, although this never
happened.[43]

Presumably all of Bucklen's trackage, built or projected, would be electrified. "That the Valley Line will some day substitute the trolley wire and
pole for the motor car and the steam engine is probable." Once electrification of the Elkhart-to-Bristol segment was completed, reports circulated that
wire would be strung over the remainder of the line. In late 1911 observers
expected Bucklen to dam the St. Joseph River near Elkhart to secure water-
power for electric generation. Then in a July 1912 news column, "Valley Line
Talk," the *La Grange Standard* noted, "Mr. Bucklen is now unloading poles and
wire along the Valley Line tracks between Bristol and Angola preliminary to
electrification." About the same time, the *Goshen News-Times* indicated that
Bucklen "has let the contract for the electrifying of the Bristol–La Grange
division to the Westinghouse Company." A year or so later overhead wires
were placed in Angola and La Grange, but electrification stalled. Expense is
the likely explanation, or Bucklen remained hopeful that internal combus-

tion or battery-powered equipment, at least for passenger, mail, and express service, would supercede the traditional trolley.[44]

As the Valley Line took shape, newspapers mentioned what seemed to be increased business, suggesting at least modest prosperity. For one thing, there were those ubiquitous specials. "Superintendent Swinehart is running special trains east on the Valley Line this week for the accommodation of the people in eastern La Grange county who have it in mind to avail themselves of money-saving opportunities in merchandising at the county seat," announced the *Standard* in early December 1907, one of many such reports. In the latter part of 1911 Bucklen told the press, "Patronage along the Valley Line has exceeded all expectations." Actually the road was at best a marginal operation. The official report for the year ending June 30, 1909, indicated that passenger earnings stood at $19,813; freight, $10,142; mail and express, $1,501, for a total of $31,456, yet operating expenses amounted to $36,119. Adding taxes and a loss-carry-forward, the earnings picture was a negative $12,383. The shaky financial situation remained mostly unchanged. For the year ending June 30, 1913, overall earnings reached $51,546 and expenses were $49,272. But when taxes were included, a small deficit resulted. Bucklen, though, did not like to reveal the financials or comment on his personal wealth. In fact, according to the *Poor's Manual of Railroads*, "The company failed to respond to requests for the 1914 report, or to file the report with the Interstate Commerce Commission to December 10, 1914." Bucklen's personal resources continued to cover the deficits. "No wonder people called the Valley railroad the 'Arnica Salve Line,'" said one wag. "Mr. Bucklen always needed to sell a lot of salve to keep it going." In 1917 an attorney for the railroad revealed that operating income amounted to less than $50,000 ($832,000 in 2008 dollars) annually while operating costs exceeded $100,000 ($167,000 in 2008 dollars), and that the company's obligations to Bucklen personally approached $2 million ($33.3 million in 2008 dollars).[45]

As with even the worst performing twilight roads in the Midwest, the presence of the Valley Line had a pronounced economic impact on its service territory. And this involved more than the wages paid to the men who built the road. Bucklen grasped the potential of increased real-estate values and was probably not surprised that the opening of the Elkhart-to-Bristol interurban, for instance, drove up nearby land prices by as much as 25 percent. Then there were the expanded summer lake resorts, especially at Lake Gage and Crooked Lake, and a new town, Berlein, on the Columbia extension. Although this townsite never developed much beyond a depot, general store, grain elevator, stock pens, and a few houses, its platting in 1911 offered additional real-estate opportunities. Early on, the Valley Line stimulated agricultural activities, including expanded operations of creameries in La Grange and Angola. Also helping farmers was development of on-line marl beds (lime-rich mud), used as a fertilizer. The railroad corridor in the various communities experienced construction of elevators, coal yards, lumberyards, stock facilities, and some light manufacturing firms. In Angola, for example, the new works of the United Machine Company, recruited by Valley Line representatives, appeared at trackside in 1909. Other businesses gravitated to the energized communities along the road, including Grubb's Sanitarium that opened in Mongo in 1912. Newspapers made clear that the railroad allowed merchants, particularly in Angola and La Grange, to tap a wider trading area. Also, the small shops of the railroad in La Grange bolstered that town's economy, providing "steady employment, the year around, for four or five men." As with all railroads there were other employees, and their earnings had a multiplier effect on a community's economy.[46]

As frequently happened with the railroads that materialized in the final period of construction, speculation developed about the possibility of a takeover. Just as rumors appeared about the Great Western acquiring the Creston, Winterset & Des Moines, or the Rock Island assuming the Ozark Short Line, the press at times believed that either the Lake Shore or Pennsylvania might be interested in the Valley Line. But the most persistent talk centered on a Wabash purchase. "It is rumored that H. E. Bucklen is dickering with the Wabash Railroad Company in a proposal to connect the Saint Joseph Valley Railway with the Wabash lines at Montpelier, Ohio," reported the *Kendallville Sun* in 1907. "That would give the Wabash a branch to La Grange." A year later the *Standard* raised the question, "Has the Valley Line been sold?" Again Wabash involvement was predicted. "Should the Wabash succeed in securing control of the road, it will be extended east to Montpelier and west to South Bend, giving it terminals that will greatly increase its earning power." For years, rumors of a possible Wabash involvement persisted. Bucklen denied that he wished to liquidate, but as red ink mounted, he might have been disposed to any reasonable offer from the Wabash or another qualified buyer. However, the likelihood of a major steam road taking over the property was remote; there is no evidence that any carrier was seriously interested.[47]

As long as Bucklen committed his wealth to the Valley Line, trains rolled along what had become a seventy-mile interstate operation. Unfortunately for patrons, the railroad began to unravel. On December 30, 1916, a steam-powered extra freight train crashed into the rear of the crowded Brill car No. 171, which had stopped at the Inverness station six miles west of Angola to discharge passengers. Two riders, a woman and her two-year-old daughter, died immediately, another passenger succumbed two weeks later, and there were more than a score who suffered injuries. While the road had maintained a reasonably good safety record, an inquiry by the Interstate Commerce Commission revealed lax procedures. "The investigation of this accident disclosed the fact that the operating practices of this railway are bad. Even the most important rules are disregarded, evidently because of lack of familiarity with them on the part of employees." Yet passengers did not blame the company. As a seriously injured man told the *Elkhart Truth*, "Terrible as this thing is, I don't believe that any one of us harbors resentment against the Valley Line for it. We know too well what H. E. Bucklen has done for us all through this part of the country to go back on him when a wreck such as is liable to happen on any line just happens to strike us." Bucklen did not hear of the tragedy, however; he lay on his sickbed in his Chicago home and died soon afterward from "complications of bladder and stomach trouble." The press reported, "Because of his condition Mr. Bucklen was kept in ignorance of the wreck."[48]

While the financial repercussions that followed the Inverness disaster negatively affected the Valley Line, it was the death of Bucklen on January 10, 1917, that doomed the road. An immediate response, though, was a great sadness expressed by employees. "One of the most beautiful tributes was a broken wheel from the employees of the St. Joe Valley traction line," noted the *Elkhart Truth*. Also, black wreaths were attached to depot doors and pieces of passenger equipment. At the time of Bucklen's burial the railroad came to a halt for ten minutes. This laudation may have been inspired by the stopping of every train on the vast Hill system for five minutes on May 31, 1916, to honor the late founder-builder James J. Hill. The tribute to Bucklen began as pallbearers lowered the casket into the grave, located on the Bucklen farm, "Redfield," outside Elkhart. A telephone connection between the farm and the station in La Grange allowed the Valley Line traffic manager to use the railroad's telephone dispatching system to notify train crews and heads of work gangs when the stoppage should begin.[49]

Some Valley Line employees and others along the road must have suspected that trouble was brewing with Bucklen's passing. Although the Valley Line founder had specified in his will that his railroad assets were to be held in trust for a ten-year period, his three children, including Herbert E. Bucklen Jr., who had become a top Valley Line official, realized that if the railroad continued, the value of the multimillion-dollar estate would be greatly diminished. Still, the road operated, albeit with cuts in service and personnel. Rumors persisted, including a report in the *Electric Railway Journal*, that the railroad would be extended beyond Columbia to bolster freight traffic and that full electrification was in the offing. While these speculations were untrue, forging a Wabash connection would have increased line-haul income. Yet there were no funds for expansion.[50]

What happened was a "friendly" receivership. On December 19, 1917, Judge J. L. Harmon of the Superior Court in Elkhart, upon request of the Bucklen heirs, sought a court-appointed receiver. Herbert Bucklen Jr. assumed that position. "The appointment became necessary because the railway company was without financial support from the estate of Herbert E. Bucklen, its promoter and builder." In order to meet immediate financial needs, which amounted to an estimated $1,300 monthly ($21,600 in 2008 dollars), Bucklen Jr. issued receiver's certificates to maintain service. As with other railroad bankruptcies, these certificates were to be paid before any other liens or liabilities.[51]

The receivership set off alarm bells. "It would be a serious loss to this town and all of the territory touched by the Valley Line," editorialized the *La Grange Standard*. "Those who would lose most would be the shippers, especially the farmers from Shipshewana to Angola." Added the newspaper, "It may become necessary for our people to come to the financial assistance of the road in some way, and even if that need does not present itself, it would be well to give some thought to what the Valley Line has done in behalf of the prosperity of the town and county."[52]

Bucklen Jr. knew that he could not save his father's railroad. The takeover of most carriers, but not the Valley Line, by the U.S. Railroad Administration (USRA) in December 1917 had generally depressed revenues for smaller roads, and management saw no way to enhance essential freight income. The company was also being squeezed by rapidly rising costs, although fortunately scrap metal prices had risen substantially because of the war. On February 22, 1918, Bucklen announced that on March 20, 1918, the property would be sold. An appraisal showed that the railroad, both the steam and electric units, possessed a value of $552,000 ($7.8 million in 2008 dollars). The court subsequently announced that "the road shall be offered for sale for two-thirds of its appraised value as a going concern, but that if it fails to sell, it shall be immediately thereafter be offered for sale as junk." When the bidding took place at the entrance to the Municipal Building in Elkhart, a single offer appeared, but M. K. Frank, a Pittsburgh, Pennsylvania, scrap dealer wanted only the non-electrified section. The bid was rejected. Finally, on April 3, 1918, both the steam and electric portions were sold to Chicago-based Benjamin Harris & Company for $390,000 ($5.5 million in 2008 dollars), somewhat higher than the amount the court had set. Specifically, Harris offered $260,000 for the steam portion and $130,000 for the electric line.[53]

As with the demise of other contemporary railroads, much discussion occurred during the final days about preserving the Valley Line, or at least the trackage between La Grange and Angola, which was considered the most important. There were a series of meetings reminiscent of those that took place about the same time to save the Creston, Winterset & Des Moines from the junk heap. "What we want is the Valley Line to run. We don't care a Billy Sunday who is the owner or operator, and what is the manner and method of operation. Let's all stand by the Valley Line!"[54]

When it appeared that there would be no way to keep the Eastern Division, the owner of the grain elevator in Orland spearheaded a small group that concentrated on maintaining freight service on the fifteen miles between Orland, Mongo, and La Grange. This would allow several shippers to retain a rail connection, allowing freight cars to move through the GR&I interchange at La Grange. "If this road means anything to you, you can save it," became the theme of these several gatherings. And this message brought a positive response. By August 1918 Orland area residents raised about $50,000 ($709,000 in 2008 dollars) and Mongo generated another $3,000 ($42,500 in 2008 dollars). Neither community wanted to revert to inland status.[55]

While discussions occurred on how to keep the Valley Line alive, the Public Service Commission of Indiana, with no interference from the USRA or the court, allowed operations to cease. On April 11, 1918, service ended between Bristol and La Grange. Since the CSB&NI did not want to continue traction operations, at midnight on April 17 the last car from Bristol pulled into Elkhart. The following day the final trains traveled between La Grange and Columbia.[56]

Yet the Valley Line was not completely dead. Although crews from Harris & Company dismantled the trolley overhead and began to lift rails and ties, shippers in Mongo and Orland, with strong community backing, remained active in their efforts to maintain freight service. A successful subscription drive, which ultimately approached $100,000 ($1.41 million in 2008 dollars), and support from politicians, USRA officials, and Pennsylvania Railroad executives led to an agreement with the junk dealer. The track would not be pulled up between La Grange and Orland, preserving service on this portion of the former Valley Line. In October the *Orland Zenith* reported what it believed to be the arrangement: "The people are to raise $117,000 as a subsidy, the Pennsylvania is to take over the road and run it not less than three times a week for a period of twenty-five years, and at the end of that time the road becomes their property."[57]

The details outlined by the Orland editor were not exactly accurate. Yes, local funding of the line segment was part of the final arrangement, the Pennsylvania's GR&I subsidiary entered the picture, and tri-weekly freights became the operational format. But a new company with a grandiose, even silly name, La Grange, Toledo & Eastern Railway (LT&E), emerged. This firm bought the trackage and contracted with the GR&I for service. Trains, however, only plied the nine miles between La Grange and Mongo; the trackage to Orland had become unsafe and repairs were not undertaken. Even though the LT&E received permission to issue $35,000 ($496,000 in 2008 dollars) of first mortgage bonds and $55,000 ($780,000 in 2008 dollars) of common stock that could have rehabilitated the entire property, these financial plans were never implemented. Although GR&I locals continued to serve Mongo until USRA control ended on March 1, 1920, service then stopped. The Pennsylvania System wanted out, and because of dismal revenues the LT&E shut down and soon liquidated its meager assets. This scheme to preserve a portion of the Valley Line had an unhappy ending. It was much different from the fate of the Detroit, Bay City & Western, when in 1925 the Detroit, Caro & Sandusky took over about half of the trackage and continued operations for nearly three decades.[58]

The last chapter of the Bucklen property had been written. Some residents along the line still hoped for a miraculous resurrection. In late 1920 reports circulated that Henry Ford, the motorcar czar, was contemplating the acquisition of the Toledo & Western and the now fully abandoned right-of-way of the Valley Line to reach South Bend and Chicago. Recently, Ford had entered the railroad business with the purchase of the 500-mile Detroit, Toledo & Ironton Railroad. But why he would want a line westward from Toledo is uncertain. The observation of the *Montpelier Leader* that this extension "would provide him with an excellent line to try out his new gasoline operated [railroad] cars" made no sense. Except for the adaptive uses for some former railroad structures, farmers and nature reclaimed the right-of-way.[59]

It is easy to criticize the Bucklen venture. After all, the two units of the St. Joseph Valley Railway lasted for less than fifteen years and except for Elkhart, with a population of 24,777, they served communities with small populations: Bristol (568), Middlebury (600), La Grange (1,772), Mongo (225), Orland (650), and Angola (3,200). Those who have commented on the Valley Line have concluded that it should never have been built, but they miss the point. During the height of interurban mania, the concept of a direct electric link between Chicago and Toledo was not fuzzy thinking. In fact, the Bucklen scheme was much more sensible than a much-discussed contemporary plan to dig a ship canal between Chicago and Toledo. The trackage that was completed filled a void; before the Bucklen road there were several communities that had inadequate or no railroad service. Furthermore, the territory through which the line crossed abounded in agricultural resources and was popular with summer vacationers. "The country is rich, the farms well cultivated, the population quite dense for a rural region, the towns connected thrifty and ambitious," boosterism yes, but true. A variety of commercial betterments followed in the wake of the train service, underscoring again the positive economic impact of twilight-era carriers. Although it had a brief life span, the Valley Line served patrons well; residents thought highly of what its builder had accomplished. "Bucklen was a man of good judgment and built wisely and for the future." Moreover, this wealthy entrepreneur sensed the potential of internal combustion motive power, being a true pioneer in the replacement technologies for steam, a contribution that has been generally ignored. Admittedly, the St. Joseph Valley possessed train-wreck qualities; however, the impact of what witty residents called the "Arnica Salve Line" was hardly insignificant or negligible.[60]

Epilogue

Legacy of Twilight Rails

As these case studies reveal, the boom in twilight railroad projects in the Midwest occurred prior to the zenith of national railroad mileage. Although 1916 was a watershed year for total trackage, construction in the region did not stop, including the opening in 1918 of the Ettrick & Northern, and the expansion somewhat later of the Electric Short Line, reconstituted in the early 1920s as the Minnesota Western.

While excitement and success were part of the experiences of twilight rails in the Midwest, these roads came with some pain. When faced with an insolvent property, supporters at times refused to accept defeat and continued to pour in resources. More dollars were lost. And it was not unusual for owners of securities to see their investments vaporize. Even decades after an abandonment, disappointment and anger might linger. In the 1980s a former resident of Montgomery County, Iowa, whose father was a farmer who had invested in the Atlantic Northern & Southern Railroad, blamed him for "being so stupid and reckless with our money." Her father had believed that the southern division of this latter-day short line, which quickly collapsed, would be both a dependable avenue of transport and a good financial investment. This agrarian and many of his neighbors in the Grant vicinity had gambled on a railroad and lost. Irrespective of the financial outcome, the public usually expressed genuine sadness when a carrier failed. Although the coming of better roads and more dependable automobiles and trucks lessened the blow, shippers might for some time be left without a practical, economical means to meet their transportation needs. Abandonment also caused hardships for employees left jobless. Fortunately, only the Ettrick & Northern of these studies liquidated during the Great Depression, and that affected but a handful of workers. The dismantling of this little pike actually provided some short-term jobs. There can be genuine sympathy for those involved with the least successful roads, although those lines that might be classified as failures did have that initial positive impact on local economies.[1]

In the 1920s, reports spread about the steady and at times sharp contraction of the railroad network. Most spectacular was the demise of interurbans, both in numbers and condition. In 1926, for example, some 689 miles were abandoned, including such relatively large and strategic midwestern roads as the Cleveland, Painesville & Eastern and the Grand Rapids, Holland & Chicago. Many remaining electrics saw a general deterioration of track and rolling stock. "As maintenance declined, the cars caused progressively more damage to the track," noted economists George Hilton and John Due, "and the rougher the track became, the greater the extent to which the cars were pulled apart." Needless to say, investors wanted out of the weakest carriers, and for scores of interurbans twilight became darkness.[2]

At the time that the interurban industry was facing a crisis, steam railroads, whether old, new, large, or small, continued to retrench, occasionally closing. In 1921 *Railway Age* lamented that during the previous year 713 miles of steam railroad track had been lifted, twenty-four miles more than in 1919, "But what is more to the point, some 400 miles more than was constructed during the same period." This report of shutdowns was just the beginning. In 1924 journalists commented extensively on the failure of the 250-mile Chicago, Peoria & St. Louis Railway (CP&StL), a road that served thirty-five cities and towns in western Illinois including Alton, Jacksonville, Peoria, and Springfield. While reaching several important interchanges, the CP&StL was handicapped because it had the heaviest grades and the longest line between competitive points. If the carrier shut down, not only would scores of shippers be left without a railroad connection, but also abandonment would depreciate property values. Even with improved roads, one commentator observed, "Without the railroad, shipments will have to be brought in by truck and this will be extremely difficult, if not impossible, during a considerable part of the year. Many [businesses] will find it necessary to close their doors." While the CP&StL disappeared as a corporation in 1926, portions of the line were saved, being purchased by new or established carriers. Most significantly, the Chicago & Illinois Midland bought the north end between Springfield and Pekin, a scenario paralleling the fate of the Handy Lines.[3]

As years passed, it became apparent that automobiles and trucks traveling along improved roadways offered the public greater flexibility in terms of time and distance. By the late 1920s vehicle ownership throughout the Midwest had become fairly common because of price and reliability. Moreover, gasoline was inexpensive and motoring, at least for automobile owners, could be a pleasant adventure. As highways improved, a host of roadside attractions appeared: filling stations, tourist courts, diners, and the like. "As the owner of an automobile does not ordinarily use his car simply as a matter of economy," noted a railroad official, "this class of competition is one which we can hardly meet." Leisurely automobile touring meant trouble, indeed. Historian Carroll Pursell put it well when he observed that the automobile reinforced "deeply rooted values of individuality, privatism, free choice, and control over one's life." Furthermore, trucks were well-suited for delivering small shipments, and these vehicles did not represent large capital investments. It became practical for an Albia, Iowa, wholesale fruit and vegetable dealer, for example, to use his Reo truck to pick up a load of perishable peaches or strawberries from growers in the Ozarks and not have to rely on a slow, complicated pattern of rail service. Just as railroads had earlier enhanced property values, road development did much the same. As early as 1908 an Illinois newspaper suggested that "wherever good roads have been built, there has been a sharp increase in the value of farm lands which all agree is due to the good roads. The increase ranges from 10 to as high as 50 per cent in some cases, the average being about 20 per cent."[4]

Notwithstanding dramatic changes in intercity transportation, the appearance of independent railroads is a process that has not ended. Most of these steam and then diesel roads have emerged from the unwanted remains of trackage, a process that accelerated rapidly following the "merger madness" of the 1960s and later. By the twenty-first century, there were scores of recently created short lines and longer regional carriers that have been carved from the carcasses of Class I roads, and they frequently have shown impressive profitability, especially when grouped together under a corporate umbrella arrangement.

New line building has also become part of twenty-first century railroading. In recent years construction has centered on tapping natural resources, although usually outside the Midwest. In 2008 a consortium of two Ohio-based energy firms began building a thirty-mile railroad to serve the Signal Peak Mine, located in the Bull Mountain coal fields of Montana, that handled its first coal train in September 2009. This multimillion-dollar project is reminiscent of the considerable mileage built in the 1980s by the Burlington Northern and Chicago & North Western (North Western) railroads in southeastern Wyoming to tap the coal-rich Powder River Basin.[5]

Even in the post–World War II era a variety of construction proposals surfaced. In the late 1940s what was likely the most ridiculous scheme involved a line between Atlanta and Savannah, Georgia, cities that already had a direct connection. E. T. Mitchell, a dreamer from Philadelphia, Pennsylvania, ballyhooed this 229-mile project. But the craziness of the concept, plus carrier and regulator opposition, torpedoed the Mitchell road. Much more sensible,

Some twilight railroads made lasting contributions to the urban landscape, including factories, warehouses, and related facilities, but other improvements diminished in size and importance or disappeared after the railroad declined or failed. When a photographer took this photo of the once-active village of Troxel, Illinois, founded by the Rockford Route, not much was left besides the general store and a few other buildings in July 1960. *Courtesy of Embree Collection, Regional History Center, Northern Illinois University.*

and a distinct possibility, has been the on-again, off-again plan to extend the Dakota, Minnesota & Eastern Railroad (DM&E), a regional carrier consisting mostly of former trackage of the Chicago & North Western in Iowa, Minnesota, and South Dakota. The objective of the DM&E, which began operations in the 1980s and was acquired by the Canadian Pacific Railway in 2007, is to haul Powder River Basin coal by constructing an extension from the West River Country of South Dakota into Wyoming and reconstructing much of its core line to accommodate heavy unit trains.[6]

It is easy to malign an unsuccessful twilight railroad project, whether in the United States or elsewhere. The last important private rail system to be built in Great Britain, the Great Central Railway, experienced financial problems early on and in time most of its trackage, including its London Extension, which opened in 1899, would be relegated to local service or abandoned. "It goes to places that do not need a railway, that never use a railway, that probably do not yet know they have a railway," opined A. G. Macdonell in his 1933 book, *England, Their England.* "It goes to way-side halts where the only passengers are milk-churns. It visits lonely platforms where the only tickets are bought by geese and ducks. It stops in the middle of buttercup meadows to pick up eggs and flowers. It glides past the great pile of willow branches that are maturing to make England's cricket-bats." Added Macdonell, "It is a dreamer among railways, a poet, kindly and absurd and lovely. The Great Central is like that old stream of Asia Minor. It meanders and meanders until at last it reaches, loveliest of English names, the Vale of Aylesbury." Such entertaining commentary was highly exaggerated and really cannot be applied fairly to the eight latter-day roads of the Midwest.[7]

Promoters and backers of twilight rails should not be blamed for building blunders; only historical hindsight provides 20/20 vision. The belief that railroads would retain their dominance indefinitely was widely held. And few, if any, citizens expected the steady and at times sharp population declines in the rural Midwest that took place in the 1920s, 1930s, and later. Although some carriers have been viewed with derision, they were appreciated by their contemporaries and did much that was good. In several cases these twilight roads for years served their on-line customers well and remnants continue to do so today.

Notes

Introduction

1   Howard Elliott, *The Truth about the Railroads* (Boston, Mass.: Houghton Mifflin Company, 1913), xv.

2   *Douglas County Herald* (Ava, Mo.), February 17, 1910.

3   *Clarinda (Iowa) Herald*, January 4, 1912; J. W. Kendrick, "Report on Valuation [of] Iowa & Southwestern Railway," April 15, 1915, John W. Barriger III papers, John W. Barriger III National Railroad Library, St. Louis, Mo., hereafter cited as Kendrick report.

4   Duncan L. Bryant, "The Pumpkin Vine," *Railroad Magazine* 28 (July 1940): 24.

5   Charles Manfred Thompson, *History of the United States: Political, Industrial, Social* (Chicago, Ill.: Benjamin H. Sanborn & Company, 1927), 443; *A Chronology of American Railroads* (Washington, D.C.: Association of American Railroads, 1957), 7; "Era of Railroad Building," *Air Line News* 1 (February 1907): 6; "Twin City–Twin Ports Line of the Soo," *Railway Age Gazette* 52 (April 12, 1912): 942; Richard S. Simons and Francis H. Parker, *Railroads of Indiana* (Bloomington, Ind.: Indiana University Press, 1977), 41.

A good example of late construction took place when the Missouri Pacific in 1925–26 built a fifty-mile extension in southwestern Texas between Raymondville and Monte Cristo and between Faysville and Edinburg. See "We Build More Railroad," *Missouri Pacific Lines Magazine* 3 (June 1926): 17–18, 121.

6   "Railroads Versus Manufacturing, as Development Investments," *Air Line News* 2 (December 1907): 7; *Report of the Public Service Commission of Ohio for the Year 1912* (Springfield, Ohio: Springfield Publishing Company, 1913), 4.

   About the time ex-Governor Larabee made his pronouncement, the miles of railroad operated by receivers had dropped to virtually nothing, 796. This was dramatically different from 1894, the most severe year of national depression, when bankruptcy courts controlled 40,819 miles.

7   *A Chronology of American Railroads*, 7; George W. Hilton and John F. Due, *The Electric Interurban Railways in America* (Stanford, Calif.: Stanford University Press, 1960), 255, 275, 287, 335, 353, 357, 359, 365–69; H. Roger Grant, "Electric Traction Promotion in the South Iowa Coalfields," *The Palimpsest* 58 (January–February 1977): 18–29; William F. Gephart, *Transportation and Industrial Development in the Middle West* (New York: Columbia University, 1909), 231–41.

8   William D. Middleton, *The Interurban Era* (Milwaukee, Wis.: Kalmbach Publishing Company, 1961), 12–13, 16–17; *Hutchinson (Minn.) Leader*, March 21, 1913; *La Grange (Ind.) Standard*, August 27, 1908.

9   Martin Dodge, "The Good Roads Movement," *American Monthly Review of Reviews* 25 (January 1902): 66–72; William H. Thompson, *Transportation in Iowa: A Historical Summary* (Ames, Iowa: Iowa Department of Transportation, 1989), 93; *Red Oak (Iowa) Express*, December 10, 1909.

10 *Clarinda Herald*, December 16, 1909; Michael Kammen, *Mystic Chords of Memory: The Transformation of Tradition in American Culture* (New York: Knopf, 1991), 48.

11 "Through Sleepers from Nome to Cape Horn," *Bulletin of the Pan American Union* 39 (November 1914): 768–71; "Construction Work Begun," *Air Line News* 1 (October 1, 1906): 1.

12 August Derleth, *The Milwaukee Road: Its First Hundred Years* (New York: Creative Age Press, 1948), 178–95; Les Standiford, *Last Train to Paradise: Henry Flagler and the Spectacular Rise and Fall of the Railroad that Crossed an Ocean* (New York: Crown Publishers, 2002).

13 "Electricity Versus Steam," *Air Line News* 6 (April 1912): 11; H. Roger Grant, *The Railroad: The Life Story of a Technology* (Westport, Conn.: Greenwood Publishing Group, 2005), 71–91; *Electric Railway Journal* 48 (September 16, 1916): 517.

14 *Clarinda Herald*, December 9, 1909.

15 "Railroads Are Swamped," *Air Line News* 1 (April 1907): 6.

16 See Richard W. Goldsmith, *Financial Intermediaries in the American Economy Since 1900* (Princeton, N.J.: Princeton University Press, 1958); *Drovers' Telegram* (Kansas City, Mo.), March 23, 1911; *Catskill Mountain News* (Margaretville, N.Y.), January 11, 1907; "The Passing of a Railway Crisis," *Railway Age Gazette* 47 (September 17, 1909): 483.

17 Kendrick report.

18 *Clarinda (Iowa) Journal*, September 25, 1913.

19 Albro Martin, *Enterprise Denied: Origins of the Decline of American Railroads, 1897–1917* (New York: Columbia University Press, 1971); "Railroad Construction in 1914," *Railway Age Gazette* 58 (January 1, 1915): 53.

20 *Clarinda Herald*, January 17, 1918; *Scientific American* 109 (September 6, 1913): 178; James J. Flink, *The Automobile Age* (Cambridge, Mass.: MIT Press, 1988), 33–39; James J. Flink, *The Car Culture* (Cambridge, Mass.: MIT Press, 1975), 67–112.

1. A Road with a Bright Future

1   *A Centennial History of Akron, 1825–1925* (Akron, Ohio: Summit County Historical Society, 1925), 469.

2   Ronald E. Shaw, *Canals for a Nation: The Canal Era in the United States, 1790–1860* (Lexington, Ky.: University Press of Kentucky, 1990), 127–29, 132; Jack Gieck, *A Photo Album of Ohio's Canal Era, 1825–1913* (Kent, Ohio: Kent State University Press, 1992), 53–54, 73–80, 200; H. Roger Grant, *Ohio on the Move: Transportation in the Buckeye State* (Athens, Ohio: Ohio University Press, 2000), 52–57, 63; Jack Gieck, *Early Akron's Industrial Valley: A History of the Cascade Locks* (Kent, Ohio: Kent State University Press, 2008), 5–20; George W. Knepper, *New Lamps for Old: One Hundred Years of Urban Higher Education at the University of Akron* (Akron, Ohio: University of Akron, 1970), 73.

3   Gieck, *A Photo Album of Ohio's Canal Era*, 278–82; Lynn Metzger and Peg Bobel, eds., *Canal Fever: The Ohio & Erie Canal from Waterway to Canal Way* (Kent, Ohio: Kent State University Press, 2009), 209–29.

4   H. Roger Grant, "The Akron, Canton & Youngstown and the Politics of Expansion, 1890–1920," *Proceedings of the Business History Conference* (Second Series, Vol. 3, 1975), 127.

5   John A. Rehor, *The Nickel Plate Story* (Milwaukee, Wis.: Kalmbach, 1965), 106–8; *Akron (Ohio) Beacon Journal*, December 4, 1900.

6   *A Centennial History of Akron*, 470; *Poor's Manual of the Railroads of the United States* (New York: H. V. and H. W. Poor, 1901), 309.

7   George W. Hilton and John F. Due, *The Electric Interurban Railways in America* (Stanford, Calif.: Stanford University Press, 1960), 255, 273; *Electric Railway Journal* 34 (October 2, 1909): 575–76; *Akron Beacon Journal*, February 15, 1901; March 30, 1907; January 27, 1910.

8   *Akron Beacon Journal*, August 21, 1907.

9   *Akron (Ohio) Beacon and Republican*, December 18, 1893; *Akron Beacon Journal*, January 23, 1897; August 21, 1907; *A Centennial History of Akron*, 627–28.

10 George W. Knepper, *Akron: City at the Summit* (Tulsa, Okla: Continental Heritage Press, 1981), 79; Michael J. French, *The U.S. Tire Industry: A History* (Boston: Twayne Publishers, 1991), 21–35; Daniel Nelson, *American Rubber Workers & Organized Labor, 1900–1941* (Princeton, N.J.: Princeton University Press, 1988), 16; *Akron Beacon Journal*, March 5, 1907; January 1, 1910.

11 David D. Van Tassel and John J. Grabowski, eds., *The Encyclopedia of Cleveland History* (Bloomington, Ind.: Indiana University Press, 1987), xxix–xliii.

12 *Akron Beacon Journal*, May 10, 1901; Herbert T. O. Blue, *History of Stark County Ohio* (Chicago: S. J. Clarke, 1928), 346–47, 357; C. Harold McCollam, *The Brick and Tile Industry in Stark County, 1809–1976* (Canton, Ohio: Stark County Historical Society, 1976), 13.

13 McCollam, *The Brick and Title Industry in Stark County*.

14 George Higley, *Youngstown: An Intimate History* (Youngstown, Ohio: United Printing Co., 1953), 92–96; Frederick J. Blue et al., *Mahoning Memories: A History of Youngstown and Mahoning County* (Virginia Beach, Va.: The Donning Company, 1995), 93–95, 119; Howard C. Aley, *A Heritage to Share: The Bicentennial History of Youngstown and Mahoning County, Ohio* (Youngstown, Ohio: Bicentennial Com-

mission of Youngstown and Mahoning County, Ohio, 1975), 196; William D. Jenkins, *Steel Valley Klan: The Ku Klux Klan in Ohio's Mahoning Valley* (Kent, Ohio: Kent State University Press, 1990), 17–19; *Akron Beacon Journal*, August 13, 1907.

15 Higley, *Youngstown*, 101–4; Hilton and Due, *The Electric Interurban Railways in America*, 273–74.

16 William S. Snyder, *The Rattlesnake & The Ramsey: The History of the Lorain, Ashland & Southern Railroad* (Ashland, Ohio: Custaloga Press, 2004), 128–31.

17 Ibid., 131.

18 Ibid., 132.

19 Ibid., 132–33. In 1901, the Mansfield Railway, Light & Power Company opened a twelve-mile interurban between Mansfield and Shelby, presumably incorporating some of the French right-of-way and grade.

20 Ibid., 134; *Akron Beacon Journal*, March 26, 1901.

21 Snyder, *The Rattlesnake & The Ramsey*, 135–36; Grant, "The Akron, Canton & Youngstown and the Politics of Expansion," 127.

22 *Akron Beacon Journal*, April 4, 1901.

23 *Summit County Beacon* (Akron, Ohio), August 29, 1901; H. Roger Grant, "Frank Augustus Seiberling," in John A. Garraty, ed., *Dictionary of American Biography, Supplement Five, 1951–1955* (New York: Charles Scribner's Sons, 1977), 617–18.

24 Snyder, *The Rattlesnake & The Ramsey*, 137–38; *Summit County Beacon*, September 26, 1901.

25 Snyder, *The Rattlesnake & The Ramsey*, 145–47; Grant, "The Akron, Canton & Youngstown and the Politics of Expansion," 127; *Akron Beacon Journal*, July 29, 1907; August 17, 1907; H. Roger Grant, *"Follow the Flag": A History of the Wabash Railroad Company* (DeKalb, Ill.: Northern Illinois University Press, 2004), 95–96.

26 Synder, *The Rattlesnake & The Ramsey*, 145, 148.

27 *Poor's Manual of the Railroads of the United States* (New York: Poor's Railroad Manual Company, 1906), 434; Synder, *The Rattlesnake & The Ramsey*, 150; *Akron Beacon Journal*, March 14, 1907.

28 Synder, *The Rattlesnake & The Ramsey*, 166–68, 352; *Akron Beacon Journal*, November 22, 1907; January 13, 1908.

29 Synder, *The Rattlesnake & The Ramsey*, 169–73; Grant, *"Follow the Flag,"* 105; *Akron Beacon Journal*, January 28, 1907; December 4, 1907.

30 Grant, "The Akron, Canton & Youngstown and the Politics of Expansion," 131; *Akron Beacon Journal*, March 23, 1907; March 26, 1907; December 19, 1907.

31 *Poor's Manual of the Railroads of the United States* (New York: Poor's Railroad Manual Company, 1913), 618; *Akron Beacon Journal*, June 28, 1907; August 1, 1907.

32 *Akron Beacon Journal*, April 8, 1907; August 17, 1907; December 19, 1907; October 17, 1908; Grant, "The Akron, Canton & Youngstown and the Politics of Expansion," 132.

33 *Akron Beacon Journal*, October 17, 1908.

34 Ibid., July 22, 1907.

35 Ibid., December 23, 1908; January 17, 1910; July 7, 1911; December 8, 1911; "Tentative Valuation Report on the Property of the Akron, Canton & Youngstown Railway Company, as of June 30, 1918," Interstate Commerce Commission, Valuation Docket No. 650, 17, hereafter cited as ICC Valuation Docket No. 650.

36 *Akron Beacon Journal,* September 22, 1908; October 5, 1908; December 1, 1908; December 26, 1908.

37 Ibid., December 26, 1908.

38 Ibid., December 10, 1908; December 26, 1908; January 30, 1909; March 23, 1909; March 24, 1909; March 30, 1909; April 19, 1909; May 12, 1909; May 25, 1909.

39 *Electric Railway Journal* 35 (May 21, 1910): 926; ibid. 38 (December 9, 1911): 1222.

40 Grant, "The Akron, Canton & Youngstown and the Politics of Expansion," 132; ICC Valuation Docket No. 650, 9.

41 Grant, "The Akron, Canton & Youngstown and the Politics of Expansion," 132; ICC Valuation Docket No. 650, 1, 4, 9; "Interstate Commerce Commission Bureau of Valuation: Engineering Report upon the Akron, Canton & Youngstown Railway Company Showing Cost of Reproduction New and Cost of Reproduction Less Depreciation as of June 30, 1918"; *A Centennial History of Akron,* 469–70; *Akron Beacon Journal,* July 19, 1909; H. Roger Grant and William D. Edson, "The Akron, Canton & Youngstown Railroad: Historical Overview and Locomotive Roster," *Railroad History* 172 (Spring 1995): 53; *Official Railway Equipment Register* 38 (April 1913): 58; *Poor's Manual of the Railroads of the United States* (New York: Poor's Railroad Manual Company, 1912), 2827; *Report of the Public Service Commission of Ohio* (Springfield, Ohio: Springfield Publishing Company, 1913), 902. "Akron, Canton & Youngstown Railway Company," March 31, 1936, in John W. Barringer III papers, Box 1, Series 1, Mercantile Library, St. Louis, Mo., hereafter cited as AC&Y report.

42 *Poor's Manual of the Railroads of the United States* (New York: Poor's Railroad Manual Company, 1915), 543; *Poor's Manual of the Railroads of the United States* (New York: Poor's Railroad Manual Company, 1917), 1107; AC&Y report.

43 Grant, "The Akron, Canton & Youngstown and the Politics of Expansion," 132–33; *Report of the Public Utilities Commission of Ohio for the Year 1913* (Springfield, Ohio: Springfield Publishing Company, 1914), 85.

44 Grant, "The Akron, Canton & Youngstown and the Politics of Expansion," 133.

45 See James D. Johnson, "A History of the Midland Continental Railroad Company, 1906–1950" (master's thesis, University of North Dakota, 1952).

46 H. Roger Grant, "Frank A. Seiberling and the Formative Years of the Midland Continental Railroad, 1912–1920," *North Dakota History* 43 (Fall 1976): 28–29.

47 Ibid., 30.

48 Ibid., 30–36; Nelson, *American Rubber Workers & Organized Labor,* 17.

49 H. Roger Grant, "Land Development in the Middle West: The Case of the Akron, Canton & Youngstown Railroad, 1913–1925," *The Old Northwest* 1 (December 1975): 362.

50 Ibid., 362–63.

51 Ibid., 363.

52 Ibid.

53 Ibid., 365; Knepper, *Akron,* 105; *Akron Beacon Journal,* June 1, 1911; Marlene Ginaven, *Not For Us Alone* (Akron, Ohio: Stan Hywet Hall Foundation, 1985), 1–2; *Poor's Manual of Railroads* (New York: Poor's Publishing Company, 1922), 1263.

54 Grant and Edson, "The Akron, Canton & Youngstown Railroad," 51; Grant, "The Akron, Canton & Youngstown and the Politics of Expansion," 133.

55 *Poor's Manual of Railroads* (1922), 1262.

56 Grant, "Land Development in the Middle West," 365–66.

57 Ibid., 368–69; Grant, "Frank Augustus Seiberling," 618.

58 *Electric Railway Journal* 48 (July 22, 1916): 166; Grant, "The Akron, Canton & Youngstown Railroad and the Politics of Expansion," 133. When the AC&Y took control of the Northern Ohio, it obtained the one-fourth interest that the Northern Ohio held in the Akron & Barberton Belt Railroad Company. The B&O, Erie, and PRR also each owned a 25 percent interest in the Belt Line's common stock.

59 Knepper, *Akron*, 103; *Wall Street Journal*, November 17, 1922; January 15, 1923; Grant, "The Akron, Canton & Youngstown Railroad and the Politics of Expansion," 134.

60 H. P. Faxon, "The Railroad That 'Holds the Pass,'" *The Annalist* 25 (March 2, 1925): 633.

61 Time Table No. 6, Akron, Canton & Youngstown Railway–Northern Ohio Railway, August 29, 1920; Time Table No. 14, Akron, Canton & Youngstown Railway–Northern Ohio Railway, September 1, 1926; Richard J. Cook, "Ohio Mixed Train," *Railroad Magazine* 56 (December 1951): 34–39.

62 *Nineteenth Annual Report of the Akron, Canton & Youngstown Railway Company–The Northern Ohio Railway Company* (Akron, Ohio: Akron, Canton & Youngstown Railway, 1932), 1; *Commercial & Financial Chronicle*, April 8, 1933; *Wall Street Journal*, April 4, 1933; August 20, 1938; *Traffic World* 59 (May 22, 1937): 1126; Grant and Edson, "The Akron, Canton & Youngstown Railroad," 51; *1944 Annual Report of the Akron, Canton & Youngstown Railroad Company* (Akron, Ohio: Akron, Canton & Youngstown Railroad Company, 1945); *Moody's Manual of Investments: Railroad Securities* (New York: Moody's Investors Service, 1948), 9–16.

63 *Moody's Manual of Investments, 1948*, 15; Grant and Edson, "The Akron, Canton & Youngstown Railroad," 52–53, 61.

64 "Erie and Erie Lackawanna in the Sterling, Akron, Kent, Ravenna Corridor," *The Diamond* 22 (2008): 12; "Locomotives of the Akron, Canton & Youngstown," *Railroad Magazine* 65 (February 1955): 46; Grant and Edson, "The Akron, Canton & Youngstown Railroad," 52, 61; H. Roger Grant and Daniel Nelson, "Alva W. Hochberg Oral History," August 14, 1973, American History Research Center, The University of Akron, Akron, Ohio, hereafter cited as Hockberg Oral History.

65 Hockberg Oral History.

66 Ibid.; *The Story of Riverlake Belt Conveyor Lines, Inc.* (n.p., n.d.); *Wall Street Journal*, March 14, 1949.

67 *Wall Street Journal*, January 11, 1962; Gus Welty, ed., *Era of the Giants: The New Railroad Merger Movement* (Omaha, Neb.: Simmons-Boardman Publishing Corporation, 1982), 89; George H. Drury, compiler, *The Historical Guide to North American Railroads* (Milwaukee, Wis.: Kalmbach, 1985), 15; *Traffic World* 120 (December 12, 1964): 105; Grant and Edson, "The Akron, Canton & Youngstown Railroad," 51–52.

68 Matt Van Hattem, "Stealing Beauty [Wheeling & Lake Erie Railway]," *Trains* 68 (July 2008): 38; Scott A. Hartley, "From Light Weight to Heavy Duty [Wheeling & Lake Erie Railway]," ibid., 58.

2. Crazy Willie & Dandy Molly

1   Ben Hur Wilson, "Abandoned Railroads in Iowa," *The Iowa Journal of History and Politics* 26 (January 1928): 3–64; William H. Thompson, *Transportation in Iowa: A Historical Survey* (Ames, Iowa: Iowa Department of Transportation, 1989), 69–77, 83–85.

2   *Forty-First Annual Report of the Board of Railroad Commissioners for the Year Ending December 2, 1918* (Des Moines, Iowa: State Printer, 1918), v, viii; *A Chronology of American Railroads* (Washington, D.C.: Association of American Railroads, 1957), 7; Don L. Hofsommer, *Steel Trails of Hawkeyeland: Iowa's Railroad Experience* (Bloomington, Ind.: Indiana University Press, 2005), 64–65; Peter Weller and Charles Franzen, *Remembering the Southern Iowa Railway* (Washington, Iowa: Privately Printed, 1992), 4–5, 14; "Electrification of Steam Road Results in Service and Success," *Electric Traction* 15 (May 1919): 290–93.

3   George W. Hilton and John F. Due, *The Electric Interurban Railways in America* (Stanford, Calif.: Stanford University Press, 1960), 3–44; H. Roger Grant, "Electric Traction Promotion in the South Iowa Coalfields," *The Palimpsest* 58 (January–February 1977), 18–29; *Current-Press* (College Springs, Iowa), May 5, 1904.

4   Hilton and Due, *The Electric Interurban Railways in America*, 363–65; *The Official Guide of the Railways* (New York: National Railroad Publication Company, June 1904), 683, 712, 732.

5   *Atlas of Madison County, Iowa* (Philadelphia, Pa.: Harrison & Warner, 1875); *A. T. Andreas Illustrated Historical Atlas of the State of Iowa* (Chicago: Lakeside Press, 1875); *History of Madison County, Iowa* (Des Moines, Iowa: Union Historical Society, 1879), 388–89; *Macksburg and Neighbors* (n.p., n.d.), Book 1, 175; *Union County Iowa History* (Creston, Iowa: Union County Historical Society, 1981), 12.

6   George A. Ide, *History of Union County, Iowa* (Chicago: S. J. Clarke, 1908), 51.

7   *Winterset (Iowa) Madisonian*, January 23, 1908; *Macksburg (Iowa) Independent*, May 8, 1919.

8   *Winterset Madisonian*, February 27, 1908; March 5, 1908.

9   *Des Moines (Iowa) Register and Leader*, September 27, 1908. Ex-Governor Shaw later became heavily involved in the financial affairs of the Atlantic Northern & Southern Railroad, a twilight Iowa carrier that struggled nearly as much as the CW&DM.

10 *Creston (Iowa) Semi-Weekly Advertiser*, January 19, 1909.

11 Ibid.

12 *Des Moines (Iowa) Capital*, March 23, 1909.

13 *Winterset Madisonian*, April 8, 1909; July 1, 1909; *Electric Railway Journal* 34 (July 3, 1909): 57.

14 *Winterset Madisonian*, July 8, 1909; *Des Moines (Iowa) Register and Leader*, July 20, 1909; *Creston Semi-Weekly Advertiser*, July 13, 1909; *Electric Railway Journal* 34 (September 18, 1909): 450; ibid. 34 (October 23, 1909): 925; ibid. 37 (March 18, 1911): 483; ibid. (November 4, 1911): 1013; *Railway World* 55 (October 13, 1911): 867; *Creston City and Union County Directory* (Des Moines, Iowa: R. L. Polk & Company, 1913), 65.

In 1910 the leadership of the company suffered when lightning struck and killed Jerry Wilson (1842–1910), who farmed thirteen hundred acres west of Macksburg. Yet the Wilson family continued to support the road, and according to one source "is largely responsible for the fact that a railroad has been extended into Macksburg." *History of Madison County, Iowa, and Its People* (Chicago: Clarke Publishing Company, 1915), 3, 138–43.

15 *Winterset Madisonian*, October 7, 1909; Wilson, "Abandoned Railroads of Iowa," 23–25; *Thirty-Eighth Annual Report of the Board of Railroad Commissioners for the Year Ending December 6, 1915* (Des Moines, Iowa: State Printer, 1915), 62–63; *Creston Semi-Weekly Advertiser*, December 29, 1910; H. Roger Grant, *"Follow the Flag": A History of the Wabash Railroad Company* (DeKalb, Ill.: Northern Illinois University Press, 2004), 91; *Clarinda (Iowa) Journal*, September 5, 1912; *Red Oak (Iowa) Express*, September 6, 1912.

A portion of the projected AN&S would be built by the Judd & Ross company and so would the Clarinda and Blanchard, Iowa, line of the Iowa & Southwestern Railway (I&SW). That short line, whose history closely paralleled that of the CW&DM, was finished on December 30, 1911, although the company did not operate fully until mid-1912. In 1917 the bankrupt I&SW ended operations and the line was later dismantled after a failed effort to save part of the trackage between Blanchard and College Springs.

16 *Clarinda (Iowa) Herald*, November 18, 1909.

17 *Winterset Madisonian*, January 27, 1910; September 29, 1910.

18 Diane Burdette, Office of Iowa Secretary of State, to author, February 6, 2008, hereafter cited as Burdette letter; *Articles of Incorporation of the Creston, Winterset and Des Moines Railroad Company*, Book C-5, 241; *Annual Report of the Creston, Winterset & Des Moines R. R. Co. to the Interstate Commerce Commission of the United States for the Year Ended June 30, 1915*, 1, Interstate Commerce Commission Records, Record Group 134, National Archives and Records Administration, College Park, Md., hereafter cited as *1915 ICC Annual Report; Creston (Iowa) Weekly Advertiser*, July 20, 1911; September 21, 1911; *Winterset Madisonian*, October 5, 1911.

19 *Winterset Madisonian*, January 31, 1912.

20 Ibid., June 12, 1912; August 7, 1912.

21 Ibid., August 7, 1912; *Page County Democrat* (Clarinda, Iowa), August 22, 1912; *1915 ICC Annual Report*.

22 *Creston (Iowa) Plain Dealer*, October 12, 1912; [Map] *Board of [Iowa] Railroad Commissioners* (Chicago, Ill., 1915).

23 *Creston Plain Dealer*, October 12, 1912; *Poor's Manual of the Railroads of the United States* (New York: Poor's Railroad Manual Company, 1915), 1990; *Official Railway Equipment Register* 30 (January 1915): 719.

24 *Winterset Madisonian*, November 6, 1912; November 20, 1912.

25 Ibid., December 25, 1912; January 1, 1913; January 8, 1913.

26 Ibid., January 8, 1913; January 22, 1913; *1915 ICC Annual Report*.

27 *Creston (Iowa) Daily Advertiser*, July 7, 1913; *Winterset Madisonian*, February 26, 1913; *Russell's Railway Guide* (Cedar Rapids, Iowa: Russell's Railway Guide Company, November 1913), 47.

28 *Creston (Iowa) Morning American*, September 28, 1913.

29 *Creston (Iowa) Advertiser-Gazette*, October 8, 1913; October 10, 1913.

30 *Creston Morning American*, September 2, 1913; November 21, 1913; November 30, 1913; *Thirty-Sixth Annual Report of the Board of Railroad Commissioners for the Year Ending December 1, 1913* (Des Moines, Iowa: State Printer, 1913), 426–29.

31 Interview with Ralph Breakenridge, Macksburg, Iowa, August 24, 2007, hereafter cited as Ralph Breakenridge interview; H. Roger Grant, ed., *Iowa Railroads: The Essays of Frank P. Donovan, Jr.* (Iowa City, Iowa: University of Iowa Press, 2000), 222; *Decisions of the Interstate Commerce Commission of the United States, No. 8936* (Washington, D.C., 1918), 377–78; *Macksburg Independent*, October 26, 1916.

32 *Winterset Madisonian*, April 16, 1913.

33 *Thirty-Sixth Annual Report of the Board of Railroad Commissioners*, 340–41; *1915 ICC Annual Report; History of Madison County Iowa and Its People* (Chicago: S. J. Clarke, 1915), I, 355.

34 *Creston Advertiser-Gazette*, January 2, 1915.

35 *Thirty-Eighth Annual Report of the Board of Railroad Commissioners for the Year Ending December 6, 1915* (Des Moines, Iowa: State Printer, 1915), 256; *1915 ICC Annual Report; Poor's Manual of Railroads* (New York: Poor's Railroad Manual Company, 1918), 1331. The financial difficulties that the CW&DM encountered did not deter a group of Creston businessmen in early 1915 from launching the Creston Connecting Railway. The CW&DM model would be followed. "The railroad will be run by steam, electricity, gas, gasoline, or any motive power." This projected dozen-mile road would provide Creston, still dominated by the Burlington, with another outlet, a connection to the southeast with the Great Western at Arispe. The Creston Connecting Railway, resembling several others in the area including the Red Oak & North Eastern Railroad, was stillborn. *Red Oak Express*, May 28, 1915.

36 *Macksburg Independent*, August 24, 1916; August 31, 1916.

37 Ibid., September 9, 1916.

38 Ibid., October 5, 1916.

39 Ibid., October 12, 1916.

40 Ibid., November 9, 1916.

41 *Annual Report of the Creston, Winterset & Des Moines Railroad Co. to the Interstate Commerce Commission for the Year Ended 31, 1917*, Interstate Commerce Commission Records, Record Group 134, National Archives and Records Administration, College Park, Md.; *Fortieth Annual Report of the Board of Railroad Commissioners for the Year Ending December 3, 1917* (Des Moines, Iowa: State Printer, 1917), 405.

42 *Macksburg Independent*, May 17, 1917; June 26, 1917.

43 Ibid., June 7, 1917; March 18, 1918; August 22, 1918.

44 Ibid., September 5, 1918; October 31, 1918. Because of high wartime scrap prices and patriotism, small railroads, both steam and electric, fell into the hands of metal dealers, including the thirty-five-mile Chicago, Anamosa & Northern Railway in eastern Iowa. See Dan Kelliher and Frances Davis, "Buys Whole Railroads to Junk'em," *Railroad Man's Magazine* 35 (April 1918): 547–56.

45 *Macksburg Independent*, November 14, 1918; December 12, 1918.

46 Ibid., December 19, 1918; October 9, 1919; November 6, 1919; November 27, 1919; April 8, 1920.

47 Burdette letter; *Macksburg Independent*, May 20, 1920; June 17, 1920.

48 *Macksburg Independent,* December 12, 1918; December 18, 1919.

49 Ibid., November 7, 1918; May 15, 1919.

50 *Creston Morning American*, October 21, 1913; *Macksburg Independent*, August 3, 1916; October 9, 1919; *Winterset Madisonian*, June 15, 1911.

51 Richard C. Overton, *Burlington Route: A History of the Burlington Lines* (New York: Knopf, 1965), 310–18; H. Roger Grant, *The Corn Belt Route: A History of the Chicago Great Western Railroad Company* (DeKalb, Ill.: Northern Illinois University Press, 1984), 89–92; William Edward Hayes, *Iron Road to Empire: The History of 100 Years of Progress of the Rock Island Lines* (New York: Simmons-Boardman, 1953), 200–205.

52 *Macksburg Independent*, January 8, 1920; interview with Georgena Breakenridge, Macksburg, Iowa, August 24, 2007.

53 Ralph Breakenridge interview.

Spaulding-area residents recalled that the CW&DM had a slightly different nickname, "Weary Willie." *Union County Iowa History*, 12.

3. The Handy Lines

1 *A Chronology of American Railroads* (Washington, D.C.: Association of American Railroads, 1957), 7.

The Michigan Railroad Commission did not count railroads that were not common carriers, and so exact mileage in the state is not known.

2 George W. Hilton and John F. Due, *The Electric Interurban Railways in America* (Stanford, Calif.: Stanford University Press, 1960), 287–89.

3 The counties that are usually included in the Thumb Country of Michigan are Huron, Lapeer, St. Clair, Sanilac, and Tuscola. See Gerald Schultz, *A Brief History of Michigan's Thumb* (Elkton, Mich., 1964).

4 *Tuscola County Advertiser* (Caro, Mich.), October 27, 1922.

5 "Descendants of Thomas Handy," manuscript in the Collection of the Bay County Historical Society–Historical Museum of Bay County, Bay City, Mich.; *Bay City (Mich.) Times-Tribune*, October 23, 1922; *Bay City (Mich.) Tribune*, January 31, 1907; *West Bay City Directory for 1890–1891* (Detroit, Mich.: R. L. Polk & Company, 1891), 84; *West Bay City Directory for 1897* (Detroit, Mich.: R. L. Polk & Company, 1897), 105.

6 Jeremy W. Kilar, *Bay City Logbook: An Illustrated History* (St. Louis, Mo.: G. Bradley Publishing, 1996), 34; Leon Katzinger, *Bay City, 1900–1940, in Vintage Postcards* (Chicago: Arcadia Publishing, 2002), 7.

7 Katzinger, *Bay City, 1900–1940*, 41, 44; George E. Butterfield, ed., *Bay City Past and Present* (Bay City, Mich., 1918), 157–58; Jeremy W. Kilar, *Michigan Lumbertowns: Lumbermen and Laborers in Saginaw, Bay City, and Muskegon, 1870–1905* (Detroit, Mich.: Wayne State University Press, 1990), 294; "Detroit, Bay City & Western

Railroad Company" (Chicago: Lawrence Mills & Company, 1916), 3, hereafter cited as Mills & Company prospectus.

8 *Bay City Times-Tribune*, October 23, 1922; *Polk's 1911 Bay City Directory* (Detroit, Mich.: R. L. Polk & Company, 1911), 412. According to Michigan railroad historian Graydon Meints, "The Pere Marquette obtained stock control and leased [the H&W] on 6 August 1903. I've never found whether the PM merged the H&W or continued the lease of it until abandonment." Graydon Meints to author, October 8, 2008.

9 *Poor's Manual of the Railroads of the United States* (New York: Poor's Railroad Manual Company, 1909), 496; *Bay City Times-Tribune*, October 24, 1922; Irl L. Baguley, "The Story of the Detroit, Bay City & Western Railroad Company, 1908–1925," (1976), copy in Indianfields Public Library, Caro, Mich.

10 *Bay City Times-Tribune*, October 24, 1922.

11 *Railway Age* 43 (May 24, 1907): 819; Meints to author, October 8, 2008.

12 *Tuscola County Advertiser*, January 23, 1910; George N. Fuller, ed., *Historic Bay County* (New York: National Historical Association, 1924), 63; John M. Kenn, "The Saint Clair River Railroad Tunnel," *Inland Seas* 31 (Fall 1975): 175–85; Jim and Dwayne Anderson, "Unseen Wonder of the World: The St. Clair Railroad Tunnel," *Chronicle* 19 (Summer 1983): 8–19; Omar Lavallee and Raymond F. Corley, "The Grand Trunk Railway: A Look at the Principal Components," *Railroad History* 147 (Autumn 1992): 28; *Bay City Times-Tribune*, October 24, 1922.

13 Augustus H. Gansser, ed., *History of Bay County, Michigan and Representative Citizens* (Chicago: Richmond & Arnold, 1905), 236; U.S. Senate, *Production and Commercial Movement of Sugar* (1906), 59th Congress, 1st Session, Document 250; "Detroit, Bay City & Western Railroad Company," 3.

14 George W. Hilton, *American Narrow Gauge Railroads* (Stanford, Calif.: Stanford University Press, 1990), 424–26; Paul Wesley Ivey, *The Pere Marquette Railroad Company* (Lansing, Mich.: Michigan Historical Commission, 1919), 373–76; Frank A. Kirkpatrick, "The Saginaw, Tuscola & Huron: An Early Railroad of the Michigan Thumb," *Michigan History* 52 (1968): 196–217.

15 *Railway Age* 43 (October 21, 1907): 1194; *Tuscola County Advertiser*, April 1, 1910; April 22, 1910.

16 *Tuscola County Advertiser*, December 10, 1909; April 1, 1910; June 17, 1910; March 17, 1911. The Handys made several amendments to the original articles of association, noting their building intentions. A 1913 amendment set Wilmot as the terminus, a 1915 amendment listed Sandusky, and amendments in 1916 first named Peck and then Port Huron.

17 Ibid., August 19, 1910; September 16, 1910; "Detroit, Bay City & Western Railroad," n.d., memorandum in Pliny Fisk Collection, John W. Barringer III National Railroad Library at the Mercantile Library, St. Louis, Mo.

18 *Fifth Annual Report of the Michigan Railroad Commission for the Year Ending December 31, 1911* (Lansing, Mich.: State Printers, 1912), 90; *Tuscola County Advertiser*, November 15, 1911.

19 Baguley, "The Story of the Detroit, Bay City & Western Railroad Company"; *Tuscola County Advertiser*, January 27, 1911; January 10, 1913; December 26, 1979.

20 *Tucsola County Advertiser*, March 10, 1911; March 21, 1913.

21 Ibid., September 30, 1910; October 14, 1910; February 10, 1911.

22 William D. Edson, "Locomotives of the Grand Trunk Railway," *Railroad History* 147 (Autumn 1982): 96, 156; *Tuscola County Advertiser*, December 16, 1910; Interstate Commerce Commission, Division of Valuation, Central District, "Detroit, Bay City & Western R.R." (June 30, 1918), hereafter cited as ICC Valuation of DBC&W; "Detroit, Bay City & Western RR., Detroit, Caro & Sandusky RR," *Midwest Railroader and Roster Journal* (August–September 1964): 18.

23 "Detroit, Bay City & Western Railroad Co.," *Official Railway Equipment Register* 28 (April 1913): 427; "Detroit, Bay City & Western Railroad Co.," *Official Railway Equipment Register* 36 (May 1921): 443.

24 *Tuscola County Advertiser*, March 17, 1911; November 3, 1911; Leslie E. Arndt, *The Bay County Story: Memoirs of the County's 125 Years* (Detroit, Mich.: Harlo Printing, 1982), 205.

25 *Tuscola County Advertiser*, August 25, 1911; April 19, 1912; December 6, 1912; October 17, 1913. Soon after the DBC&W reached Akron, residents of Akron Township and adjoining Fairgrove Township voted overwhelmingly to incorporate their community, "advancing [Akron] to a proper place among Michigan villages." *Tuscola County Advertiser*, September 23, 1910; December 12, 1910. The Akron townsite had been platted in 1882. See Walter Romig, *Michigan Place Names* (Detroit, Mich.: Wayne State University Press, 1986), 13.

26 "Detroit, Bay City & Western Railroad"; *Tuscola County Advertiser*, March 31, 1911; September 1, 1911; November 29, 1912.

27 *Tuscola County Advertiser*, June 23, 1911.

28 Ibid., March 25, 1910; G. R. Stevens, *Canadian National Railways: Towards the Inevitable, 1896–1922* (Toronto, Ontario: Clarke, Irwin & Company, 1962), 249–54; "The 'Titanic' Disaster," *Railway Age Gazette* 52 (April 19, 1912): 891; Don L. Hofsommer, *Grand Trunk Corporation: Canadian National Railways in the United States, 1971–1992* (East Lansing, Mich.: Michigan State University Press, 1995), 16, 18–21.

29 *Tuscola County Advertiser*, December 16, 1910; November 3, 1911.

30 Baguley, "The Story of the Detroit, Bay City & Western Railroad Company, 1908–1925."

31 George H. Burgess and Miles C. Kennedy, *Centennial History of the Pennsylvania Railroad Company* (Philadelphia, Pa.: Pennsylvania Railroad, 1949), 538–40.

32 Mills & Company prospectus; *Tuscola County Advertiser*, November 8, 1912.

33 *Tuscola County Advertiser*, May 30, 1913; *Railway Age Gazette* 55 (November 28, 1913): 1004.

34 *Tuscola County Advertiser*, November 7, 1913; December 19, 1913; Romig, *Michigan Place Names*, 149.

35 *Tuscola County Advertiser*, October 25, 1912; January 3, 1913; ICC Valuation of DBC&W.

36 *Tuscola County Advertiser*, August 8, 1913.

37 Ibid., December 19, 1913.

38 *Poor's Manual of the Railroads of the United States* (New York: Poor's Railroad Manual Company, 1915), 658.

39 *Population, 1920 Vol. I* (Washington, D.C.: Department of Commerce, 1921), 467; *Railway Age Gazette* 55 (November 28, 1913): 1004.

40 *Railway Age Gazette* 59 (November 12, 1915): 922; *Tenth Annual Report of the Michigan Railroad Commission for the Year Ending December 31, 1916* (Lansing, Mich.: State Printers, 1917), 5.

41 *Tenth Annual Report of the Michigan Railroad Commission*, 46–47.

42 Ibid., 47.

43 *The Official Guide of the Railways* (New York: National Railway Publication Company, May 1917), 581.

44 Mills & Company prospectus, 3; *Tuscola County Advertiser*, April 15, 1915; LeRoy Barnett, *A Drive Down Memory Lane: The Named State and Federal Highways of Michigan* (Allegan Forest, Mich.: Priscilla Press, 2004), 111–12.

45 William N. Boyd, "Historical Record of Construction of the Port Huron & Detroit Railroad," n.d., in possession of G. Y. Duffy Jr., Port Huron, Mich., hereafter cited as PH&D History; Romig, *Michigan Place Names*, 356; *Poor's Manual of Railroads* (New York: Poor's Publishing Company, 1920), 2122.

46 PH&D History; Jack E. Schramm and William H. Henning, *When Eastern Michigan Rode the Rails, II: The Rapid Railway and Detroit-Port Huron by Rail-Ship-Bus* (Glendale, Calif.: Interurban Press, 1986), 121, 175–76.

47 PH&D History.

48 *Eleventh Annual Report of the Michigan Railroad Commission for the Year Ending December 31, 1917* (Fort Wayne, Ind.: Fort Wayne Printing Company [contractors for Michigan State Printing and Binding], 1919), 97.

49 *Bay City Times-Tribune*, October 23, 1922; Schramm and Henning, *When Eastern Michigan Rode the Rails, II*, 176; PH&D History.

50 Schramm and Henning, *When Eastern Michigan Rode the Rails, II.*, 120–21, 176–77.

51 Ibid., 177.

52 *Wall Street Journal*, August 24, 1921; *Tuscola County Advance*, March 25, 1921.

53 *Bay City Times-Tribune*, January 1, 1922; October 23, 1922; *Tuscola County Advertizer*, January 13, 1922; *Cass City (Mich.) Chronicle*, October 27, 1922. The receivership for the DBC&W officially began on September 29, 1922.

    For many Bay City residents Thomas Handy would be remembered for the land that he donated for construction of Thomas L. Handy Junior High School, later Thomas L. Handy High School, located on Handy Street. In 1990 the school board closed this large structure.

54 *Bay City Times-Tribune*, October 2, 1922; *Tuscola County Advertiser*, October 6, 1922.

55 *Tuscola County Advertiser*, October 7, 1921; January 26, 1923; February 16, 1923; Baguley, "The Story of the Detroit, Bay City & Western Railroad Company."

56 *Tuscola County Advertiser*, January 4, 1924; January 25, 1924.

57 *Bondholders' Protective Agreement, Dated October 2, 1922, of Detroit, Bay City and Western Railroad Company; The Official Guide of the Railways* (New York: National Railway Publication Company, October 1923), 1138.

58 *Tuscola County Advertiser*, October 31, 1924; January 2, 1925; January 16, 1925; *Wall Street Journal*, August 8, 1923; November 15, 1924. The official approval by the ICC for abandonment came on March 24, 1925. See ICC Finance Docket No. 3171, *ICC Reports*, Vol. 94, p. 666.

59 *Wall Street Journal*, January 1, 1924; Schramm and Henning, *When Eastern Michigan Rode the Rails, II*, 176.

60 *Tuscola County Advertiser*, February 27, 1925; April 3, 1925; April 24, 1925; May 1, 1925; "Michigan 'Tom Thumb' Railroad Is Calling It Quits," typed manuscript in Fred C. Olds Sr. Collection, Box 1, Michigan State Archives, Lansing, Mich., hereafter cited as Olds Collection; *Times Herald* (Port Huron, Mich.), December 3, 1972.

61 "Michigan 'Tom Thumb' Railroad Is Calling It Quits"; *Times Herald*, December 3, 1972; *Moody's Manual of Investments: Railroad Securities* (New York: Moody's Investors Service, 1933), 813; *Moody's Manual of Investments: Railroad Securities* (New York: Moody's Investors Service, 1947), 88; *Annual Report of the Detroit, Caro & Sandusky Railway Company to the Public Service Commission of the State of Michigan, for the Year Ended December 31, 1951.*

62 Clipping from *Bay City Times*, Olds Collection, Box 1.

63 Interstate Commerce Commission, Finance Docket No. 1783; Olds Collection, Box 30.

64 *Times Herald*, December 3, 1972.

65 *Electric Railway Journal* 36 (November 26, 1910): 1084. The *Tuscola County Advertiser* of November 11, 1910, made these remarks about the interurban project: "No better country is to be found in Michigan than that through which the proposed line would run and is not now properly supplied with railroads."

4. Luce Line

1 *Thirty-Second Annual Report of the Railroad and Warehouse Commission of the State of Minnesota, for the Year Ending November 30, 1916* (Minneapolis, Minn.: Syndicate Printing Company, 1917), 333, 374; *Minneapolis Star-Journal*, July 6, 1946.

2 Gary Lenz, "The Minnesota Western Railroad," *North Western Lines* 26 (Fall 1999): 42; *Hutchinson (Minn.) Leader*, December 13, 1912; January 1, 1913; May 1, 1914; April 4, 1919; Marion Daniel Shutter, ed., *History of Minneapolis: Gateway to the Northwest* (Chicago: S. J. Clarke Publishing Company, 1923), 366–70.

3 *Thirtieth Annual Report of the Railroad and Warehouse Commission of the State of Minnesota, for the Year Ending November 30, 1914* (Minneapolis, Minn.: Syndicate Printing Company, 1915), 596; Stan Mailer, "The Blue Dragon of Golden Valley," *Railfan and Railroad* 4 (July 1982): 44.

4 Lenz, "The Minnesota Western Railroad," 42–43; *Electric Railway Journal* 36 (November 5, 1910): 975; *Hutchinson Leader*, May 10, 1912; November 1, 1912; November 22, 1912; January 24, 1913; January 23, 1914; Richard S. Prosser, *Rails to the North Star* (Minneapolis, Minn.: Dillon Press, 1966), 48; "Electric Short Line Railway," Interstate Commerce Commission Docket 998, 4.

5 *Hutchinson Leader*, October 15, 1915; Charles Byron Kuhlmann, *The Development of the Flour-Milling Industry in the United States* (Boston: Houghton Mifflin, 1929), 165–82.

6 *Hutchinson Leader*, March 10, 1916; September 29, 1922; *Handy Railroad Maps of the United States* (New York: Rand McNally & Company, 1928), 25; Franklyn

Curtiss-Wedge, ed., *History of McLeod County Minnesota* (Chicago: H. C. Cooper Jr. & Company, 1917), 295.

7 *Hutchinson Leader*, August 30, 1912.

8 *Railway Age Gazette* 58 (January 23, 1915): 171; ibid. 59 (November 26, 1915): 1031; "Electric Short Line Railway," 4, 8.

9 *Hutchinson Leader*, January 24, 1913; January 29, 1915; October 8, 1915; October 15, 1915; Lenz, "The Minnesota Western Railroad," 45. There were reports that the Luces hoped to build southwest from the Minneapolis area to Sioux City, Iowa, serving such towns as Sleepy Eye, Mountain Lake, and Jackson, Minnesota, and Spirit Lake, Iowa. See *Spirit Lake Centennial* (Spirit Lake, Iowa: Spirit Lake Centennial Committee, 1979), 91–92.

10 *Hutchinson Leader*, February 14, 1913; February 28, 1913; August 1, 1913; December 19, 1913; October 8, 1915.

11 Electric Short Line public timetable, May 19, 1918; Russell L. Olson, *The Electric Railways of Minnesota* (St. Paul, Minn.: Minnesota Transportation Museum, 1976), 524; *Official Railway Equipment Register* 36 (May 1921): 593; *Hutchinson Leader*, May 19, 1916; "Electric Short Line Railway Company," 1.

12 *Hutchinson Leader*, March 14, 1913; July 11, 1913.

13 Ibid., January 21, 1916; April 21, 1916; May 5, 1916; October 27, 1916; November 3, 1916; November 10, 1916; December 8, 1916.

14 Lenz, "The Minnesota Western Railroad," 45; *Railway Age Gazette* 63 (December 14, 1917): 1106; *Wall Street Journal*, June 12, 1919; *Hutchinson Leader*, June 22, 1917; December 20, 1918.

15 *Hutchinson Leader*, July 11, 1919; May 14, 1920; Curtiss-Wedge, ed., *History of McLeod County Minnesota*, 496.

16 William D. Middleton, "The Strange, Successful Story of the Railroad that Was Once Named for a Race Horse," *Trains* 19 (June 1959): 16–22; Steve Glischinski, "MN&S: Unique and Colorful Well Beyond Its Size," *Classic Trains* 6 (Summer 2005): 16–19.

17 Ibid.

18 *Hutchinson Leader*, May 27, 1921; *Minneapolis Journal*, October 16, 1922.

19 *Hutchinson Leader*, October 13, 1922; November 17, 1922; December 22, 1922; *Railway Age Gazette* 59 (September 10, 1915): 457.

20 *Hutchinson Leader*, December 29, 1922.

21 Ibid., October 6, 1922; October 27, 1922; December 8, 1922; May 11, 1923.

22 Ibid., June 22, 1923; *Cosmos (Minn.) News*, July 31, 1925; August 11, 1925.

23 *Hutchinson Leader*, November 3, 1922; April 6, 1923.

24 Ibid., June 8, 1923; June 29, 1923.

25 Ibid., May 25, 1923; March 20, 1925; December 10, 1926; *Lake Lillian (Minn.) Echo*, January 21, 1926; March 4, 1926; July 29, 1926.

26 *Minneapolis Tribune*, June 25, 1923; *Hutchinson Leader*, June 29, 1923.

27 *Hutchinson Leader*, February 29, 1924; April 18, 1924.

28 Ibid., April 18, 1924

29 Ibid.

30 Ralph W. Hidy et al., *The Great Northern Railway: A History* (Boston: Harvard Business School Press, 1988), 177; H. Roger Grant, "Missouri Southern: History

of a Shortline," *Bulletin of the Railway & Locomotive Historical Society* 123 (October 1970): 48; "Bus Operations by Electric Railways and Subsidiary Companies," *Electric Railway Journal* 69 (January 1, 1927): 34–35. See also "Co-ordination in Portsmouth, Ohio," *Electric Railway Journal* 69 (June 26, 1927): 1133–35.

31 *Hutchinson Leader*, October 24, 1924; November 28, 1924.

32 Ibid., December 5, 1924.

33 Ibid., January 2, 1925; February 13, 1925.

34 Ibid., October 10, 1925.

35 Ibid., July 2, 1926; *Wall Street Journal*, July 2, 1926.

36 *Hutchinson Leader*, October 8, 1926.

37 Ibid., October 19, 1926; August 12, 1927; *Lake Lillian Echo*, September 27, 1926; *Minneapolis Journal*, February 1, 1927.

38 *Hutchinson Leader*, August 12, 1927; October 28, 1927; November 4, 1927; November 11, 1927; *Montevideo (Minn.) American*, November 11, 1927; *Montevideo (Minn.) News*, August 26, 1927.

39 Lenz, "The Minnesota Western Railroad," 47; *Montevideo News*, August 26, 1927; March 3, 1928; Wayne G. Broehl Jr., *Cargill: Trading the World's Grain* (Hanover, N.H.: University Press of New England, 1992), 269.

40 *Montevideo News*, September 23, 1927; October 28, 1927; *Hutchinson Leader*, October 28, 1927.

41 *Hutchinson Leader*, February 4, 1927; *Montevideo American*, December 12, 1927; *Minneapolis Tribune*, December 6, 1927; Lenz, "The Minnesota Western Railway," 47; *Official Guide of the Railways* (New York: National Railway Publication Company, October 1923), 1120; *Moody's Steam Railroads* (New York: Moody's Investors Service, 1930), 27.

42 Olson, *The Electric Railways of Minnesota*, 524; *Wall Street Journal*, January 23, 1933; *Poor's Railroad Manual* (New York: Poor's Publishing Company, 1940), 1715.

43 Broehl, *Cargill*, 622–29, 743–44, 771.

44 Olson, *The Electric Railways of Minnesota*, 524; Broehl, *Cargill*, 779; Don L. Hofsommer, *The Tootin' Louie: A History of Minneapolis & St. Louis Railway* (Minneapolis, Minn.: University of Minnesota Press, 2005), 266–67; "M. & St. L. Buys Minnesota Western," *The Express* 1 (February 1956): 1; *Annual Report of the Minneapolis & St. Louis Railway Company, 1955* (Minneapolis, Minn.: Minneapolis & St. Louis Railway, 1956), 3; *Annual Report of the Minneapolis & St. Louis Railway Company, 1956* (Minneapolis, Minn.: Minneapolis & St. Louis Railway, 1957), 8–9.

45 Lenz, "The Minnesota Western Railroad," 50–51; *Prairie Herald Journal* (Winsted–Lester Prairie, Minn.), April 29, 2002.

5. Ettrick & Nothing

1 Merle Curti, *The Making of an American Community: A Case Study of Democracy in a Frontier Society* (Stanford, Calif.: Stanford University Press, 1959), 8–11, 36.

2 Franklyn Curtiss-Wedge, compiler, and Eben Douglas Pierce, ed., *History of Trempealeau County Wisconsin* (Chicago: H. C. Cooper, Jr. & Company, 1917), 261–66;

Chicago and North Western Railway Company and Components to April 30, 1910 (Chicago: Chicago & North Western Railway Company, 1910), 27–28; Stan Mailer, *Green Bay & Western: The First 111 Years* (Edmonds, Wash.: Hundman Publishing, 1989), 25–34.

3   Mailer, *Green Bay & Western*, 34; *GBW: Wisconsin's Historic East-West Railroad* (North Freedom, Wis.: Mid-Continent Railway Historical Society, 1986), 4–6; Ray and Ellen Specht, "The Story of the Green Bay and Western," *Bulletin of the Railway and Locomotive Historical Society* 115 (October 1966): 23–24; *Wisconsin Blue Book* (Madison, Wis.: Industrial Commission, 1917), 386–87; George W. Hilton and John F. Due, *The Electric Interurban Railways in America* (Stanford, Calif.: Stanford University Press, 1964), 353.

4   Wedge and Pierce, *History of Trempealeau County Wisconsin*, 266, 279–80; *Blair (Wis.) Press*, June 17, 1920; Leland R. Drangstveit, "The Ettrick and Northern Railroad," manuscript in Ettrick Public Library, Ettrick, Wis.; telephone interview with Arild Englien, Trempealeau, Wis., January 28, 2008.

5   Wedge and Pierce, *History of Trempealeau County Wisconsin*, 266.

6   Drangstveit, "The Ettrick and Northern Railroad"; *Ettrick (Wis.) Advance*, December 11, 1936.

7   H. Roger Grant, *Self-Help in the 1890s Depression* (Ames: Iowa State University Press, 1983), 74–100.

8   *Blair Press*, February 17, 1916; Charles C. Nelson, "Wisconsin & Northern Railroad," *Bulletin of the Railway and Locomotive Historical Society* 116 (April 1967): 7–21.

9   Wedge and Pierce, *History of Trempealeau County Wisconsin*, 423–24, 485–86, 490–91, 626–27, 674–76; *Blair Press*, December 11, 1936; *Poor's Manual of Railroads* (New York: Poor's Publishing Company, 1922), 485; Articles of Incorporation, Ettrick and Northern Railroad Company, June 17, 1915, State of Wisconsin, Department of State; *Railway Age Gazette* 59 (September 10, 1915): 487.

10   *Blair Press*, November 4, 1915; Drangstveit, "The Ettrick and Northern Railroad."

11   *Osseo (Wis.) News*, September 30, 1915; *Blair Press*, September 23, 1915; *Poor's Manual of Railroads* (1922), 485.

12   *Blair Press*, October 28, 1915; December 16, 1915.

13   Ibid., September 23, 1915; November 18, 1915; March 1, 1917.

14   Ibid., July 27, 1916.

15   Mailer, *Green Bay & Western*, 267; *Blair Press*, August 31, 1916; November 3, 1916; July 19, 1917; Drangstveit, "The Etttrick and Northern Railroad;" *Railway Age* 61 (October 6, 1916): 619.

16   *Blair Press*, December 11, 1936.

17   Ibid., December 20, 1917; December 27, 1917; December 24, 1936.

18   Ibid., April 18, 1918; *Biennial Report of the Railroad Commission of Wisconsin* (Madison, Wis., 1920), 32.

19   Mailer, *Green Bay & Western*, 267; *Ettrick Advance*, December 5, 1919; January 7, 1921.

20   Mailer, *Green Bay & Western*, 267–68; *Blair Press*, January 30, 1919; April 27, 1922.

21   *Blair Press*, May 8, 1919; *Ettrick Advance*, October 3, 1919; December 5, 1919; Drangstveit, "The Ettrick and Northern Railroad."

22   *Ettrick Advance*, November 11, 1919; January 7, 1921; *Blair Press*, February 10, 1921.

23 *Blair Press*, February 15, 1917; *Ettrick Advance*, November 14, 1919; November 28, 1919; March 4, 1921.

24 *Ettrick Advance*, October 3, 1919; *Blair Press*, September 4, 1919.

25 *Blair Press*, September 23, 1920.

26 Ibid., October 17, 1918; October 24, 1918; March 24, 1919; May 1, 1919; *Ettrick Advance*, May 14, 1920; October 8, 1920.

27 *Ettrick Advance*, October 10, 1919.

28 *Poor's Manual of Railroads* (New York: Poor's Publishing Company, 1923), 200.

29 Ibid.

30 *Ettrick Advance*, April 22, 1921.

31 *Blair Press*, July 7, 1921; November 3, 1921.

32 Ibid., March 21, 1921; August 10, 1922; *Ettrick Advance*, October 27, 1922.

33 *Ettrick Advance*, October 27, 1922; *Poor's Manual of Railroads* (1923), 200.

34 *Blair Press*, August 10, 1922; *Ettrick Advance*, August 4, 1922; November 16, 1923.

35 *Ettrick Advance*, October 27, 1922.

36 *Poor's Manual of Railroads* (1923), 200; *Ettrick Advance*, June 28, 1923; November 9, 1923; April 18, 1924; December 25, 1924; December 24, 1926.

37 *Blair Press*, April 12, 1928.

38 Ibid., March 1, 1928; March 15, 1928.

39 Ibid., March 29, 1928; telephone interview with Arild Engelien, Trempealeau, Wis., January 7, 2008, hereafter cited as Engelien interview, January 7, 2008.

40 *Blair Press*, April 26, 1928; June 28, 1928.

41 Ibid., May 17, 1928; Articles of Incorporation, Ettrick Railroad Company, filed November 3, 1928, State of Wisconsin, Department of State.

42 *Blair Press*, May 17, 1928; Mailer, *Green Bay & Western*, 268.

43 *Ettrick Advance*, December 11, 1936; Mailer, *Green Bay & Western*, 268; C. M. Sherwood to the Whitcomb Locomotive Co., March 19, 1932, copy in Ettrick Public Library.

44 Engelien interview, January 7, 2008.

45 *Blair Press*, July 27, 1937; *Ettrick Advance*, April 23, 1937; July 30, 1937.

46 *Ettrick Advance*, August 20, 1937; Gordon Odegard, "A Railroad You Can Model: Ettrick & Northern RR," *Model Railroader* (September 1987): 84; Drangstveit, "The Ettrick and Northern Railroad." Shortly before the final abandonment of the railroad, the town of Ettrick finally paid off the last of the construction bonds. *Ettrick Advance*, March 5, 1937.

47 Mailer, *Green Bay & Western*, 267; William Norris Leonard, *Railroad Consolidation under the Transportation Act of 1920* (New York: Columbia University Press, 1946), 311, 328.

48 Drangstveit, "The Ettrick and Northern Railroad."

6. The Rockford Route

1 *A Chronology of American Railroads* (Washington, D.C.: Association of American Railroads, 1957), 7.

2   George W. Hilton and John F. Due, *The Electric Interurban Railways in America* (Stanford, Calif.: Stanford University Press, 1960), 136–37, 335–36, 346–49.

3   "The Burlington's Entrance into the Southern Illinois Coal Fields," *Railway Age Gazette* 50 (April 14, 1911): 900–902; Richard C. Overton, *Burlington Route: A History of the Burlington Lines* (New York: Knopf, 1965), 277–79; H. Roger Grant, *The North Western: A History of the Chicago & North Western Railway System* (DeKalb: Northern Illinois University Press, 1996), 90–91.

4   *Thirty-Sixth Annual Report of the Railroad and Warehouse Commission of the State of Illinois* (Springfield, Ill.: Phillips Brothers, State Printers, 1907), 11.

5   *Poor's Manual of the Railroads of the United States* (New York: Poor's Railroad Manual Company, 1917), 44–46; *Official Guide of the Railways* (New York: National Railway Publication Company, May 1917), 598–99.

6   *Moody's Manual of Railroads and Corporation Securities* (New York: Moody Publishing Company, 1905), 608; *Sycamore (Ill.) True Republican*, February 4, 1903; Illinois, Iowa & Minnesota Railway clippings in Pliny Fisk Collection, John W. Barriger III National Railroad Library, St. Louis, Mo., hereafter cited as Pliny Fisk Collection; *Railway Age* 38 (July 1, 1904): 27.

7   P. B. Wolfe, ed., *Wolf's History of Clinton County, Iowa, Vol. 2* (Indianapolis, Ind.: B. F. Bowen & Company, 1911), 1093; *Clinton (Iowa) Herald*, December 15, 1941.

8   *New York Times*, December 16, 1941; *Waterways Journal* 55 (December 20, 1941): 10.

9   *Dubuque (Iowa) Tribune*, December 15, 1941; Wolfe, *Wolfe's History of Clinton County*, 1094; Thomas R. Bullard, *South from Gary* (Oak Park, Ill.: Privately Printed, 1992), 4, 6–7.

10   Bullard, *South from Gary*, 17–20; *Electric Railway Journal* 38 (July 15, 1911): 139.

11   Illinois, Iowa & Minnesota Railway clippings in Pliny Fisk Collection.

12   Bullard, *South from Gary*, 8; *DeKalb (Ill.) Evening Chronicle*, November 16, 1904; December 21, 1904.

13   *DeKalb Evening Chronicle*, March 28, 1904; September 8, 1904; September 21, 1904; September 29, 1904; October 17, 1904; October 25, 1904.

14   Ibid., October 10, 1904; October 25, 1904; November 2, 1904.

15   *Railway Age* 39 (April 21, 1905): 659; H. H. Field, *History of the Milwaukee Railroad, 1892–1940* (Chicago: Chicago, Milwaukee, St. Paul & Pacific Railroad, 1940), 52.

16   *DeKalb Evening Chronicle*, June 13, 1904; October 25, 1904.

17   Ibid., July 27, 1904; August 30, 1904; September 15, 1904; October 26, 1904; November 21, 1904; May 4, 1908; *Report on Chicago, Milwaukee & Gary Railway with Proposed Extension from Rockford, Illinois, to Milwaukee, Wisconsin and Momence, Illinois to Gary, Indiana* (Chicago, Ill., Chicago, Milwaukee & Gary Railway, July 1, 1908), 35–37.

18   *Report on Chicago, Milwaukee & Gary Railway*, 66; *DeKalb Evening Chronicle*, October 25, 1904; James Buckley, "Aurora, DeKalb & Rockford Electric Traction Co.," manuscript in possession of author; *DeKalb Evening Chronicle*, January 26, 1905.

19   *Rockford To-Day* (Rockford, Ill.: The Clark Company Press, 1903), 12; Jon W. Lundin, *Rockford: An Illustrated History* (Rockford, Ill.: Windsor Publications,

1989), 107–110; Pat Cunningham, *Rockford: Big Town, Little City* (Rockford, Ill.: Rockford Newspapers, 2000), 15–16; *Rockford (Ill.) Republic*, June 9, 1909; February 15, 1910.

20 *Official Guide of the Railways* (New York: National Railway Publication Company, June 1906), 623, 644, 759, 870; Hilton and Due, *The Electric Interurban Railways in America*, 343.

21 *Railway Age* 39 (February 3, 1905): 162; *Report on Chicago, Milwaukee & Gary Railway*, 66; *DeKalb Evening Chronicle*, December 22, 1904; March 1, 1905.

22 *DeKalb Evening Chronicle*, May 17, 1905.

23 *Report on Chicago, Milwaukee & Gary Railway*, 66.

24 *Railway Age* 40 (July 28, 1905): 119; ibid. (September 15, 1905): 334; *DeKalb Evening Chronicle*, May 17, 1905; April 25, 1906; *Report on Chicago, Milwaukee & Gary Railway*, 63–65.

25 *DeKalb Evening Chronicle*, November 14, 1905; March 22, 1906; August Derleth, *The Milwaukee Road: Its First Hundred Years* (New York: Creative Press, 1948), 207; *Railway Age* 39 (June 23, 1905): 1144; ibid. 40 (November 17, 1905): 644.

26 *DeKalb Evening Chronicle*, March 2, 1905; *Official Guide of the Railways* (June 1906), 878.

27 *DeKalb Evening Chronicle*, August 12, 1905; July 23, 1906.

28 Charles A. Church, *Past and Present of the City of Rockford and Winnebago, County, Illinois* (Chicago: S. J. Clarke Publishing Company, 1905), 140.

29 *Decisions and Opinions of the Railroad and Warehouse Commission of the State of Illinois* (Springfield.: Illinois State Journal Company, 1912), vol. 3, 451; *DeKalb Evening Chronicle*, September 18, 1906; September 27, 1906; August 5, 1909; Hilton and Due, *The Electric Interurban Railways in America*, 339–41.

30 *Decisions and Opinions of the Railroad and Warehouse Commission*, 450–52.

31 *DeKalb Evening Chronicle*, July 19, 1906; *Railway Age* 39 (April 14, 1905): 624; *Official Equipment Register* 38 (April 1913): 528.

32 *Decisions and Opinions of the Railroad and Warehouse Commission*, 451; *Report on the Chicago, Milwaukee & Gary Railway*, 2, 6; clippings in Pliny Fisk Collection.

33 *DeKalb Evening Chronicle*, September 23, 1905; *Rockford Republic*, October 29, 1909; George W. Hilton, "The Chicago, Cincinnati & Louisville Railroad," *Bulletin of the Railway and Locomotive Historical Society* 114 (April 1966): 10; clippings in Pliny Fisk Collection.

34 Clippings in Pliny Fisk Collection; *Report of the Chicago, Milwaukee & Gary Railway*, 1–2, 16–18.

35 *Report of the Chicago, Milwaukee & Gary Railway*, 3; "Seeking Entrance into Gary," *Air Line News* 3 (April 1909): 3.

36 *Report of the Chicago, Milwaukee & Gary Railway*, 51–53, 61–63; *DeKalb Chronicle*, November 11, 1907; Raymond A. Mohl and Neil Betten, "The Failure of Industrial City Planning: Gary, Indiana, 1906–1910," *Journal of the American Institute of Planners* 38 (July 1972): 203–4; "The Great Steel City of Gary," *Air Line News* 1 (September 1907): 12–13.

37 Clippings in Pliny Fisk Collection.

38 Ibid.; *The Biographical Directory of the Railway Officials of America* (New York: Simmons-Boardman Publishing Company, 1922), 488; *Forty-Second Annual*

Report of the Railroad and Warehouse Commission of the State of Illinois (Springfield: Illinois State Journal Company, State Printers, 1912), 290; Bullard, *South from Gary*, 12.

39 *DeKalb Daily Chronicle*, June 14, 1909; Charles H. Stats, "The Railroads of DeKalb, Sycamore, and Cortland, Illinois: The Second Era of Railroad Expansion in the DeKalb Area," *North Western Lines* 19 (Spring 1992): 37; clippings in Pliny Fisk Collection.

40 *Poor's Manual of Railroads* (New York: Poor's Publishing Company, 1923), 768–69; *Railway Age* 71 (July 13, 1921): 164; Max Lowenthal, *The Investor Pays* (New York: Alfred A. Knopf, 1933), 41; F. Stewart Graham, "Initials, Brickbats, and Sobriquets," *Bulletin of the Railway & Locomotive Historical Society* 118 (April 1968): 88.

41 Lowenthal, *The Investor Pays*, 42.

42 Field, *History of the Milwaukee Road*, 62; *Fifty-Seventh Annual Report of the Chicago, Milwaukee, St. Paul Railway Company* (Chicago: Chicago, Milwaukee & St. Paul Railway, 1922), 5; *New York Times*, January 6, 1922.

43 Derleth, *The Milwaukee Road*, 198–225.

44 Lowenthal, *The Investor Pays*, 37.

45 Ibid., 42.

46 Ibid., 44–48; "St. Paul Hearings," *Railway Age* 80 (April 17, 1926): 1083–84; "The St. Paul," *Time* (April 19, 1926).

47 *Sycamore True Republican*, December 19, 1923; *DeKalb Evening Chronicle*, August 30, 1926; Time Table No. 25, Chicago, Milwaukee & St. Paul Railway, September 28, 1925; Field, *History of the Milwaukee Road*, 63–64.

48 Field, *History of the Milwaukee Road*, 63.

49 *Sycamore True Republican*, June 21, 1940; *DeKalb Chronicle*, April 16, 1947; Jerrold F. Hilton, "The Rockford Route: Chicago, Milwaukee and Gary," *Bulletin of the National Railway Historical Society* 41 (1976): 30.

50 Frederick K. Plous, "Unclogging Chicago," *Railroad History* 196 (Spring–Summer 2007): 4. More than a century after the concept of the Rockford Route was put forward, Chicago remains the railroad center of North America and still suffers from traffic congestion. Presently the Windy City is the only place where all six Class 1 carriers meet to exchange cars, and approximately one-third of all freight in the country originates in, terminates in, or passes through Chicago. Since Chicago is a bottleneck for the speedy flow of freight, a coalition of carriers, governments, and other interested groups has recently conceived a plan to forge five rail express corridors across metropolitan Chicago. The plan involves construction of more than fifty miles of main line track and likely comes with a price tag of $1.5 billion. If a completed Rockford Route existed today, part of the work of the Chicago Region Environmental and Transportation Efficiency Program (CREATE) would surely be easier and less expensive.

7. Ozark Short Line

1   Paul W. Gates, "The Railroads of Missouri, 1850–1870," *Missouri Historical Review* 26 (January 1932): 126–41; Edward J. White, "A Century of Transportation in Missouri," *Missouri Historical Review* 15 (October 1920): 152.

2   A Houston, Missouri, editor noted the meaning of the "Ozark Short Line," explaining "not that the line is to be short, but it means a short line to southern Missouri." See *Houston (Mo.) Herald*, May 4, 1911.

3   *Houston Herald*, December 24, 1908; *Texas County Star* (Houston, Mo.), December 24, 1908.

4   *Rolla (Mo.) New Era*, March 14, 1885; *Texas County Star*, August 20, 1908; November 26, 1908; *Houston Herald*, January 9, 1881; January 31, 1909; *Licking (Mo.) News*, January 29, 1909; July 29, 1910.

5   George W. Hilton and John F. Due, *The Electric Interurban Railways in America* (Stanford, Calif.: Stanford University Press, 1960), 3, 186, 368–69; H. Roger Grant, "The Excelsior Springs Route: Life and Death of a Missouri Interurban," *Missouri Historical Review* 65 (October 1970): 37–50; *Houston Herald*, December 10, 1908; *Electric Railway Journal* 35 (February 19, 1910): 336.

6   *Houston Herald*, February 25, 1909; March 4, 1909.

7   *Licking News*, February 26, 1909; "State Penitentiary Register," 1911–1913, Missouri State Archives, Jefferson City, Reel 5230, 8 A–B; *Texas County Star*, February 25, 1909; *Rolla (Mo.) Herald-Democrat*, March 11, 1909; *Houston Herald*, February 15, 1909.

8   *Houston Herald*, March 11, 1909; May 6, 1909; *Texas County Star*, February 25, 1909.

9   *Licking News*, February 26, 1909.

10 "Articles of Incorporation of the Missouri Inland and Southern Railway Company," copy in Western Manuscripts Collection, Missouri University of Science and Technology, Rolla, Mo.; *Railroad Age Gazette* 46 (June 4, 1909): 1187. The selection of Rolla as the northern terminus disappointed residents of nearby St. James. In early 1909 the *St. James Journal* reported that the community had formed a committee to bring the electric railroad to town. That prompted a sympathetic *Licking News* to editorialize, "St. James is not asleep on the railroad proposition, and when the proper time comes She will be up for action." *Licking News*, March 12, 1909.

11 *Licking News*, May 21, 1909; *Houston Herald*, April 22, 1909; May 13, 1909; September 23, 1909; March 12, 1987; "Articles of Incorporation of the St. Louis & Houston Mineral Belt Railway Company," copy in Western Manuscripts Collection, Missouri University of Science and Technology.

12 *Licking News*, May 21, 1909; June 11, 1909.

13 Ibid., May 7, 1909; May 14, 1909. It is difficult to know if Hugh Palmer was a credible participant, although he was a dedicated interurban enthusiast. Later, though, Palmer served as the electrical engineer for the Cienfuegos, Palmira & Cruces Electric Railway & Power Company in Cuba.

14 *Houston (Mo.) Republican*, May 21, 1909; June 10, 1909.

15 *Licking News*, July 30, 1909; August 13, 1909.

16   *Licking News*, July 2, 1909; July 15, 1909; November 12, 1909; *Houston Herald*, June 17, 1909; June 24, 1909; December 12, 1909.

17   *Licking News*, July 23, 1909.

18   Ibid., July 16, 1909.

19   Ibid., October 15, 1909.

20   Ibid.

21   *Houston Republican*, December 23, 1909; *Houston Herald*, September 22, 1910; William Edward Hayes, *Iron Road to Empire: The History of the Rock Island Lines* (New York: Simmons-Boardman, 1953), 177–89.

22   *Houston Herald*, November 25, 1909.

23   *Licking News*, January 21, 1910.

24   Ibid., March 18, 1910.

25   Ibid., January 28, 1910; *Rolla Herald*, February 3, 1910; *Texas County Star*, January 12, 1916; *Houston Herald*, January 16, 1908.

26   *Licking News*, March 18, 1910; June 10, 1910; July 15, 1910; July 22, 1910; *Houston Herald*, July 28, 1910.

27   *Houston Herald*, July 22, 1910; July 29 1910; August 5, 1910; *Licking News*, August 5, 1910; *Rolla Herald*, August 18, 1910.

28   *Rolla (Mo.) Times*, June 16, 1910; November 17, 1910; November 24, 1910; *Rolla Herald*, June 2, 1910; *Licking News*, September 23, 1910; *Houston Herald*, November 17, 1910; *St. Louis Globe-Democrat*, December 4, 1910.

29   *Houston Herald*, December 15, 1910; January 19, 1911; March 2, 1911; *Houston Republican*, March 16, 1911; April 6, 1911.

30   *Texas County Star*, April 27, 1911; *Houston Herald*, April 27, 1911; *Houston Republican*, April 27, 1911; "Articles of Incorporation of the Missouri, Arkansas & Gulf Railway Company," copy in Western Manuscripts Collection, Missouri University of Science and Technology; *Missouri, Arkansas & Gulf Railway: Ozark Short Line* (Rolla, Mo., 1911), 2.

31   *Texas County Star*, January 12, 1911; *Houston Herald*, January 12, 1911; May 4, 1911; *Houston Republican*, February 9, 1911; May 25, 1911.

32   *Houston Herald*, July 20, 1911; *Houston Republican*, July 21, 1911.

33   *Houston Herald*, July 20, 1911.

34   Ibid., July 20, 1911; August 3, 1911.

35   *Houston Republican*, September 7, 1911; September 21, 1911; October 12, 1911; *Houston Herald*, September 14, 1911.

36   *Houston Republican*, October 19, 1911; *Houston Herald*, November 23, 1911.

37   *Houston Republican*, November 30, 1911; *St. Louis Republic*, January 7, 1912; *Licking News*, July 5, 1912.

38   *Houston Herald*, January 25, 1912; April 4, 1912; *Licking News*, February 16, 1912; July 5, 1912; *Houston Republican*, March 7, 1912; *Houston Republican*, August 1, 1912. In late fall 1912 workers finished the Houston depot. "This structure is built with concrete, with commodious waiting room, etc.," observed the *Houston Republican* on December 5, 1912, "and we must say it is a better depot than graces many of our neighboring towns."

39   *Houston Herald*, March 28, 1912; August 29, 1912; September 26, 1912; November 7, 1912; January 23, 1913; *Houston Republican*, January 22, 1914.

40 John F. Bradbury Jr., "The Ozark Short Line: Electric Railway from Rolla to Houston," *Newsletter of the Phelps County Historical Society* (October 1997): 6; *Houston Herald*, November 26, 1912; December 19, 1912; February 20, 1913; *Rolla Times*, May 29, 1913; "State Penitentiary Register."

41 *Houston Herald*, March 13, 1913; *Houston Republican*, March 20, 1913.

42 *Houston Herald*, March 12, 1987; *Houston Republican*, May 21, 1914; *Licking News*, January 2, 1914.

43 "Articles of Incorporation for Standard Gauge Railway: Rolla, Ozark & Southern Railway Company," copy in Western Manuscripts Collection, Missouri University of Science and Technology; *Licking News*, April 24, 1914.

44 Bradbury, "The Ozark Short Line," 1, 10.

45 *Missouri, Ozark & Gulf Railway*, 10–11; *Poor's Manual of Railroads* (New York: Poor's Publishing, 1921), 2089; William D. Edson, compiler, *Railroad Names* (Potomac, Md., 1989), 95.

46 Bradbury, "The Ozark Short Line," 10; *Licking News*, March 28, 1913; July 2, 1915; August 6, 1915; July 13, 1917; *Houston Republican*, July 17, 1913; *Houston Herald*, July 2, 1914. The growing interest in better public roads even involved the Ozark Short Line. The idea was floated that grading the railroad right-of-way should be finished, but rather than install ties and rails, the roadway should be used as a highway. See *Licking News*, July 4, 1913.

8. The Arnica Salve Line

1 "Bucklen's Arnica Salve," n.d., typed manuscript in possession of the Elkhart County Historical Society, Bristol, Indiana.

2 Ibid.; *Elkhart (Ind.) Truth*, January 10, 1917; *The Book of Chicagoans: A Biographical Dictionary of Leading Living Men in Chicago* (Chicago: Albert Nelson Marquis, 1911), 98; Samuel Hopkins Adams, *The Great American Fraud* (New York: P. F. Collier & Son, 1907), 45–47, 159; James Harvey Young, *The Toadstool Millionaires: A Social History of Patent Medicines in America before Federal Regulation* (Princeton, N.J.: Princeton University Press, 1961), 93–110. In 1912 Bucklen left the patent medicine business when he sold his interests "for a consideration of one million dollars" to the Pfefer Chemical Company of St. Louis, Missouri. However, he retained ownership of his Chicago factory building and leased the facility to the new owner. *La Grange (Ind.) Standard*, August 15, 1912.

3 George W. Butler, *The Manual of Elkhart* (Privately Printed, 1889); *The Book of Chicagoans*, 98; *Chicago Tribune*, January 11, 1917; William S. Locke, *Elcar and Platt Automobiles: The Complete History* (Jefferson, N.C.: McFarland & Company, Publishers, 2000), 9–10; *La Grange Standard*, October 4, 1917; *Elkhart Truth*, August 19, 1916; January 10, 1917. Stories about Bucklen's skill in the business world were legendary. "Of the thousands of examples of Mr. Bucklen's acumen the one which stands out foremost occurred in 1876 when by competitive bidding he secured the soda water concession at the Philadelphia Centennial Exposition. Here he not only accumulated a small fortune but incidentally advertised his proprietary

medicines. Every patron received a pamphlet telling of the various medicines' virtues. As a result a demand was created in foreign countries while the business in this country increased by great strides." See *Elkhart Truth*, January 10, 1917.

4   J. Harold Kiracofe, "A History of the Elkhart & Western Railroad Company: 'The Bucklen Line,'" *Bulletin of the Railway and Locomotive Historical Society* 90 (May 1954): 115.

5   *Poor's Manual of the Railroads of the United States* (New York: H. V. & H. W. Poor, 1895), 152; Kiracofe, "A History of the Elkhart & Western Railroad Company," 115, 117–21; *The Weekly Truth* (Elkhart, Ind.), August 31, 1893; September 7, 1893.

6   Craig Sanders, *Limiteds, Locals, and Expresses in Indiana, 1838–1971* (Bloomington: Indiana University Press, 2003), 250; Kiracofe, "A History of the Elkhart & Western Railroad Company," 128.

7   Kiracofe, "A History of the Elkhart & Western Railroad," 120; *The Weekly Truth*, August 24, 1893; *Travelers' Official Railway Guide for the United States, Canada and Mexico* (New York: National Railway Publication Company, July 1895), 288.

8   Kiracofe, "A History of the Elkhart & Western Railroad Company," 121, 130. It would not be until the formative years of the twentieth century that self-propelled handcars became widely used, and the power would be gasoline and not steam. See John H. White, "A History of the Railroad Hand Car," *Railroad History* 127 (October 1972): 65–95.

9   Ibid., 125, 131; *South Bend (Ind.) Tribune*, March 25, 1979.

10 George W. Hilton and John F. Due, *The Electric Interurban Railways in America* (Stanford, Calif.: Stanford University Press, 1964), 276.

11 Ibid., 275.

12 Ibid., 264, 276, 281–82; Bob Sell and Jim Findlay, *The Teeter & Wobble: Tales of the Toledo & Western Railway Co.* (Blissfield, Mich.: Blissfield Advance, 1993), 15–16; *La Grange Standard*, February 8, 1906.

13 Joseph A. Galloway and James J. Buckley, *The St. Joseph Valley Railway* (Chicago, Ill.: Electric Railway Historical Society Bulletin No. 16, 1955), 6–7.

14 Richard S. Simons and Francis H. Parker, *Railroads of Indiana* (Bloomington, Ind.: Indiana University Press, 1997), 219; H. Roger Grant, *"Follow the Flag": A History of the Wabash Railroad Company* (DeKalb: Northern Illinois University Press, 2004), 78–80; St. Joseph Valley Railway Co. public timetable, August 30, 1913.

15 *La Grange Standard*, March 3, 1904.

16 Richard S. Simons, "St. Joseph Valley Railway," *National Railway Bulletin* 52 (1987): 28–29. Only a few traction companies, including the Portland-Lewiston Interurban, were financed without public sale of securities. See Hilton and Due, *The Electric Interurban Railways in America*, 19.

17 *La Grange Standard*, April 28, 1904; July 7, 1904; August 11, 1904; July 26, 1906.

18 Ibid., April 13, 1905.

19 Ibid., June 9, 1904; September 1, 1904; November 17, 1904.

20 Ibid., March 21, 1905; April 13, 1905; May 11, 1905.

21 Ibid., March 16, 1905.

22 Ibid., March 30, 1905; June 1, 1905; August 23, 1906; Galloway and Buckley, *The St. Joseph Valley Railway*, 7–8.

23 *La Grange Standard*, April 27, 1905.

24 Ibid., May 4, 1905; June 15, 1905.

25 Ibid., June 29, 1905; July 13, 1905.

26 Ibid., September 14, 1905; Galloway and Buckley, *The St. Joseph Valley Railway*, 9.

27 *La Grange Standard*, July 27, 1905; September 7, 1905; *Angola (Ind.) Herald*, January 1, 1919; Galloway and Buckley, *The St. Joseph Valley Railway*, 32–34; Glen A. Blackburn, "Interurban Railroads of Indiana," *Indiana Magazine of History* 20 (December 1924): 439.

28 *La Grange Standard*, January 25, 1906; March 1, 1906; July 5, 1906.

29 Ibid., May 31, 1906; June 21, 1906; September 16, 1906; April 11, 1907; May 2, 1907; May 9, 1907; August 22, 1907; September 5, 1907.

30 Ibid., March 8, 1906; July 26, 1906.

31 Ibid., August 1, 1907; December 12, 1907; January 21, 1909; James Buckley, "Aurora, DeKalb & Rockford Electric Traction Co.," manuscript in possession of author; Simons, "St. Joseph Valley Railway," 30–31, 33, 35; *Official Railway Equipment Register* 38 (April 1913): 430. For several decades the Sheffield firm, operating under the name of George S. Sheffield & Company, had been in the railroad-equipment business, making mostly handcars. In 1918 Fairbanks, Morse & Company absorbed this manufacturer based in Three Rivers, Michigan.

    By 1915 the Valley Line had reduced its freight equipment fleet from thirty-four to just nineteen units, namely eleven boxcars and eight flat cars. See *Official Railway Equipment Register* 40 (January 1915): 430. Later, though, the company acquired a small fleet of gondolas for the movement of marl fertilizer.

32 *DeKalb (Ill.) Daily Chronicle*, November 29, 1909.

33 *La Grange Standard*, June 15, 1911; June 19, 1913; Simons, "St. Joseph Valley Railway," 30–31, 35; Galloway and Buckley, *The St. Joseph Valley Railway*, 24.

34 Galloway and Buckley, *The St. Joseph Valley Railway*, 11.

35 *La Grange Standard*, February 15, 1906; August 30, 1906; September 13, 1906; November 22, 1906; February 21, 1907; September 26, 1907.

36 Ibid., May 28, 1908.

37 Ibid., November 26, 1908; July 29, 1909; September 23, 1909.

38 Galloway and Buckley, *The St. Joseph Valley Railway*, 10; *Electric Railway Journal* 35 (June 11, 1910): 1045; *La Grange Standard*, September 14, 1911.

39 *La Grange Standard*, October 20, 1910; November 10, 1910; November 24, 1910; January 19, 1911; June 22, 1911; July 20, 1911; July 27, 1911.

40 Galloway and Buckley, *The St. Joseph Valley Railway*, 21.

41 Ibid., 21, 23; Hilton and Due, *The Electric Interurban Railways in America*, 263–64; *Electric Railway Journal* 38 (November 18, 1911): 1084; *La Grange Standard*, June 15, 1911.

42 "Electric Railroad Building," *Air Line News* 5 (January 1911): 88–89.

43 *Electric Railway Journal* 36 (September 24, 1910): 488; *La Grange Standard*, September 22, 1910; July 27, 1911; February 1, 1912; Graydon M. Meints, "The Fruit Belt Line: Southwest Michigan's Failed Railroad," *Michigan Historical Review* 31 (Fall 2005): 117–48; Hilton and Due, *The Electric Interurban Railways in America*, 289. Bucklen may not have pursued a route to Kalamazoo because other promoters had a similar project in mind, namely construction of the Kalamazoo, Elkhart &

South Bend Traction Company between Kalamazoo and South Bend. See *Electric Railway Journal* 36 (November 19, 1910): 1049.

44 *La Grange Standard*, May 4, 1911; November 16, 1911; June 27, 1912; July 4, 1912; July 11, 1912; Galloway and Buckley, *The St. Joseph Valley Railway*, 24–25.

45 *La Grange Standard*, December 5, 1907; November 2, 1911; March 15, 1917; *Poor's Manual of the Railroads of the United States* (New York: Poor's Railroad Manual Company, 1910), 881–82; *Poor's Manual of the Railroads of the United States* (New York: Poor's Railroad Manual Company, 1915), 1944–45; Dwight Boyer, "There Never Was a Line Like It," *Railway Progress* (February 1955): 10.

46 Galloway and Buckley, *The St. Joseph Valley Railway*, 10; *La Grange Standard*, April 8, 1909; April 15, 1909; July 1, 1909; April 4, 1911; August 4, 1917; August 30, 1917; Sandy Yoder, *A Pictorial History of La Grange County, Indiana* (Virginia Beach, Va.: The Donning Company, 1996), 141.

47 *La Grange Standard*, September 19, 1907; July 2, 1908.

48 Ibid., January 4, 1917; January 18, 1917; *Elkhart Truth*, January 2, 1917; January 3, 1917; January 9, 1917; Galloway and Buckley, *The St. Joseph Valley Railway*, 25, 38–42; Elmer G. Sulzer, *Ghost Railroads of Indiana* (Bloomington: Indiana University Press, 1998), 127–29.

49 *Elkhart Truth*. January 11, 1917; January 12, 1917; January 13, 1917; Albro Martin, *James J. Hill and the Opening of the Northwest* (New York: Oxford University Press, 1976), 614.

50 *La Grange Standard*, January 18, 1917; January 25, 1917; February 22, 1917; March 15, 1917; *Electric Railway Journal* 48 (September 9, 1916): 471; *McGraw Electric Railway List* (New York: McGraw-Hill Company, 1918), 44.

51 *La Grange Standard*, December 20, 1917; Galloway and Buckley, *St. Joseph Valley Railway*, 29.

52 *La Grange Standard*, December 12, 1917.

53 Ibid., February 22, 1918; March 8, 1918; March 22, 1918; April 5, 1918.

54 Ibid., March 29, 1918.

55 Ibid., August 9, 1918.

56 Galloway and Buckley, *The St. Joseph Valley Railway*, 27.

57 *La Grange Standard*, August 16, 1918; October 18, 1918; October 25, 1918; November 1, 1918.

58 Ibid., November 29, 1918; January 17, 1919; May 9, 1919; *Angola Herald*, March 14, 1919.

59 *Angola Herald*, August 15, 1919; December 3, 1920; December 31, 1920; *La Grange Standard*, May 30, 1919. See also Yoder, *A Pictorial History of La Grange County, Indiana*.

60 Galloway and Buckley, *The St. Joseph Valley Railway*, 6; Simons, "St. Joseph Valley Railway," 35; *Akron (Ohio) Beacon Journal*, November 1, 1911; *La Grange Standard*, May 11, 1905; March 29, 1918.

Epilogue

1   "An Unfortunate Railroad Project," in *The Railway Library* (Chicago: Stromberg, Allen & Company, 1916), 69–70; interview with Geraldine "Gerry" Slemmons, Akron, Ohio, October 2, 1980.

2   George W. Hilton and John F. Due, *The Electric Interurban Railways in America* (Stanford, Calif.: Stanford University Press, 1960), 214, 245.

3   "Railway Lines Abandoned During the Year," *Railway Age* 70 (January 7, 1921): 151–52; "What About the Patrons of an Abandoned Road?" *Railway Age* 76 (May 3, 1924): 1077–79; George H. Drury, *The Historical Guide to North American Railroads* (Milwaukee, Wis.: Kalmbach Books, 1985), 93–95; Richard R. Wallin et al., *Chicago & Illinois Midland* (San Marino, Calif.: Golden West Books, 1979), 84–94.

4   George W. Hilton, *The MA & PA: A History of the Maryland & Pennsylvania Railroad* (Berkeley, Calif.: Howell-North, 1963), 91; Carroll Pursell, *The Machine in America: A Social History of Technology* (Baltimore, Md.: Johns Hopkins University Press, 1995), 239; *DeKalb (Ill.) Chronicle*, January 30, 1908.

5   *Billings (Mont.) Gazette*, September 10, 2009; Andy Cummings, "Construction Begins on 30-mile Coal Spur," *Trains* 68 (November 2008): 14–15.

6   H. Roger Grant, *Rails through the Wiregrass: A History of the Georgia & Florida Railroad* (DeKalb: Northern Illinois University Press, 2006), 208–9; H. Roger Grant, *The North Western: A History of the Chicago & North Western Railway System* (DeKalb: Northern Illinois University Press, 1996), 225–31; Andy Cummings and Jerry Huddleston, *Dakota, Minnesota & Eastern: A Modern Granger Railroad* (David City, Neb.: South Platte Press, 2005).

7   Michael Soar, ed., *The New Line to London of the Great Central Railway* (Nottinghamshire, England: Rook Books, 1999), 3–14; A. G. Macdonell, *England, Their England* (New York: Macmillan Company, 1933), 221–22.

Index

H. Roger Grant is Kathryn and Calhoun Lemon Professor of History at Clemson University. He has written and edited twenty-six books, most on railroad and transportation history.